THE CONFEDERATION OF EUROPE

THE CONFEDERATION OF EUROPE

A STUDY OF THE EUROPEAN ALLIANCE, 1813–1823
AS AN EXPERIMENT IN THE INTERNATIONAL
ORGANIZATION OF PEACE

BY

WALTER ALISON PHILLIPS

NEW YORK

Howard Fertig

1966

First published in 1914 by Longmans,
Green and Co. Limited

Second edition 1920

HOWARD FERTIG, INC. EDITION
reprinted from the Second edition in 1966
by arrangement with Longmans, Green and Co. Limited

Library of Congress Catalog Card Number: 66-24350

PRINTED IN THE UNITED STATES OF AMERICA
BY NOBLE OFFSET PRINTERS

PREFACE

TO

THE SECOND EDITION

SINCE the first edition of this work was published, in the spring of 1914, the Great War has led to immense changes in the conditions affecting the particular problems with which it was concerned. When the question of preparing a new edition arose I was, therefore, faced with the question of whether the book would not need a more or less drastic alteration in order to adapt it to these new conditions. A book, if it have any vitality at all, is always an organic whole, the product of a particular point of view at a particular time, and the attempt to adapt it to changed circumstances requiring a fresh outlook may easily result in depriving it of such permanent value as it may possess, even if this be no more than that of a milestone marking the progress of opinion. I had, then, to make up my mind as to how far the changed conditions brought about by the war necessitated a change in my own attitude towards the problems which I had discussed before the war.

I came to the conclusion that, though the change in conditions has been immense, it has not been fundamental ; that nothing has happened, or is likely to happen, to deprive of its value, either by way of warning or of example, the history of the attempt made a hundred years ago to set up an international organization for the maintenance of peace, and that the lessons which I drew from this history are still, generally speaking, valid and applicable. I decided, however, that they needed re-stating in the light of what has since happened and is still happening. I have therefore largely modified the introductory section of the first edition, and I have re-written the concluding section. As for the body of the book, which is almost purely historical in character, I have subjected this to a careful revision. The greater part remains substantially untouched ; but I have made considerable alterations in the sections on the Congress of Vienna and the Conference of Aix-la-Chapelle, and that on the Spanish Colonies I have practically rewritten.

The original edition of the book was criticized in certain quarters as falling short of that full and scholarly account of the period of the Congresses which had been expected of me. But, as I stated in the Preface, my object was a limited one. During a prolonged visit to the United States in 1911 I had been impressed with the danger likely to arise from the shallow and uninformed idealism of the pacifist movement—a danger which is now obvious to everybody—and my object was to counter this by an appeal to the relevant facts of history. Such an attitude may be condemned as ' journalistic ' by the straiter sect of historians, but I confess that for me the chief value of history lies precisely in the light which it can throw on the problems of the present ; and I consider that the divorce between journalism and scholarship—only too obvious in our newspapers—is a serious danger. An exhaustive study of the period covered by this book would require facilities which have not been at my command, and in any case it is a task which I must now leave to younger men.

Fortunately, the younger school of English historians have in recent years devoted more and more attention to a period of history long neglected, but of immense importance to the understanding of the great questions at issue at the present day. Among those who, since the Foreign Office records covering the period after 1815 were thrown open to scholars, have drawn their materials from this rich quarry are Mr. H. V. E. Temperley, notably in his admirable ' Life of Canning,' and Professor C. K. Webster in a series of brilliant monographs contributed from 1912 onwards to the 'Transactions' of the Royal Historical Society and the ' English Historical Review.' Unfortunately, owing to the fact that I was abroad when the earlier of these papers appeared, I happened not to see them and was ignorant of their existence when I wrote the first edition of this book, greatly to its loss. The defects due to this cause I have in the present edition studied to remedy, and I am anxious to acknowledge my great obligations to Mr. Webster's work.   In the revision of the section of the Congress of Vienna I have made some use of his ' England and the Polish-Saxon Question at the Congress of Vienna ' ; elsewhere I have found his ' Some Aspects of Castlereagh's Foreign Policy ' helpful and suggestive ; but I have, above all, expanded the section on the Spanish Colonies with the aid of his two articles on ' Castlereagh and the Spanish Colonies ' [1] I have not made any actual use of his short history of the Congress of Vienna, recently published for the Historical Section of the Foreign Office, but I should like to express my admiration for this clear and scholarly presentation of a difficult and complicated subject.

Of the innumerable books and brochures advocating a League of Nations which have been issued since the beginning of the war I do not think it necessary to speak. I have read many of them, and they have left my own standpoint unchanged.   But, lest this should be interpreted as a sign of hardness of heart, I may perhaps be allowed a word of personal explanation.   I have been described on at least one pacifist platform as ' the English Bernhardi '—in other words, as an apostle of the gospel of war.   I hate war.   I regard it as a horrible calamity

[1] *English Historical Review*, xxvii. p. 78, 1912 ; and xxx. p. 631, 1915.

and a monstrous folly. But the mass of men are not wise, and all history seems to me to prove that they need an occasional calamity to teach them wisdom. The long centuries of Roman peace did not produce a wholesome world ; sensitive souls fled from the corruption of it, fled in hundreds and in thousands to the peace of utter negation in the desert. Before the war our own civilization seemed to be perishing of fatty degeneration ; men of good will watched with misgiving the monstrous growth of luxury, the decay of old moral standards, the increasing desertion of all shrines save those of Mammon. The war has brought untold misery and suffering ; but it has brought something more as well. It has turned the minds of men back violently to the realities of life and to its responsibilities ; it has, by its revelation of the illimitable capacity of human nature for heroic endurance and self-sacrifice, given to the mass of men a new faith in themselves and in the destiny of the race ; it has opened the path to a new and more strenuous age in which there will be no place for the once popular preachers of a cynical hedonism. Whether the modern gospel of Labour will succeed in imposing a new discipline upon the world which will make that of war unnecessary, I do not know. Perhaps it will. But, as a historian, I am concerned not with the world as it may be, but with the world as it has been and is.

W. ALISON PHILLIPS.

TRINITY COLLEGE, DUBLIN,
  July 1919.

PREFACE

TO

THE FIRST EDITION

THE lectures here reproduced were delivered at Oxford during Trinity Term of 1913. Though included among the courses falling under the Faculty of History, their object and scope, as I explain more fully in the introductory lecture, are not purely historical. Their intention is, briefly, to illustrate from a particular period of history the problems involved in the practical application of the principles of International Law, and my hope is that they may serve a useful purpose in helping to create a sound opinion upon questions which are too often discussed from a standpoint wholly out of touch with the realities of life.

Apart from the modern movement for the organization of peace, there is another question, of even greater practical importance, upon which the study of the experiment in international government during the period under review throws no little light. This is the question, or series of questions, involved in recent developments of the Monroe Doctrine, about which so much is now being heard in connection with the relations of the United States with the Republics of Latin America. The doctrine, inspired by Canning, formulated by John Quincy Adams, and embodied by President Monroe in his famous Message to Congress in

1823, was originally a protest against the principle of
intervention consecrated by the Troppau Protocol. It
has passed since then through many phases, and not the
least singular is the latest, by which it has itself been
made to consecrate the principle of intervention. The
'Lodge Resolution' of 1912, by which it was declared
that the United States would regard as an infraction of
the Monroe Doctrine any concession made by a Latin
American State to a foreign corporation of a maritime
base or of territory in the neighbourhood of the
Panama Canal, involved the assertion of the right of
the North American Federation to interfere with the
free discretion of sovereign States, a principle embodied
in drastic form in the draft Treaty concluded with
Nicaragua in 1913 ; and still more striking, from our
present point of view, is the refusal of President Wilson
to recognize an 'illegitimate' Government in Mexico
and his reservation of the ultimate right of intervention
for the purpose of restoring order. Thus the United
States, itself a confederation of sovereign States, would
seem to be playing in the New World the part played in
the Old by the 'Confederation of Europe.' The analogy,
of course, is not perfect ; no historical analogy ever is
so ; but it is sufficiently close to enable the lessons
derived from the earlier experiment to be applied to
the problems involved in the later. Especially is this
true of the central problem of all, namely, how to reconcile
a system of paternal supervision over a somewhat unruly
family of nations with due regard to their sovereign
rights. The Holy Alliance, in its inception at least, was
coloured by a lofty idealism, and it ended by stinking in
the nostrils of all lovers of liberty. To the Latin American
nations the Monroe Doctrine, once the palladium of their
liberties, is rapidly becoming a portentous bugbear, and,
as once the Holy Alliance, so now 'Monroism' is denounced as threatening them with an alien and hateful
domination.

So far as other matters of purely historical interest

of my lectures are concerned, I think I may claim to
have thrown some fresh light on the question of the
origins of the Holy Alliance. These have been
sought by various writers in various places, and the
analogy of previous projects of peace has not been lost
sight of. But hitherto no one, so far as I am aware, has
recognized in the Instructions to Novosiltsov the ' missing
link ' in the evolution of the Emperor Alexander's idea
of a Confederation of Europe from these earlier peace
projects. I have also been able to shed some new light
on two of the most conspicuous figures of this period,
namely, the Emperor Alexander and Lord Castlereagh.
With regard to the former, I am under great obligations
to the recent work on the Emperor by H.I.H. the Grand
Duke Nicholas Mikhailovich, and to M. Muhlenbeck's
' Étude sur les origines de la Sainte-Alliance,' but I have
been able to supplement these most fascinating studies
by many vivid touches of characterization from letters
preserved in the Foreign Office records. As for Castlereagh, in the ' Cambridge Modern History ' (vol. x. chap. i.)
I had already attempted to reverse the shallow judgments
passed upon him and his work by the prejudice and
ignorance of earlier generations ; the present work will,
I hope, serve to make still clearer the debt of gratitude
which Great Britain and Europe owe to him.

The central theme of the lectures now published is
practically the same as that of an article on ' The Peace
Movement and the Holy Alliance ' contributed by me
to the *Edinburgh Review* in April 1912, and much of the
purely historical part covers the same ground as my
chapter on the Congresses in the ' Cambridge Modern
History.' As regards the former, the theme is now illustrated with a wealth of material impossible to include
within the narrow compass of a review article. As regards
the latter, while the present studies include much that
is not in the ' Cambridge Modern History,' there has
necessarily been some repetition ; but my readers will
find it useful to refer to the ' History ' for the general

affairs of the period, of which in these lectures I had
to assume a knowledge in my audience.

Substantially the lectures are here printed as they
were delivered, with a few modifications of form.
The last of the series, however, which was unduly cramped
by the necessary time limit, I have taken this opportunity
of expanding.   In preparing them I have drawn mainly
on the unpublished records of the Foreign Office, so far
as the period from the Conference of Châtillon to that of
Verona is concerned.   References to these are necessarily
cumbersome, as the volumes are not permanently
numbered and the full title (*e.g.* F.O. : Congress, France,
M. Talleyrand, etc., June 1814–June 1815) has usually
to be given in order to make the reference clear.   I
need not repeat here the concise indication of the
contents of these volumes for the period from the
second Peace of Paris to the Conference of Verona given
in the bibliography to my chapter on the Congresses in
the ' Cambridge Modern History ' (x. 787), to which I
refer my readers as possibly useful to them.   The numerous published works and collections of documents on
which I have drawn are sufficiently indicated by references
in footnotes.

WALTER ALISON PHILLIPS.

January 1914.

CONTENTS

I

THE CONCEPTION OF THE CONFEDERATION

PAGE

I. INTRODUCTORY. German political morality a survival—
The eighteenth century and the Reason of State—The State and
statecraft—Influence of Machiavelli—The Revolution and the
Reason of State—The conception of war as an appeal to the judgment of God—Rise of nationalism and its effect in increasing the
horrors of war—Influence of Grotius—International Law and
Diplomacy—The Holy Alliance and its motives—The fiction of a
golden age of international law—Practical effect of such fictions—
The ' Confederation of Europe' an example of this—Result of the
Hague Conferences on international morality—Their influence
on the growth of an international conscience—Danger of exaggerating the effect of this—Conflict between the national and international consciousness—Mixed motives of the peoples taking part
in the Great War—The United States and the Fourteen Points—
Mr. Roosevelt's repudiation of President Wilson's claim—Persistence of national group-consciousness—A balance of power
necessary to any international organization—Objects of the
present book   3

II. EARLIER PROJECTS OF PEACE. The Truce of God—The
ideal of the mediæval Empire—Rise of the conception of States
as sovereign and independent—The Reason of State—Effect of the
institution of permanent diplomatic agents—Development of
International Law—Conception of the European commonwealth
based on a balance of power—Projects for developing this into a
true confederation for the preservation of peace—Influence of the
tradition of the Holy Roman Empire—The Grand Design of
Henry IV of France—Éméric Crucé's 'Nouveau Cynée'—The
project of the Abbé de St. Pierre—Its relation to later peace
projects—Criticisms of Leibnitz, of Voltaire, and of Rousseau—
Effect of the French Revolution—Kant's 'Zum ewigen Frieden'
—Saint-Simon on the Holy Alliance   18

III. THE PEACE PROJECT OF ALEXANDER I OF RUSSIA. Its
probable inspiration—Novosiltsov's mission to England in 1804—

CONTENTS

His instructions—Scheme for European reconstruction and a European Confederation—Reply of Pitt—His remarks on the proposed 'general system of public law'—The proposal embodied in the Anglo-Russian Treaty of 1805—The common danger from France—The principle of collective intervention—Circular of Kaunitz, 1791—Burke's view   33

II

THE BIRTH OF THE CONFEDERATION

I. THE EMPEROR ALEXANDER I. Czartoryski and Polish nationalism—Influence on Alexander's project—Alexander falls from grace—Friedland and Tilsit—Napoleon and Alexander—Effect on the campaign of 1812—Character of Alexander—His education—Influence of La Harpe—'Jacobin' views of the young Alexander—Plans for a democratic Russia—Influence of Paul I's militarism — Effect on him of Paul's murder — His religious mysticism — Religious character of the age — The coming millennium—Influence of Golitsin and Koshelev—Effect on Alexander of the burning of Moscow—Napoleon as 'the Beast'—Alexander's mission as the world's peace-maker—He crosses the Niemen   45

II. THE GRAND ALLIANCE. Alexander's proclamation—Treaty of Kalisch—Appeal to the principle of nationality—Renewed influence of Czartoryski—Alexander and Poland—Partial alliances of Teplitz and Reichenbach—Capo d'Istria—Alexander revives the idea of a Universal Union—Questions involved in a territorial 'restoration': France, Germany, Italy, Poland—Threatened disruption of the Alliance—Mission of Castlereagh   .   .   .   58

III. THE TREATY OF CHAUMONT. Castlereagh at Langres—The British policy defined—Contrast with Alexander's views—Divisions in the Alliance—Austria and Russia—Conferences at Châtillon — Effect of Napoleon's victories — 'Criminations and recriminations'—General character of Austrian policy—Metternich—Fear of Alexander's designs on Poland—Mediation of Castlereagh—Treaty of Chaumont—Declaration of Châtillon .   68

III

THE PREPARATION OF THE CONFEDERATION

I. THE FIRST PEACE OF PARIS. The fall of Paris—The abdication of Napoleon—Disquieting attitude of Alexander—Russia and the Balance of Power—Castlereagh aims at 'grouping' Alexander—Justification of the policy of maintaining the Alliance—

PAGE

Question of its legitimate sphere of influence—This to be confined
to Europe—Question of Asia, the British Empire, the United
States and Latin America—Immediate questions : Germany,
Switzerland, Italy, Spain—The first Treaty of Paris—The future
Alliance ; question of its constitution—Talleyrand urges a wider
Alliance, to include France—The principle of ' legitimacy '—
The Allies and the French claim—Exclusion of France   .   .   81

II. THE CONGRESS OF VIENNA. Its general character—
Dictatorship of the Great Powers—Talleyrand leads the oppo-
sition of the lesser Powers—He champions ' justice and public
law ' against the particularist ambitions of the Powers—Questions
of Poland and Saxony—Attitude of Alexander and its causes—
Threatened break-up of the Alliance—Diplomacy of Castlereagh
—Talleyrand admitted to the Conferences—Secret Treaty of
January 3, 1815—Harmony restored—The Vienna Final Act—
General analysis of its provisions from the point of view of a basis
of an international system—The return of Napoleon from Elba—
Revival of the Quadruple Alliance   93

IV

THE CONSECRATION OF THE CONFEDERATION

I. THE CONVERSION OF ALEXANDER. The Second Restoration—Divergent views as to the fate of France—Action of
Wellington and Castlereagh—Popularity of Louis XVIII's restoration—But weakness of the King's position—Napoleon's troops
hold out in the fortresses—Excesses of the Allies—Danger of a
disruption of the Alliance—Question of Alexander's attitude—
This determined by his 'conversion' —The Baroness von Krüdener
—The interview at Heilbronn—The Imperial prayer-meetings—
Alexander arrives in Paris—The Alliance re-cemented   .   .   119

II. THE SECOND TREATY OF PARIS. Problems of the settlement with France—The question of dismemberment—Attitude
of Castlereagh and Wellington ; of Alexander ; of the German
Powers—Compromise embodied in the second Treaty of Paris ;
the limits of 1790   128

III. THE HOLY ALLIANCE. Question of the future of the
Alliance—Proclamation of the Holy Alliance—A revival of the
idea of a universal union—Comparison with the ' instructions ' of
1804—Renewal of the Treaty of Chaumont agreed upon—Differences as to necessary modifications—The Russian project—Castlereagh's counter-project—The Treaty of Alliance of November 20,
1815—Analysis of this—Article VI the basis of the future Concert
of Europe   141

CONTENTS

V

THE CULMINATION OF THE CONFEDERATION

PAGE

THE CONFERENCE OF AIX-LA-CHAPELLE. Unsettled questions
—The reaction in Europe—Ambiguous attitude of the Emperor
Alexander—Metternich suggests an Austro-British Alliance—
Refusal of Castlereagh — Conditions in France — Rumoured
Franco - Russian Alliance — Conference of Aix - la - Chapelle—
Evacuation of France concerted—The future of the Alliance—
Question of the admission of France to the Alliance—This opens
the question of the future form of the European Concert—
Alexander revives the idea of a Universal Union—Attitude of
Austria and Prussia—Opposition of Great Britain—The principle
of non-intervention — Outcome of the negotiations — Fresh
proposals for a treaty of guarantee defeated by Great Britain—
General character of the Conference—Its proceedings illustrate
the difficulty of an international system 151

VI

THE BREAK-UP OF THE CONFEDERATION

I. REVOLUTION AND REACTION. The Treaty of Frankfort—
Alexander and Liberalism—The Constitution of Poland—Enigmatic attitude of Alexander—Russian propaganda in Italy—
Metternich and the Tsar's Jacobinism—Liberal reaction in France
—Attitude of the Powers—Murder of Kotzebue—The Carlsbad
decrees—Alexander champions German Liberalism—Change in
his views—Revolution in Spain—Murder of the Duc de Berri—
Alexander suggests intervention in Spain—Opposition of Austria
and Great Britain—Revolution in Naples—Metternich and Alexander—The idea of the universal union revived—Question of
intervention—Attitude of Great Britain—Castlereagh and Metternich on intervention   185

II. THE CONFERENCES OF TROPPAU AND LAIBACH. Alexander
recants his Liberalism—Conversation with Metternich at Troppau
—Mutiny of the Semyonovski regiment—The Holy Alliance
becomes an instrument of reaction—Rift between the Autocratic
and Constitutional Powers of the Alliance—The Troppau Protocol
—Consecration of the principle of intervention—Metternich's
explanations—Protest of Castlereagh—Effect on the Powers—
Adjourned Conference at Laibach—Continuation of the controversy—The British objections overriden—Breach in the Alliance . 205

III. THE EASTERN QUESTION. Alexander and the Christians
in Turkey—Suggestions to Pitt—Agreement of Tilsit—Treaty of
Bucharest—Turkey and the Congress of Vienna—Exclusion of

PAGE

Turkey from the Holy Alliance—Effect of the Greek insurrection
—Metternich keeps Alexander 'grouped' at Laibach—Insurrection
in the Morea—*Rapprochement* of Great Britain and Austria—Meeting of Metternich and Castlereagh at Hanover—Peril of Russian
intervention—Alexander and Capo d'Istria—The Holy Alliance
v. Russia—Alexander agrees to a Conference—Death of Castlereagh—George Canning—No breach in the continuity of British
policy—Castlereagh's ' instructions ' as plenipotentiary at the
Conference—These handed unaltered to Wellington—Definition
of the attitude of Great Britain towards the questions to be
raised—Wellington at Vienna—Dismissal of Capo d'Istria—
The Eastern Question shelved   219

IV. THE QUESTION OF SPAIN AND HER COLONIES. The
Spanish colonial system—The Latin American revolutions—
Monarchies or Republics ?—Misgivings in Europe—Conflicting
interests of the Powers—France and Great Britain—Castle-
reagh's policy—Rivalry of Spain and Portugal on the River
Plate threatens a European war—Russian intrigues in Paris
and Madrid—Spain invites the intervention of the Alliance
against her colonies—Successful protest of Great Britain—
Attitude of the United States—Reasons for their delay in
recognizing the independence of the Latin American States—
Question of the Spanish colonies discussed at Aix-la-Chapelle
—Proposal to invite the United States to co-operate with the
Allies—Opposition of Great Britain to the principle of inter-
vention—Triumph of Castlereagh's diplomacy—French intrigue
for setting up a Bourbon king in Buenos Aires—Revolution
of 1820 in Spain—Strained relations between the Allies—
Recognition of the Latin American States by the United
States—Castlereagh takes the first steps towards recognition
—The question on the eve of the Congress of Verona—France
and intervention in Spain — Wellington and the Emperor
Alexander at the preliminary conferences in Vienna   .   .   233

V. THE CONGRESS OF VERONA. Character of the Congress—
Subjects for discussion—The Spanish colonies—The Spanish
Revolution — France proposes intervention — Montmorency's
questions to the Congress—Answers of the Powers—Alexander
proposes concerted intervention — Attitude of Austria and
Prussia—Wellington withdraws from the Conferences—Attempts
at compromise—The policy of identical notes—Protest of Great
Britain—Open breach of the Alliance—Views of Canning on this   252

VI. THE GENESIS OF THE MONROE DOCTRINE. The French
invasion of Spain—Ferdinand VII restored to power—The
question of the Spanish colonies—A Congress *ad hoc* proposed—
Attitude of the Emperor Alexander—Russia as an American
Power—Russian overtures at Washington—Attitude of Canning—
He suggests a concert between Great Britain and the United
States—Suspicious attitude of the American Minister—The

xviii CONTENTS

PAGE

question at Washington—Favourable attitude of President Monroe
—Influence of the Russian proposals—John Quincy Adams—
Victory of the principle of the isolation of the Americas—
President Monroe's Message of December 2, 1823—The Monroe
Doctrine—Effect on the Allied Powers 265

VII

THE FEDERATION OF THE WORLD

THE LEAGUE OF NATIONS. Criticism of pacifist proposals
before the war—Danger of an international system to national
liberties—The principle of intervention—President Wilson and
Mexico—Comparison with the action of the reactionary Powers
at Troppau—Light thrown by the international experiment
after 1815 on the programme of the League of Nations—Parallel
between the proceedings at Paris and those at Vienna—The
' dictatorship exercised by the Great Powers '—Criticism of the
Covenant of the League—Objections by British statesmen to
similar proposals a hundred years ago—The reservation of the
Monroe Doctrine—Significance of this—Criticism of President
Wilson's claim that the United States have been *par exce lence*
the champions of the principle of ' self-determination '—The
Monroe Doctrine as a doctrine of conquest—The American
attitude defined in the controversy with Colombia—Reason
why the United States, in spite of their policy of expansion,
have not developed into a military power—The history of the
United States does not show that democracies are pacific—A
democratic international government would not necessarily
make for peace—Mirabeau on the warlike temper of popular
assemblies—A democratic international system is inconsistent
with nationalism—Falseness of the analogy between the suggested international federal system and such federations as the
United States—The cosmopolitan ideal conceived as the culmination of the historical process of human grouping—Criticism of
this—The stability of any international system must always
depend on the balance of power—Limits of willingness to obey
law, whether national or international—Criticism of the principle
of ' self-determination ' as a guarantee of peace — A vivid
sense of the community of interests between nations the only
guarantee of peace—The only proof of this would be universal
free trade — Danger of surrendering or curtailing national
sovereignty in the absence of such a guarantee . . . 279

APPENDIX. Text of the Act of the Holy Alliance . . . 305

INDEX 307

I

THE CONCEPTION OF THE CONFEDERATION

As for the philosophers, they make imaginary
laws for imaginary commonwealths, and their
discourses are as the stars, which give little
light because they are so high.—BACON.

Et jura li Dus hautement,
Et tuit li Barons ensement,
C'en jurerent que paix tendroient,
Et celle Trieves garderoient,
Pour la paix tout temps remembrer,
Qui tout temps devoit mês durer.

Roman de Rou.

I

INTRODUCTORY

German political morality a survival—The eighteenth century and
the Reason of State—The State and statecraft—Influence of
Machiavelli—The Revolution and the Reason of State—The conception of war as an appeal to the judgment of God—Rise of
nationalism and its effect in increasing the horrors of war—
Influence of Grotius—International Law and Diplomacy—The
Holy Alliance and its motives—The fiction of a golden age of
international law—Practical effect of such fictions—The ' Confederation of Europe ' an example of this—Result of The Hague
Conferences on international morality—Their influence on the
growth of an international conscience—Danger of exaggerating
the effect of this—Conflict between the national and international
consciousness—Mixed motives of the peoples taking part in the
Great War—The United States and the Fourteen Points—Mr.
Roosevelt's repudiation of President Wilson's claim—Persistence
of national group-consciousness—A balance of power necessary
to any international organization—Objects of the present book.

THE German Chancellor von Bethmann-Hollweg made
his name immortal by a single phrase, blurted out in
the moment of surprise and consternation caused by the
British declaration of war. For the world of Germany's
enemies the ' scrap of paper ' became a symbol and a
war-cry ; and the Chancellor's subsequent defence in
the *Reichstag* of the violation of Belgian neutrality, on
the ground that ' necessity knows no law,' was taken as
yet another proof of Germany's lapse from accepted moral
standards.

The German attitude was not the result of a lapse,
but of a survival. The rest of the Western world, under
the influence of a hundred years of liberal development,

had evolved new moral standards, not perhaps very exalted, but at least free from the unblushing cynicism which had marked those of the age preceding the French Revolution. Prussia, conservative by instinct and by the pressure of her institutions, remained true to the old standards ; for in Berlin the tradition of Frederick the Great survived as a living force, and it was upon his model that the statesmanship of Prussia-Germany was avowedly based.[1] It was the model most approved in the eighteenth century of our era, which unaffectedly admired Frederick as the most perfect and successful exponent of its political principles. British statesmen, indeed, in an age which had reduced the practice of diplomatic chicane to a fine art, maintained a certain reputation for exceptional honesty ; but if so careful an observer as Montesquieu could describe them as ' un peu plus honnêtes gens ' than the rest, this was due, in his opinion, not to their superior virtue, but to the fact that they had to report to Parliament and were therefore deprived of the facilities for double-dealing provided by an absolutely secret diplomacy. For the rest, the practical statesmen of the eighteenth century held it to be a self-evident truth that, to quote Count Ludwig von Cobenzl, in affairs of State ' interest ought to outweigh every other consideration, regardless of justice ' ; and this ' reason of State ' was justified by the Baron de Bielfeld as being no more than the maxim *salus populi suprema lex*, on which all peoples both ancient and modern had always acted.

The truth of this had been admitted, at least in practice, ever since the mediæval ideals of the universal Empire and the universal Church had given place to the modern conception of the territorial sovereign State. It was in the Italy of the Renaissance that this new conception first took its shape and name. It was in Italy also that the new ' statecraft ' was first

[1] See Ellis Barker, *The Foundations of Modern Germany*, and ' The Ethics of Prussian Statecraft,' by the present writer, in the *Quarterly Review* for October 1918.

systematized, and its rules and maxims had affected
the practice of all Europe even before the publication in
1515 of Machiavelli's ' Prince,' which for three centuries
to come was to serve as the political text-book of
statesmen.

The immense influence of this wonderful book was
not due to anything novel in the principles, or want of
principles, which it proclaimed. Old-fashioned moralists,
like Cardinal Pole, might still appeal to ' the law of
nature and the writings of learned and pious men ' ; but
for the new statesmen of the type of Thomas Cromwell,
who had served his political apprenticeship in Italy, ' in
these matters a few sentences from a man of experience are worth whole volumes written by a philosopher
who has no such experience.' [2] That which men praised
in Machiavelli, and gave him his lasting influence,
was that he held up the mirror to the world in which
he lived—a world in which might was right and the
virtù which was esteemed the highest of human qualities had certainly very little in common with virtue.
For the great jurist Albericus Gentilis, whose political
principles were in advance of his age, the service
rendered by Machiavelli was that he told the truth about
princes—for the instruction of the peoples.[3] Bacon,
on the other hand, was less concerned with Machiavelli's
motives than with his method. Only men of large
experience in affairs, he says, ought to discuss them, and
' it is for this reason that we give thanks to Machiavelli
and writers of this kind, who openly and without dissimulation set out what men are wont to do, not what
they ought to do.' [4] Wicquefort, whose treatise on the
ambassador and his functions became a text-book of
eighteenth-century diplomacy, says the same thing in
almost the same words : ' Machiavelli nearly everywhere

[2] Cardinal Pole's *Apologia ad Carolum Quintum*, abstracted in
Brewer's essay on the Royal Supremacy.
[3] *De legationibus libri tres* (ed. 1585), lib. iii. cap. ix. p. 110.
[4] *De augmentis scientiarum* (ed. Louvain, 1652), p. 503.

says what princes do, and not what they ought to do.'[5]

If, then, the name of Machiavelli has become synonymous with that of a crudely cynical *Realpolitik*, this is only because his genius standardized and set the seal of authority on the practice of his time, presenting it as a model to all who would achieve dominion over men and render this dominion secure. His practical maxims, more or less modified to suit the changing standpoint of the times, remained and remain valid wherever this motive prevailed or prevails. In the seventeenth and eighteenth centuries it was open and avowed. Machiavelli had praised the instinct of acquisition as laudable in itself ; the seventeenth century began to conceive aggrandizement to be not only the right but the duty of princes, ' since the weak are at the mercy of the strong, and the legitimate frontiers of a State are those necessary to its own conservation.'[6] This was the principle which, whatever their pretext, underlay most of the diplomacy and the wars of this period. It consecrated in the eyes of Frenchmen the aggressions of Louis XIV., since these were directed to securing for France her ' natural frontiers ' of the Alps, the Pyrenees and the Rhine. It was the excuse of Frederick the Great for all his violations of right, from the invasion of Silesia to the crowning international crime of the partition of Poland. Nor did the men of the Revolution break with this tradition, for all their loud profession of cosmopolitan principles. For them too, as Sorel has made clear, the Reason of State was supreme ; and the world knows well how short a time it took to change the Revolutionary gospel of peace into the Revolutionary doctrine of conquest, and how, in the end, ' Napoleon sprang armed from the Revolution, as Minerva from the brow of Jove.'

Out of the welter of the Revolutionary epoch there

[5] *L'ambassadeur et ses fonctions* (La Haye, 1680), i. 174.
[6] Céleste, ' Louis Machon, apologiste de Machiavel.' Quoted by Sorel, *L'Europe et la Révolution française*, i. 20.

emerged a new conception, that of the peoples conceived as homogeneous groups or ' nations ' and, as such, entitled to form separate bodies politic. This principle of nation‑ality, though almost wholly modern, was accepted by nineteenth-century Liberalism as based on the laws of eternal justice, and its universal application, regardless of the fitness of nations for self-government, was pro‑claimed as the most perfect basis for lasting peace. But the whole history of the hundred years following the settlement of 1815, culminating in the great world war, has proved that peoples are no less aggressive than princes, and that the principle of nationality was but a new force making for war, and for war on an incomparably vaster scale, and more terrible in its incidents, than any which had been waged in· the days of mere dynastic rivalry. After all, most of the wars of the eighteenth century were of the nature of the old ordeal by battle ; they were deliberate appeals to the arbitrament of God, in the absence of any court competent to decide disputes between sovereigns [7]; they were fought by small professional armies according to fixed rules ; they were ended, when one side or the other felt the cost to be excessive, by treaties which, more often than not, represented a com‑promise, and in their forms studiously respected the dignity of the defeated party. Nationalism brought back into the conduct of war the old cruel and uncom‑promising spirit of the wars of religion ; for with the genuine spirit of nationality no compromise is possible. ' No man has the right to fix boundaries to the march of a nation,' cried the Irish leader Parnell, and the words are engraved in letters of gold on his monument in Dublin. The logical corollary is supplied by the Pan-German Dr. Paul Rohrbach. ' In every great and power‑ful nation,' he wrote in his 'Der Deutsche Gedanke,' ' the instinct of self-preservation reveals itself in a natural pressure to expand, which only finds its frontiers

---

[7] See, e.g., Jean Domat, *Les lois civiles dans leur ordre naturel* (ed. Paris, 1745), chap. viii. § iv. I. p. 10.

where it meets other national - political counteracting forces strong enough to resist it.' The truth of this is proved by the record of the nations in both hemispheres during the last hundred years ; it is a truth which has been but imperfectly disguised by the cosmopolitan professions of the Paris Conference. And in this bitter competition of the nations which has replaced the old rivalry of kings there seems to have been as little room for nice distinctions of morality as in the bitter competition of modern commerce. The conventions must be observed ; but, in the long run, business is business, and might is right.

The political gospel according to Machiavelli, then, is still preached, and there has been no break in the apostolic succession of the great Florentine. What of the other political doctrine, that of the rights and reciprocal obligations of nations, of which Grotius is reverenced as the father ? The great Dutchman, too, had his apostolic succession ; his principles had been glossed and interpreted and expanded by generations of international jurists ; generations of statesmen and politicians had done lip-service to them before ever President Wilson proclaimed the rule of universal morality to a reverent world. But the devil, if theologians may be believed, is never so dangerous as when he persuades people that he does not exist. To denounce Machiavelli has always been a last refinement of Machiavellism. Frederick the Great announced the publication of his ' Anti-Machiavel ' just eight days before, in the pure spirit of the ' Prince,' he invaded Silesia [8] ; and in doing so he was but following old precedent. ' It doth to me a little relish of paradox,' said a seventeenth-century writer, ' that wherever I come, Machiavel is verbally cursed and damned, and yet practically embraced and asserted ; for there is no kingdom but hath a race of men that are ingenious at the peril of

---

[8] *Nouvelles privilégiées de Berlin*, no. lxx., jeudi, 8 décembre, 1740 : ' A la Haye chez Jean van Duren est imprimée Examen du Prince de Machiavel avec des Notes historiques et politiques, in-octavo.' Frederick crossed the frontier on the 16th.

the public . . . and in all the strugglings and disputes that have of late years befallen this corner of the world, I found the pretence fine and spiritual, yet the ultimate end and true scope was gold, and greatness, and secular glory.' [9]

This suspicious temper, for which there was so much justification in the traditions of the old diplomacy, survived and survives.[10] A hundred years ago it was given loud and contemptuous expression in the language of contemporaries about the experiment in international government made after the close of the Napoleonic wars. In the concert of the Allies themselves a deep note of mutual suspicion sounded a diapason through all their surface harmony, which in the end it dominated and broke into a discord ; and the note has boomed in the ears, and to a certain extent dazed the judgment, of some of the most conspicuous historians of the period. It was the Liberal fashion in the Victorian age to pour scorn on the whole conception of the Alliance, to stigmatize the motives which directed it as wholly obscurantist and reactionary, and to vilify the memory of Lord Castlereagh as the statesman responsible for the adhesion of Great Britain to a system conceived as fundamentally opposed to liberty. This attitude, in the light of evidence now available, can no longer be maintained, and the experiment in the international organization of peace after the downfall of Napoleonic militarism must be studied from quite a different point of view. It has, indeed, since the Great War and the emergence of the ideal of the League of Nations into the sphere of practical politics, gained far more than a merely historical interest, and it has become more than ever necessary to study it, the motives which underlay it, and the results which it achieved.

Were, then, the motives of the parties to the Quadruple Alliance wholly selfish ? Was the so-called Treaty of the Holy Alliance no more than a hypocritical device

---

[9] W. Blois, *Modern Policies taken from Machiavel.*

[10] For earlier theorists of the ethics of diplomacy see my article ' Diplomacy ' in the *Encyclopædia Britannica* (11th ed.), viii. 297d.

for deceiving the world, and the object of its author, Alexander of Russia, only—as the Austrian Baron Vincent suggested—to ' disguise under the language of evangelical self - abnegation schemes of far - reaching ambition ' ? Was it, as the Whig Opposition in Parliament declared, the consecration of a conspiracy of despots against national and popular liberties ?   Or was it, as Metternich said, only ' a loud-sounding nothing ' which, according to the Swiss historian, Professor Alfred Stern, remained ' an ineffective piece of paper that has had no influence on any noteworthy affairs, whether in the internal or external life of States ' ? [11]

Sorel, whose great work is coloured throughout by his French prejudices, and who has the Frenchman's love for clear-cut characterization, has no doubt whatever as to Alexander's motives. ' Not for an instant,' he says, ' did he lose sight of his design, conceived in his youth, of reconstituting Europe and taking in the supremacy of the Continent the place usurped by Napoleon.' [12] As for the principles of the Holy Alliance, from their first appearance in the preamble to the Treaty of Kalisch in February 1813 to their solemn consecration in the act of September 26, 1815, they were no more than a politic fiction, that religious faith and the inviolability of treaties were to consecrate the return to the sacred principle of a former system of law. Now, as Sorel rightly points out, these principles had never prevailed in the past, and international law had only been known ' through the declamations of publicists and its violation by the Governments.' ' In default of the guarantees to the peoples of the silver age promised them,' he says scornfully, ' the next best thing is to invoke the legend of a golden age which they have never experienced, but of which the imaginary memory gives substance to all the illusions of hope.' [13]

We may admit the truth of this, yet deny its impli-

[11] Geschichte Europas, i. 41.
[12] L'Europe et la Révolution française, viii. 185.   [13] Ibid. vii. 65.

cation, affirming, with equal truth, that it is precisely such ' legends ' and ' imaginary memories ' that have been the impelling forces of nearly all great human movements :—the great religions of the world ; the doctrines of the divine right of kings and the fundamental rights of the people ; Rousseau's ' state of nature ' and ' social contract,' with their outgrowth, the revolutionary fictions of the brotherhood of men and of liberty and equality as the birthright of all ; and lastly, in flat contradiction to revolutionary cosmopolitanism, the modern doctrine of the prescriptive and inalienable rights of nationalities. The significance of these legends lies, not in the fact that they are wholly or largely based on ' imaginary memories,' but in the fact that they secure widespread belief, govern the motives of men, and so exercise a practical effect upon the world.

This is the case with the legend of a European juridical system which the Revolution had violently overthrown. No such system had in fact existed. But whatever their motives, the Powers, in appealing to it, consecrated the principle of an international law, and gave to it a wholly new sanction by committing themselves to the task of acting in concert for the maintenance of the sanctity of treaties. The significance of the European Coalition during the eight years that followed the signature of the Treaty of Chaumont is that it represented, whatever the motives of the several Allies may have been, an experiment in international government, an attempt to solve the problem of reconciling central and general control by a ' European Confederation ' with the maintenance of the liberties of its constituent states, and thus to establish a juridical system. The attempt failed ; but it left certain permanent effects : — the tradition of respect for the obligation of international engagements, the impetus thereby given to the study and application of international law, and the abiding hope of the ultimate establishment of an effective international system.

Substance seemed to be given to this hope by the work of the Peace Conferences held at The Hague in 1899 and 1907, and it is interesting to note that, whatever the immediate motive, it was the memory of the Holy Alliance that inspired the famous rescript of the Emperor Nicholas II. to which their convocation was due. In his opening address to the first Conference the President, M. de Beaufort, spoke of the desire of its august originator ' to realize the desire expressed by one of the most illustrious of his predecessors, the Emperor Alexander I.—that of seeing all the nations of Europe united for the purpose of living as brethren, aiding each other to their reciprocal needs.' How far the Conferences were from realizing this ideal is now abundantly clear. It was less clear at a time when the Hague Conventions could still be regarded as having a binding force at least *in foro conscientiae*. The more extreme pacifists, indeed, loudly expressed their disappointment with the results achieved at The Hague. They clamoured for the immediate establishment of a supernational system, with a central executive, a supreme court of arbitration to which all disputes between nations were to be compulsorily submitted, and an international army to enforce its decrees— in short, for the whole mechanism of what is now known as the League of Nations. Both President Wilson and Lord Grey of Falloden have committed themselves to the opinion that these demands were justified, and that had a League of Nations existed in July 1914 there would have been no war. But it should surely now be clear enough that any attempt, before the war, to base an international system on the territorial *status quo*—the only possible foundation for a juridical system— would have been foredoomed to failure, and that any collective effort to reform the world's political geography, so as to make it a reasonably secure foundation for peace, would merely have resulted in resolving the League into its elements. That the world was not ripe for such a settlement was, in fact, the opinion of many of the most eminent persons connected with the peace movement, who did not share the disappointment of the extremists at the results actually achieved.

On paper, indeed, these results looked impressive enough. The Convention of October 18, 1907, for the regulation of international disputes, was signed by the representatives of fourty-four States. The preamble ran as follows :—

The Sovereigns and the Chiefs of State of the signatory Powers, represented at the Second Peace Conference.

Animated by the firm intention of acting together for the maintenance of the general peace ;

Resolved to encourage by all their efforts the friendly settlement of international disputes ;

Recognize the solidarity which unites the members of the Society of the civilized Nations.

This was hailed as establishing in the whole world the empire of Right. M. Léon Bourgeois, who was later to have a weighty share in preparing the draft scheme for the League of Nations at Paris, declared that the Society of Nations had been created, that it was ' very much alive.' But elsewhere and a little later he somewhat modified this estimate. The Society of Nations had become conscious of itself ; it was alive ; but it lived as yet, not so much in the practical world of politics, as in the moral consciousness of mankind. The principles unanimously accepted by The Hague Conference were, he admitted, not embodied in binding agreements, but only in declarations and *vœux* ; they represented, however, a moral force which would in time impose them upon the Governments.[14] It was the growth of this moral force, bearing fruit in a long series of arbitration treaties, which Sir Thomas Barclay also recognized as one of the most valuable outcomes of The Hague meetings ; for, like Kant in his ' Zum ewigen Frieden,' he saw in the growth of the moral idea, as

[14] Preface to M. Ernest Lémonon's *La seconde conférence de la paix* (Paris 1909).

opposed to mere *Staatsklugheit* (the Machiavellian principle), the provision of that sanction which alone can
make international law effective, i.e. in the accepted
sense of ' law ' as ' a body of rules enforceable in the
courts.' [15]

The sequel has proved that they were right who saw
in the impulse given to the growth of an international
conscience the most valuable and permanent outcome of
The Hague Conferences. The conventions, the declarations and the *vœux* were blown into space, with other
' scraps of paper,' by the first blast of the hurricane of
war. But the moral indignation of the world, aroused
by Germany's cynical violation of her treaty obligations,
was a new factor ; for in the eighteenth century, and
even in the greater part of the nineteenth, any such
manifestation of an international conscience would have
been inconceivable. It is, however, possible to exaggerate the significance of this manifestation, and there
is a danger in such exaggeration. It may be true, as
President Wilson said at Manchester, that there has
never before in the history of the world been such a
keen international consciousness as there is now ; but
it would be extremely unsafe to assume that this consciousness, the outgrowth of a sense of common interests
in the face of a common peril, constitutes such a general
and reasoned consent to the subordination of national
interests as alone would provide a firm and lasting foundation for a supernational system. A similar international
consciousness was the result of the last great general
war in Europe. Then, too, ' men promised themselves
an all-embracing reform of the political structure of
Europe, guarantees for universal peace, in one word,
the return of the golden age ' ; and in 1814 all eyes were
fixed on Vienna, as in 1919 they were fixed on Paris.
If these hopes were disappointed, this was doubtless
partly due to the short-sightedness and selfishness of
sovereigns and statemen ; but it was also due to the

[15] *Encyclopædia Britannica* (11th ed.), article ' Peace.'

fact that the international consciousness faded away with the memory of the causes which had produced it, giving place to that exaggerated nationalism which it was the pride of nineteenth-century Liberalism to encourage.

The Great War which opened in 1914 was essentially the culmination of the conflict of nationalities and of national ideals which had been going on during the century which succeeded the epoch of the French Revolution. But it was also a struggle between two rival and irreconcilable conceptions of a ' right ' which transcends the bounds of nationality. The motives which led the various peoples to join in the struggle were, in different proportions, compounded of both these elements, and no peace settlement can be a lasting one in which due allowance is not made for both. The main difference between the supporters of the League of Nations and its critics is in their views as to the relative value, strength and permanence of the national and international consciousness respectively. President Wilson saw in the new ' vision of the people,' the outcome of the terrible sufferings of the war, the guarantee of a wholly new spirit in international relations, of the permanent subordination of national hatreds and rivalries to ' the mandate of humanity.' ' Those who suffer see,' he said ; and then proceeded, with a strange inconsistency, to claim a special clarity of vision for the people of the United States, which of all the belligerent nations had suffered least.

Now it is doubtless true, as the President affirmed, that the American troops went to the war in the spirit of crusaders ; the same is equally true of the French or the British ; but it is equally untrue of all to pretend that they fought ' with their eyes fixed on heaven ' for the abstract rights of humanity. ' It is sheer nonsense,' said the late Mr. Roosevelt, in reply to President Wilson's claim, ' to maintain that the American army is fighting for his fourteen points. There is not one American in a thousand who has ever heard of them. The American army is fighting Germany, and the American people want Germany smashed.' [16] The truth is that, though the Americans and the British alike fought for a principle, it was not because of a principle that they entered the war, but because their honour and their vital interests left them no alternative. And this was affirmed at the outset in quite unequivocal language by President Wilson himself. ' I have again and again stated,' he said, ' the very serious and long-continued wrongs which the Imperial German Government have perpetrated against the rights of commerce and the citizens of the United States. The list is long and overwhelming. No nation that respected itself or the rights of humanity could have borne these wrongs any longer.' [17]

I have insisted on these points in order to show that the elements of national self-respect, and still more perhaps of national self-interest, remain the most powerful forces in the field of international politics. After all, a nation is in its essence a group consciously separated from other groups by a vivid sense of its common and separate interests. The problem of preserving peace then remains, after as before, the old one of holding the balance between these groups ; and the problem of international organization is that of creating and keeping in order a mechanism by which this balance shall be kept steady. The task of the allied and associated nations at the present time, that is to say, is the same as that which confronted the Allied Powers at the Congress of Vienna and during the succeeding years ; and, though in many respects the conditions have changed, the problem remains essentially the same.

The original purpose of the lectures which formed the foundation of this book was to study the history of the European Coalition which succeeded to Napoleon's dictatorship in Europe, in order to see what light this threw on the feasibility of those peace projects to the

[16] *The Times*, December 5, 1918.   [17] *Ibid.*, May 24, 1917.

promulgation of which so great an impetus had been given by The Hague Conferences of 1899 and 1907. The acceptance by the Powers in conference in Paris of the Covenant of the League of Nations has once more seemed to give hope of the realization of the ideal of an international system for the preservation of peace. It is, then, still not without practical value, in helping to estimate the nature of the problems that will confront the League of Nations, to examine from this point of view the history of the period during which, in very similar circumstances, a serious effort was made to realize the same ideal.

The ideal itself is a very old one, and for centuries past men of good will have laboured for its realization. By way of introduction to my subject I propose to give a sketch of some of the more important 'projects of peace' which saw the light during the seventeenth and eighteenth centuries, and to show how these came to influence the mind of the Emperor Alexander and, through him, the counsels of Pitt and of the European Coalition.

II

EARLIER PROJECTS OF PEACE

The Truce of God—The ideal of the mediæval Empire—Rise of
the conception of States as sovereign and independent—The
Reason of State—Effect of the institution of permanent diplo-
matic agents—Development of International Law—Conception
of the European commonwealth based on a balance of power—
Projects for developing this into a true confederation for the
preservation of peace—Influence of the tradition of the Holy
Roman Empire—The Grand Design of Henry IV of France—
Éméric Crucé's 'Nouveau Cynée'—The project of the Abbé de
St. Pierre—Its relation to later peace projects—Criticisms of
Leibnitz, of Voltaire, and of Rousseau—Effect of the French
Revolution—Kant's 'Zum ewigen Frieden'—Saint-Simon on the
Holy Alliance.

IT is nine hundred years since the bishops of France,
justly shocked by the universal misery caused by the
never-ceasing feudal warfare, combined in establishing
the first league to enforce peace. The Truce of God,
as it was called from 1041 onward, was to be observed
on certain days of the week and during certain holy
seasons. All were to take an oath to observe it, under
penalty of anathema, and to compel others to do the
same. It is recorded that Bishop Gerard of Cambrai
at first opposed the plan, as likely to lead to perjury
rather than to peace.[18] His objections were overruled,
but the upshot fully justified his misgivings, and is
not without a moral for our own day. For, as the
chronicler sadly records, 'scarcely a very few escaped
the crime of perjury.'

[18] *Gesta pontificum Camaracensium*, ascribed to Baldric of Thérou-
anne, lib. iii. cap. 27, quoted in Du Cange, *Glossarium*, s.v. ' Treuga Dei.'

But though, in those turbulent times, all men—to quote a chronicler of somewhat later date [19]—were mad with warlike fury, the ideal of universal peace was never wholly lost to sight. Even during the anarchic period that followed the break-up of the Roman Empire the *pax romana* lived on as a memory and a hope ; and throughout the middle ages the Holy Roman Empire continued to represent in the world the principle of political unity. The world-dominion of the Empire existed, of course, only in theory, even in the days of its greatest power ; but the fact that the theory was consistently upheld and universally accepted at least preserved through long ages of savage conflict the ideal of a great European or Christian commonwealth. This ideal seemed to be finally shattered by the disruptive forces unloosed by the Reformation and the Renaissance, culminating in the Thirty Years' War. The new States which had been built up out of the ruins of the feudal system, intensely conscious of their separate interests, evolved a new theory to give a juridical sanction to their *de facto* independence—the theory of the State as self-sufficient and sovereign, i.e. supreme, both in its internal and its external relations. All idea of common obligation — to say nothing of a common allegiance—seemed to be lost. To the ' great and pacific Emperor,' reduced now to playing the most conspicuous part in a venerable but empty pageant, no more than an honorary precedence was given. For the rest, the States, big and little, arrogated to themselves all the prerogatives of the Roman *majestas* ; conceived themselves as placed by virtue of their supremacy above the moral law ; and, applying to the service of their own ambitions the ancient maxim *salus populi suprema lex*, proceeded to a ruthless prosecution of their own interests, wholly regardless of those of their neighbours, and justified aggressive war and an unscrupulous diplomacy by the plea of the *raison d'état*.

[19] Conrad Usperg, *anno* 1116, quoted in Du Cange.

So early as the sixteenth and seventeenth centuries,
however, during this war of all against all, forces were
at work which tended to develop new and more wholesome ideas as to the nature of the States system and
the mutual relations of its constituent members.   The
first of these was the gradual establishment of the system
by which sovereigns were represented at foreign courts
by accredited agents permanently resident.   It is true
that at the outset these agents were regarded as ' spies
rather than ambassadors,' and with much justification ;
but the existence of a permanent diplomacy, none the
less, tended to increase the sense of interdependence
between the States, while the negotiations conducted
through these regular channels led to the accumulation of
a mass of rules and precedents which served as materials
for the jurists who, during this period, were laying the
foundations of international law.   The second was the
exhaustion caused by the Thirty Years' War and the
object-lesson of the great Westphalian Congress by which,
in 1648, this war was concluded.   The work of the
Congress, indeed, dissolved for ever the illusion of the
universal Empire.   But it was the first time that the
representatives of many States had met together for a
great general purpose ;   the treaties concluded by it
seemed in some sort to be the code of a new law of nations ;
and there were many who saw in it the beginning of that
European commonwealth of which, in the darkest days,
the ideal had never been abandoned.

In the opinion of certain eighteenth-century theorists,
indeed, this European commonwealth had already
a substantial existence.   ' Europe,' wrote the jurist
Emerich de Vattel, ' constitutes a political system, a
body politic, in which everything is bound up together
by the relations and various interests of the nations
which inhabit this part of the world.   It is no longer, as
formerly, a confused mass of isolated pieces, of which
each one thought himself little interested in the fate
of the others, and rarely troubled about matters which

did not affect it immediately.   The continuous attention of the sovereigns, ministers permanently in residence, perpetual negotiations, make of modern Europe a sort of Republic, of which the members, independent yet bound together by ties of common interest, combine to preserve the order and freedom.   It is this that has given birth to that celebrated idea of the political equilibrium, or balance of power.' [20]   By the balance of power, he said, is understood such an arrangement of things that no Power is in a position to dominate over and give the law to the rest.

Friedrich von Gentz, writing half a century later under the influence of his passionate opposition to the spirit of French imperialism, went so far as to speak of the European States system of the eighteenth century as a ' confederacy,' united for certain common ends on certain well-defined principles.   ' The proper character of a union of States,' he said, ' such as has existed in modern Europe, and the triumph of its constitution, is that a certain number of States, possessing various degrees of power and wealth, shall remain untroubled within their own confines, under the protection of a common league.' He admitted, indeed, that the organization of this league was imperfect, owing to the absence of any central executive and judicial authority ; but he claimed that its objects had to a large extent been attained by the gradual development and consistent application of the principle of the balance of power, owing to which, during three troubled centuries, no one had succeeded in prescribing laws to Europe and ' the political constitution, as it was framed in the sixteenth century, remained so entire in all its members till the end of the eighteenth (when all ancient ordinances were abolished), that none of the independent powers, which originally belonged to the confederacy, had lost their political existence.' [21]   For the balance of power was not a question of the equalization

[20] *Droit des gens* (ed. 1758), livre iii. chap. 3, I. p. 40.
[21] *Fragments on the Balance of Power* (ed. 1806), p. 65.

of the power of States, but of a system by which ' the smallest as well as the greatest is secured in the possession of his right ' against ' lawless power.' If this system had been violently overthrown, this was due, in the first instance, to the betrayal of their trust by the Powers who had conspired to partition Poland, an act ' incomparably more destructive to the higher interests of Europe than previous acts of violence, because it originated in the very sphere from which was expected to flow nothing but benefits, namely, a union of regents.' [22]

Gentz's essay was, of course, a *pièce de circonstance*, directed to persuading the Powers to draw together against Napoleon, in order to restore in Europe the balance which he had overthrown. From our present point of view it is interesting less as an accurate presentation of the principles of eighteenth-century politics, which it can hardly be said to be, than as a proof of the persistence, not only among theorists but among men in close touch with affairs, of the idea of Europe as in some sense forming a political community. That it was not a complete body politic, in the sense of a fully-developed State, Gentz of course fully realized. ' Among independent nations,' he said, ' there is neither an executive nor a judicial power ; to create the one or the other has been long a fruitless, pious wish, and the object of many a vain, well-meaning effort.' Some of these efforts, which though vain exercised an influence which is not yet exhausted, I now propose to examine.

In view of what has been said of the age-long predominance of the idea of the Holy Roman Empire as the centre of political unity, it is the more strange, and perhaps the more significant, that the first of the long series of projects of perpetual peace—the Grand Design which Sully ascribes to Henry IV of France—was directed quite frankly, so far as it had any substance at all, *against* the Empire ; was, in fact, in its idea at least, little more than a strategical move in the secular conflict between

[22] *Fragments on the Balance of Power* (ed. 1806), p. 76.

France and Austria. Yet, though Sully says that its
realization would have dealt a mortal blow at the
Imperial authority,[23] the Emperor was to be the chief or
first magistrate of this new ' Christian Republic ' ; but,
in order to put an end to Habsburg dominance, he was
not to be chosen from the same house twice in succession.[24]
For the rest, the ' Grand Design,' which Sully says was
first suggested by Queen Elizabeth, was a singular anti-
cipation of certain modern developments. Italy, for
instance, was to be unified as a ' Republic of the Church '
under the Pope (one remembers Gioberti's dream), and
the dukes of Savoy were to become kings of Lombardy ;
while the independence of Belgium under a foreign
dynasty is foreshadowed by the singular idea that the
Low Countries should be carved into a series of fiefs for
English princes or ' milords.' [25]

As for the General Council of Europe, over which
the Emperor was to preside, this was to be modelled,
with certain necessary modifications, on the Amphictyonic Council of Greece, and to consist of a perpetual
Senate of sixty-four commissioners or plenipotentiaries,
four from each Great Power, two from each lesser Power,
renewable every three years. The function of this Senate
was to be to deliberate on affairs as they arose ; to discuss matters of common interest ; to settle disputes ;
to examine into and determine all civil, political, and
religious suits either in Europe itself or arising out of
the relations of Europe with the world outside.

Such was the Grand Design, which Sully recommended in language which anticipates that of the
rescript of the Emperor Nicholas II. ' He found the
secret of persuading all his neighbours that his only
object was to spare himself and them these immense
sums which it costs them to maintain so many thousands of fighting men, so many fortified places, and
other military expenses ; to deliver them for ever from

---

[23] Sully, *Mémoires* (ed. 1814), v. 31.   [24] *Ibid.* v. 303 *seq.*
[25] *Ibid.* v. 279 *seq.*

the fear of bloody catastrophes, so common in Europe ; to secure for them an unalterable repose, so that all the princes might henceforth live together as brothers.'

It is on this Grand Design that all other projects of peace, directly or indirectly, consciously or unconsciously, are based—from that which Éméric Crucé gave to the world under the title of ' Le Nouveau Cynée,' two years before Grotius published his ' De jure belli et pacis,' to the latest programme of the modern Peace Societies. It inspired the ' Projet de paix perpétuelle ' of the Abbé de St. Pierre, and through him the Emperor Alexander I's idea of a universal Holy Alliance. It may have played its part in forming the schemes of one whose name is not usually associated with projects of peace—Napoleon. Among the conversations of the great Emperor recorded by the Comte de Las Cases, in his ' Mémorial de Sainte Hélène,' is one in which Napoleon explains the grand design which had underlain all his policy. He had aimed, he said, at concentrating the great European peoples, divided hitherto by a multiplicity of artificial boundaries, into homogeneous nations, which he would have formed into a confederation bound together ' by unity of codes, principles, opinions, feelings, and interests.' At the head of the League, under the ægis of his Empire, was to have been a central assembly, modelled on the American Congress or the Amphictyonic Assembly of Greece, to watch over the common weal of ' the great European family.' Whether this plan had ever been seriously contemplated or not, it is easy to recognize in it the source of its inspiration.

The ' Projet de traité pour rendre la paix perpétuelle ' of the Abbé de St. Pierre was published in 1713, immediately after the signature of the Treaty of Utrecht. Its immediate effect was, of course, insignificant. The Abbé, Rousseau scornfully said, was trying to do by publishing a book what Henry IV had failed to do with the power of France behind him, and with the aid of the universal dread of Austrian ambitions, which supplied a stronger motive than any care for common interests. But the Abbé's project was destined to exert considerable practical influence later, and this gives to his proposals and to the comments of his critics a permanent interest.

The social order of Europe, he argues, is still largely determined by the passions rather than by reason. We are in civil relations with our fellow-citizens, but with the rest of the world we are in the state of nature. Thus we have only abolished private wars in order to set aflame general wars, which are a thousand times more terrible ; and in forming partial alliances we make ourselves in effect enemies of the human race. Now Christianity, he argues, has given to the nations of Europe, in religion, morals, and customs, and even in laws, the impress of a single society—to such a point that those peoples which, like the Turks, have become European in a geographical sense without becoming Christians, have been regarded as strangers ; and between the members of this Christian commonwealth ' the ancient image of the Roman Empire has continued to form a sort of bond.'

But the public law of Europe, not being established or authorized in concert, having no foundation of general principle, and varying incessantly in different times and places, is full of contradictory rules, which can only be reconciled by the right of the stronger. Now, every society is based on a consciousness of common interests, while all divisions are caused by interests that are opposed, and both common and private interests may vary with a thousand changes of circumstance. In every society, then, it is necessary that there should be a coercive power to command and concert the movements of its members, and to form a solid and durable European confederation it would be necessary to place all its constituent states in such a condition of mutual dependence that no one of them should be in a position to resist the rest. If, under the system of the Balance of Power, states are limited in their opportunities for aggression, what would their position be when there is a great armed league, ever ready to prevent those who might wish to destroy or resist it ?   Such a league would not waste its time in idle deliberations, but would form an effective power, able to force the ambitious to keep within the terms of the general treaty.

The nucleus or model of such a league was already in existence in the ' Germanic Body,' as constituted by the Treaty of Westphalia—the ' conservative force of Europe,' since it was strong for defence but powerless for attack. Now since the Treaty of Westphalia was the basis of the European system—the Abbé argued —German public law was in a sense that of all Europe. His project was then, in effect, to remodel Europe somewhat on the lines of the Empire as it was after 1648. Its provisions are as follows :

1. The sovereigns are to contract a perpetual and irrevocable alliance, and to name plenipotentiaries to hold, in a determined spot, a permanent diet or congress, in which all differences between the contracting parties are to be settled by arbitration or judicial decision.

2. The number of the sovereigns sending plenipotentiaries to the congress is to be specified, together with those who are to be invited to accede to the treaty. The presidency of the congress is to be exercised by the sovereigns in turn at stated intervals, the order of rotation and term of office being carefully defined. In like manner the quota to be contributed by each to the common fund, and its method of collection, are to be carefully defined.

3. The Confederation thus formed is to guarantee to each of its members the sovereignty of the territories it actually possesses, as well as the succession, whether hereditary or elective, according to the fundamental laws of each country. To avoid disputes, actual possession and the latest treaties are to be taken as the basis of the mutual rights of the contracting Powers, while all future disputes are to be settled by arbitration of the Diet.

4. The Congress is to define the cases which would involve offending states being put under the ban of Europe.

5. The Powers are to agree to arm and take the offensive, in common and at the common expense, against any state thus banned, until it shall have submitted to the common will.

6. The plenipotentiaries in congress, on instructions from their sovereigns, shall have power to make such rules as they shall judge important with a view to securing for the European Republic and each of its members all possible advantages.

It is impossible to examine this project without being struck by the fact that there is scarcely one of its provisions which does not emerge, at least as a subject of debate among the Powers, during the years of European reconstruction after 1814. This fact is, perhaps, not the least striking on what may be called its negative side. In the Abbé de St. Pierre's project there is no provision made for even an honorary pre-eminence of the Emperor ; there is also no provision made for any representation other than that of the sovereigns. From this vision of perpetual peace the venerable phantom of the Holy Empire has vanished all but completely ; this churchman and apostle of international union has as little use as the Powers of the Grand Alliance for ' the centre of political unity,' against the abolition of which at the Congress of Vienna Cardinal Consalvi was to protest in the name of the Roman Church. He knows nothing too of nationality as the term came to be understood in the nineteenth century ; for him, as later for Metternich, a ' nation ' is but the aggregate of people bound together by allegiance to a common sovereign—a conception which, I may add, would greatly facilitate the establishment of an international system, did it but answer to the facts. Of popular rights, as developed by the Revolution, he of course knew nothing.

Apart from the generally contemptuous reception which the Abbé's project met with in that age of machiavellian statecraft, the omissions above noted met with particular criticism during the eighteenth century. Leibnitz, to whom the Abbé submitted his scheme, held that in its general idea it was both feasible and desirable. He had, he said, seen similar proposals made in the ' Nouveau Cynée ' and in a book by the Landgrave Ernest of Hesse-Rheinfels entitled ' Le Catholique discret ' ; and Henry IV, though his scheme was aimed at Austria, had clearly believed it to be practicable. For Leibnitz, however, the subordination of the Empire was a serious blot. It had been a maxim of international law for centuries that the Emperor was the temporal head of Christendom, and jurisconsults had reasoned on this basis. The Empire had become weak, partly owing to the Reformation, partly owing to the alienation of its revenues and its consequent incapacity to enforce the decisions of the courts. But the dignity and pre-cedence of the Emperor survived, and he still possessed some rights of direction in Christendom. ' I do not think it would be just,' he says, ' to destroy all at once the authority of the Roman Empire, which has lasted so many centuries. . . . Jurisconsults know that one does not lose one's rights, nor even their possession, because there has been no occasion to exercise them ; and that it is not necessary even to insist on them, save where those who owe these rights declare that they wish to repudiate their obligation.' [26]

He goes on to point out certain respects in which the system of the Empire is superior to that suggested by St. Pierre. The Tribunal of the Imperial Chamber (*Reichskammergericht*), for instance, consists of judges and assessors who are free to follow their consciences, not being bound by the instructions of the princes and states which nominated them. Moreover, in the Abbé's project there is no provision for the hearing of the com-plaints of subjects against their sovereigns, while in the

[26] *Observations sur le projet de paix. Œuvres*, t. 4, p. 328 (Paris, 1832).

Empire subjects can plead against their princes or their magistrates.

The comment of Leibnitz is interesting because it anticipates the objection which, a hundred years later, Castlereagh considered fatal to the system of guarantees, precisely similar to that suggested in the third article of St. Pierre's project, which the reactionary Powers sought to formulate at Aix-la-Chapelle and did formulate in the Troppau Protocol. The Abbé de St. Pierre pointed out how the proposals in this article would not weaken but strengthen the princes, by guaranteeing to each of them ' not only their states against all foreign invasion, but also their authority against all rebellions of their subjects.' In a Memorandum on the Treaties presented to the Powers at Aix-la-Chapelle, Castlereagh wrote :

The idea of an *Alliance Solidaire* by which each state shall be bound to support the state of succession, government and possession within all other states from violence and attack, upon condition of receiving for itself a similar guarantee, must be understood as morally implying the previous establishment of such a system of general government as may secure and enforce upon all kings and nations an internal system of peace and justice. Till the mode of constructing such a system shall be devised, the consequence is inadmissible, as nothing could be more immoral, or more prejudicial to the character of government generally, than the idea that their force was collectively to be prostituted to the support of established power, without any consideration of the extent to which it was abused.

In writing this, Castlereagh was unconsciously repeating and expanding a comment on the Abbé's third article made long before by Rousseau, who in his ' Jugement sur la paix perpétuelle ' had written :

One cannot guarantee princes against the revolt of their subjects without at the same time guaranteeing subjects against the tyranny of princes. Otherwise the institution could not possibly survive.

With Rousseau we come to the eve of the Revolutionary age ; universal peace is to be the outcome, not of a fraternal union of princes, but of the brotherhood of an enlightened humanity. ' The " Projet de paix perpétuelle,"' Voltaire wrote, ' is absurd, not in itself, but in the manner of its proposal.' ' The peace imagined by the Abbé de St. Pierre is a chimera, which will not subsist between princes any more than between elephants and rhinoceroses, between wolves and dogs. Carnivorous animals will always tear each other to pieces at the first opportunity.' Wars of ambition will cease when the mass of people realize that it is only a few generals and ministers who have anything to gain by them ; wars of commerce will cease with the universal establishment of free trade ; wars of religion with the spread of the spirit of tolerance. As for questions of succession, these are for the people to decide. ' The establishment of a European Diet,' he continues, ' might be very useful for deciding controversies about the extradition of criminals or the laws of commerce, or for settling the principles on which cases in which the laws of different nations are invoked should be decided. The sovereigns should concert a code according to which such disputes would be settled, and should engage to submit to its decisions or to the final arbitrament of their sword :—the necessary condition for the establishment, durability, and usefulness of such a tribunal. It is possible to persuade a prince, who commands two hundred thousand men, that it is not to his interest to defend his rights or his pretensions by force; but it is absurd to propose to him to renounce them.' [27] Elsewhere Voltaire asks : ' What is necessary in order to govern men, one's brothers (and what brothers !), by right ? ' And he answers : ' The free consent of the peoples.' [28]

[27] *De la Paix perpétuelle. Œuvres*, t. 29 (1785 ed.), note.
[28] ' Pour gouverner de droit ses frères, les hommes (et quels frères !), que faut-il ? Le consentement libre des peuples.'—*Les Droits des hommes et les usurpations des papes. Œuvres*, t. 29, p. 76.

The outbreak of the French Revolution, then—as the triumph of popular forces over those of the divine right of kings—was hailed by many as heralding the dawn of an era of universal peace. A single quotation may serve to illustrate a widespread hope which was destined to be so utterly belied. At a meeting of the Revolution Society to celebrate the first anniversary of the capture of the Bastille, Dr. Price—the first object of Burke's attack in the 'Reflections'—thus apostrophized the leaders of the French Revolution : ' O heavenly philanthropists, well do you deserve the admiration, not only of your own country, but of all countries ! You have already determined to renounce for ever all views of conquest and all offensive wars. This is an instance of wisdom and attention to human rights which has no example. But you will do more ; you will invite Great Britain to join you in this determination and to enter into a compact with you for promoting peace on earth, good will among men. . . . Thus united the two kingdoms will be omnipotent. They will soon draw into their confederation Holland and other countries on this side of the globe, the United States of America on the other,' and so on.[29]

Five years later, in 1795, Immanuel Kant published his treatise ' On Perpetual Peace ' (*Zum ewigen Frieden*), an essay in the construction of an international system on a philosophical basis. This basis he finds in the development of enlightened self-interest among the peoples and the growth of the moral idea, which has already made men open to the influence of the mere conception of law, as though this in itself possessed physical power. Perpetual peace will thus, he argues, ultimately be guaranteed by nature itself, through the mechanism inherent in human inclinations. ' Seek first,' he says, ' the kingdom of pure practical reason and its justice, and your goal (the benefit of perpetual peace) will be added unto you of itself.'

But this moral idea and this pure practical reason

[29] Morgan's *Life of Price*, pp. 161-63.

can, in Kant's opinion, only be developed fully under republican institutions, because the people will never vote for war ! His practical suggestions for an international organization, therefore, include these articles :

1. The civil constitution in every state is to be republican. But this republicanism is not to be` democracy, which is opposed to liberty. The true republican government is representative.

2. The law of nations is to be established on a federation of free states. Such a great federal republic, if once established, would gradually attract other states and so ultimately include all.[30]

It is perhaps not wholly without significance that a French translation of Kant's treatise was published at Paris in 1814 during the first occupation by the Allies. It is also interesting to note that in this same year was published the ' Réorganisation de la Société européenne ' of the Comte de Saint-Simon, who later on was to proclaim his appreciation of the benefit conferred upon Europe by the Holy Alliance. The language in which he does so is, I think, worth quoting here. In the third of his ' Opinions philosophiques à l'usage du XIXme siècle,' he writes :

The interests and the most widespread opinion of Europe called upon the kings to unite, in order to exercise the supreme direction over the social interests of Europe. In order that the transition from the feudal regime to the industrial system might take place in a peaceful manner, it was necessary that a supreme power should be established. The Holy Alliance fulfils this condition to perfection ; it dominates all spiritual and temporal powers. . . . Finally, thanks to the formation of the Holy Alliance, European society is in a position to reorganize itself very securely, from the moment that a clear public opinion shall have been formed as to the institutions which correspond to the present state of its civilization.[31]

[30] *Zum ewigen Frieden. Werke*, Band 6 (1868 ed.), p. 408 *seq.*

[31] *Quelques opinions philosophiques. Œuvres de Saint-Simon*, t. 39, pp. 100, 101 (Paris, 1875).

THE PEACE PROJECT OF ALEXANDER I
OF RUSSIA

Its probable inspiration—Novosiltsov's mission to England in 1804—
His instructions—Scheme for European reconstruction and a
European Confederation—Reply of Pitt—His remarks on the pro-
posed 'general system of public law'—The proposal embodied
in the Anglo-Russian Treaty of 1805—The common danger from
France—The principle of collective intervention—Circular of
Kaunitz, 1791—Burke's view.

PROJECTS of peace, then, were clearly in the air during
the War of Liberation, and played their part in disposing
men's minds to hope at least for a ' silver age ' as the
outcome of the European Alliance against the common
enemy, a hope which was encouraged by the language
of the proclamations to the peoples issued by the Powers,
from the moment when, in 1813, Alexander of Russia
crossed the borders of his Empire and offered to all the
peoples who should abandon the cause of Napoleon his
disinterested assistance.

Were these proclamations entirely hypocritical ?
Was there in the Tsar's mind no idea but that of throwing
dust in the eyes of the nations and using them as the
blind agents of his own ambitions ? Of Alexander's
enigmatical character I shall have a good deal more to
say later. He was a creature of impulse, imaginative,
impressionable, egoistic, vain, capable of large generosities
—so that the credit were his. The Grand Design of
Henry IV was eminently fitted to appeal to his soaring

imagination ; nor is it difficult to see how he may have come to harbour the thought of reviving it. The works of Rousseau, which he had studied under La Harpe's guidance, contained an elaborate exposition and criticism of the Project of the Abbé de St. Pierre. Now Rousseau's main objection to this project was that the means suggested by its author for putting it into practice were ' childish ' ; the plan, he argued, was absurd ' without a Henry IV or a Sully to carry it out.' The whole circumstances of the time, at the beginning of Alexander's reign, recalled those which had first evoked the idea of a federated Europe. The peril was no longer from Austria, it is true, but from France ; from that very France of the political *philosophes* to which the young Alexander had looked to aid him in establishing the universal sway of enlightenment. In 1802 La Harpe had returned from Paris and had presented to the Tsar his ' Reflections on the Consulship for Life.' ' The veil has fallen ! ' replied Alexander ; ' Napoleon is no true patriot. He himself has stripped himself of his best glory, which may prove fatal to him, a glory which alone it remained for him to acquire, that of proving that, setting aside all personal views, he was working solely for the honour and glory of his country and remaining loyal to the Constitution to which he himself took the oath, by resigning after ten years the authority which was in his hands. Instead of this, he has preferred to ape a Court in addition to violating the Constitution of his country.'[32] The murder of the Duc d'Enghien confirmed this opinion ; the Russian Court went into mourning, and broke off diplomatic relations with Paris. Then came the proclamation of Napoleon as Emperor of the French, and the decision of Russia to go to war, not indeed against France, but against Napoleon. The Third Coalition was in process of formation. It was, then, natural that Alexander

[32] Shilder, *Imperator Aleksander I*, iii. 117, cf. note 186. The letter, dated July 7, 1813, is given in full in the Grand Duke Nicholas Mikhailovich's *L'Empereur Alexandre Ier* (1912), i. 336.

should see a vision of himself as another Henry IV, with his friend Czartoryski as his Sully, realizing the grand design of converting the temporary alliance against France into a permanent Christian Republic, with himself, of course, as the arbiter of its destinies.

The idea was embodied in instructions addressed, on September 11, 1804, by Alexander to his friend Nikolai Nikolaievich Novosiltsov, envoy on special mission to London, who was to lay it before Pitt.[33]   The document, which was drawn up by Czartoryski and is printed in his 'Memoirs,' is too long to quote in full ; but, though it has often been quoted in part,[34] it is so important for the development of my thesis that I shall deal with it somewhat at length.

An absolute condition, the Tsar wrote, of any cordial union between Russia and England for the overthrow of Napoleon was that it should not lead to any set-back to humanity. The Governments were to agree not to re-establish ancient abuses in the countries liberated from the yoke of Bonaparte, but were to study to ensure them liberty based upon sound foundations. 'It is on this principle,' the Tsar said, 'that, according to my ideas, the Powers should act, and their conduct, their language, and their proclamations should consistently conform to it.'

He goes on to outline his plan for the reconstitution of Europe. The King of Sardinia should be restored to his dominions, and should have additions made to them, the Powers at the same time engaging him to grant a Constitution to his peoples. Switzerland ·was to be re-established and enlarged, with a Constitution adapted to the localities and conformable to the will of

[33] The Grand Duke (*op. cit.* p. 38) says that there is no evidence in the archives as to who inspired this mission, ' which left Czartoryski and Novosiltsov sceptical.'   It was, he says, probably Alexander's own idea, and the first evidence of independent action on his part in foreign affairs.

[34] Tatishchev, *Alexandre Ier et Napoléon*, 1801–1812, pp. 82, 84, 85 ; *Cambridge Modern History*, x. 3.   Curiously enough, it is not mentioned by Shilder.

the inhabitants.   Holland was to be made independent, under an hereditary Stadtholder with powers constitutionally limited.   As for France, it was to be made clear that the Allies were not at war with the French nation, but only with Napoleon, and that their object was to liberate France from the yoke under which she had so long groaned, and to leave her free to choose the government she might desire.   This government, indeed, must be monarchical, but whether under a Bourbon or any other dynasty was indifferent.

As to the forms of government to be established in the various countries, the only definite principle that could be laid down was that ' everywhere they must be founded on the sacred rights of humanity.'

The principles enunciated by him as the basis of the intimate concert between the two Powers, the only ones, perhaps, on which the power of France could be restrained within its just limits, would also singularly contribute towards fixing on firm and lasting foundations the future peace of Europe.   ' It seems to me,' wrote the Tsar, ' that this great aim cannot be looked upon as attained until, on the one hand, the nations have been attached to their governments by making these incapable of acting save in the greatest interest of the peoples subject to them, and, on the other, the relations of states to each other have been fixed on more precise rules, and such as it is to their mutual interest to respect.   The conclusions of profound thinkers and the experience of centuries sufficiently prove that these two results cannot be attained save when internal order shall have been founded on a wise liberty, which seems to consolidate the governments, surrounding them with a barrier against the passions, the unbridled ambition, or the madness which often drives out of their senses the men at their head ; and when at the same time the law of nations, which regulates the relations of the European Confederation, shall have been re-established on true principles.'

' If Europe be saved, the union of the two Government which has achieved these great results ought to last on, in order to preserve and augment them. Nothing would prevent, at the conclusion of peace, a treaty being arranged, which would become the basis of the reciprocal relations of the European states. It is no question of realizing the dream of perpetual peace, but one could attain at least to some of its results if at the conclusion of the general war, one could establish on clear, precise principles the prescriptions of the rights of nations. Why could one not submit to it the positive rights of nations, assure the privilege of neutrality, insert the obligation of never beginning war until all the resources which the mediation of a third party could offer have been exhausted, until the grievances have by this means been brought to light, and an effort to remove them has been made? On principles such as these one could proceed to a general pacification, and give birth to a league, of which the stipulations would form, so to speak, a new code of the law of nations, which, sanctioned by the greater part of the nations of Europe, would without difficulty become the immutable rule of the cabinets, while those who should try to infringe it would risk bringing upon themselves the forces of the new union.'

Particularly significant of future developments in the Emperor's policy are his references to the Ottoman Empire. ' It is impossible to deny,' he says, ' that its weakness, the anarchy of its régime, and the growing discontent of its Christian subjects, are so many elements tending to encourage speculative ambitions, and are diametrically opposed to the principles which have been advanced in these instructions as the only ones capable of securing a stable peace in Europe.' He urges that, in the event of Turkey joining France, the two Powers should concert beforehand what was to be done with the Ottoman territories, if their joint attack should succeed in overthrowing the Turkish Empire.

The least that should be done would be to secure a more tolerable existence for the Christian peoples who groaned under Turkish tyranny.

Significant, too, is Alexander's suggestion that, after the conclusion of peace, the two Powers should continue a certain degree of preponderance in the affairs of Europe, as being ' the only ones who by their position are invariably interested in the reign there of order and justice, the only ones who by their position can maintain it, and, being free from conflicting desires and interests, will never trouble this happy tranquillity.'

I have dwelt on these instructions at such length because we have in them the final link in the chain of cause and effect connecting the Holy Alliance with the projects of peace of the seventeenth and eighteenth centuries. In them we have suggested all the elements of the European system as established at the Peace of Paris and the Congress of Vienna. In the Tsar's communication these elements, it is true, are somewhat vaguely defined and somewhat ideally coloured. A clearer definition and a more immediately practical application was given to them by Pitt in a note of January 19, 1805, in response to these overtures.

He begins by expressing his satisfaction that the views of the Emperor in respect of the deliverance of Europe and of its future peace and security agree entirely with those of His Britannic Majesty. This being so, His Majesty is anxious, with a view to a close concert, to enter into the frankest explanations, with a view to forming with the Russian Emperor a union of such a nature as to induce the other great military Powers to join it. For this purpose it is necessary to define as clearly as possible the objects at which this concert is directed. These he divides into three main groups : (1) To release from the domination of France the territories conquered since the Revolution ; (2) to form out of the countries thus released, with due regard to their peace and happiness, a barrier against future

French aggression ; (3) to establish, after the restoration of peace, a convention and guarantee for the mutual protection and security of the different Powers, and to establish in Europe a general system of public law.

Of these objects the first was, of course, for Pitt the most immediately important, though it need not detain us. The second also, he said, contained matter for more than one important consideration. The countries taken from France ought, as far as possible, to be restored to their ancient rights, and regard ought to be had to establishing the well-being of their inhabitants ; but the general security should not be lost sight of, and on this even this particular object ought to depend. It is at this point that the views expressed by Pitt and by the Emperor Alexander diverge, and in a way significant of future developments. On the question of a barrier against future French aggressions both were agreed, and also on the nature of this barrier, such as a restored and strengthened Holland, and an accession of territory to the Crown of Sardinia. But the Tsar, with Poland in his mind, had put forward the modern principle of nationality in his scheme, contending that in any rearrangement of Europe consideration should be given to the question of homogeneity of population as well as to that of natural boundaries. This Pitt simply ignores, putting forward the purely conservative principle of a restoration of ancient rights.[35] This principle it would be possible, however, to apply only in some cases ; for some states had been too utterly crushed out, and others were too weak to re-establish, and he suggests a territorial settlement which anticipated that actually made at Vienna, the main features being the creation or strengthening of the Netherlands and

[35] This accounts for Czartoryski's condemnation of Novosiltsov's weakness in not insisting on the ' just demands ' of Russia and abandoning affairs to take the direction which England desired (*Mem.* i. 376). That the mission was not so fruitless as the Grand Duke Nicholas Mikhailovich supposes (*op. cit.* i. 38) I hope to show.

Savoy as barrier states against France, the establishment of Prussian power on the Rhine, and the augmenta-
tion of Austrian power in Italy, at the expense of the
weaker German and Italian states respectively.

Most interesting, however, from our present point
of view, are Pitt's remarks on the third proposal. Much,
he says, will have been done for the repose of Europe
by the carrying out of the proposed territorial rearrange-
ments, but ' in order to make this security as perfect
as possible, it seems necessary that at the time of the
general pacification a treaty should be concluded, in
which all the principal European Powers should take
part, by which their possessions and their respective
rights, as then established, should be fixed and recognized ; and these Powers should all engage reciprocally
to protect and support each other against all attempts
to violate it. This treaty would give to Europe a general
system of public law and would aim at repressing, as
far as possible, future attempts to trouble the general
tranquillity, and above all to defeat every project of
aggrandizement and ambition, such as those which
have produced all the disasters by which Europe has
been afflicted since the unhappy era of the French
Revolution.' [36]

The first ' separate and secret ' article of the Treaty
of April 11, 1805, between Russia and Great Britain
embodied these views in a formal engagement. ' Their
Majesties,' it ran, ' who take the most lively interest
in the discussion and precise definition of the law of
nations and in the guarantee of its observance by general
consent and by the establishment in Europe of a federa-
tive system, to ensure the independence of the weaker
states by erecting a formidable barrier against the

---

[36] Comte de Garden, *Histoire générale des traités de paix*, viii. 323.
Garden did not know of the instructions to Novosiltsov, and he therefore ascribes to Pitt the suggestion that the peace should be followed
by the establishment of a European system for mutual guarantee of
possessions. M. Muhlenbeck (*Sainte-Alliance*, p. 328) refers to Garden,
but also says nothing of Novosiltsov's mission.

ambition of the more powerful, will come to an amicable understanding among themselves as to whatever may concern these objects, and will form an intimate union for the purpose of realizing their happy effects.' [37]

Thus Pitt committed himself to the Grand Design. That in doing so his mind was preoccupied by the immediate peril from France is clear ; and in this he was but following precedent. It was this which, according to Sorel, had given birth to the idea of the Concert of Europe in the circular letter of July 17, 1791, in which Count Kaunitz had impressed upon the Imperial ambassadors the duty of all the Powers to make common cause for the purpose of preserving ' public peace, the tranquillity of states, the inviolability of possessions, and the faith of treaties,' and had based his appeal on the fact that the nations of Europe, united by ties of religion, institutions, and culture, formed but a single family.[38] It was in the Declaration of Pillnitz, inspired by the same motive, and issued in 1792 by the Emperor Leopold and King Frederick William of Prussia, that, in 1821, the Abbé de Pradt was to see the ' first germ ' of the Holy Alliance.[39] Finally, it was the peril from France which, in 1796, had inspired Burke to find a juridical basis for the principle of European intervention.[40] How far Pitt would have gone in the attempt to realize

[37] F.O. Treaties, Ser. 1, No. 217. The French text is printed in Holland Rose's *Select Despatches . . . relating to the Third Coalition against France*, Appendix, p. 273. Compare Art. 2 of the Convention of Bartenstein of April 26, 1807, between Russia and Prussia : ' Rendre à l'humanité les bienfaits d'une paix générale et solide, établie sur la base d'un état de possession enfin assuré à chaque puissance et mis sous la garantie de toutes, voilà le but de la guerre ' (Garden, *op. cit.* x. 405).

[38] *L'Europe et la Révolution française*, ii. 232. Compare Burke, *Letters on a Regicide Peace*, ii. *Works* (ed. 1887), v. 344.

[39] *L'Europe et l'Amérique en 1821* (Paris, 1822).

[40] ' *Vicini vicinorum facta præsumuntur scire.* The principle, which . . . is true of nations as of individual men, has bestowed on the grand vicinage of Europe a duty to know and a right to prevent any capital innovation which may amount to the erection of a dangerous nuisance ' (*Letters on a Regicide Peace*, i. *Works* (ed. 1887), v. 323).

the Confederation of Europe, with the principle of intervention necessary to its maintenance, it is perhaps idle to speculate. The Third Coalition was shattered at Austerlitz, and Pitt's dying thoughts were not of Europe but of his country. It is probable that, had he lived to take the lead in the rearrangement of Europe after Napoleon's fall, he would have followed much the same course as Castlereagh, who carried on the tradition of his policy with a courage and a constancy equal to his own. He would certainly have found, as did Castlereagh, that the principle of the European union of guarantee was calculated to produce more and greater evils than it cured, and that even the blessing of peace may be too dearly bought at the price of liberty.

II

THE BIRTH OF THE CON-
FEDERATION

The time will come when treaties shall be
more than truces, when it will again be
possible for them to be observed with that
religious faith, that sacred inviolability, on
which depend the reputation, the strength,
and the preservation of empires.—Preamble
to the Treaty of Kalisch.

I

THE EMPEROR ALEXANDER I

Czartoryski and Polish nationalism—Influence on Alexander's project —Alexander falls from grace—Friedland and Tilsit—Napoleon and Alexander—Effect of the campaign of 1812—Character of Alexander—His education—Influence of La Harpe—' Jacobin ' views of the young Alexander—Plans for a democratic Russia— Influence of Paul I's militarism—Effect on him of Paul's murder —His religious mysticism—Religious character of the age—The coming millennium—Influence of Golitsin and Koshelev—Effect on Alexander of the burning of Moscow—Napoleon as ' the Beast ' —Alexander's mission as the world's peace-maker—He crosses the Niemen.

CZARTORYSKI in his ' Memoirs ' says that his object in putting forward the principles embodied in the instructions to Novosiltsov was to conciliate the traditional Russian policy of aggrandizement with generous ideas, by making the Russian passion for glory and supremacy serve the purposes of the general good of humanity. ' My wish was,' he says, ' that Alexander should become in some sort the arbiter of peace for the civilized world ; the protector of the weak and oppressed ; the guardian of international justice ; that his reign should begin a new era in international politics ; politics henceforth based on the general good and on the rights of all and each.' [1]

The scheme was, he adds, stillborn. It was, indeed, by its very remoteness, calculated to captivate Alexander, who delighted in giving free play to

[1] *Mémoires*, i. 370.

his imagination and in forming all sorts of plans, so long as there was no immediate necessity to realize them, and loved general principles and the terms in which they were expressed, without ever going deep into the practical issues involved. But Alexander was the only man in his empire capable of adopting such a plan from conviction. The influence of Czartoryski might carry him a certain distance ; but, this influence removed, he would be isolated among counsellors who, like the future Chancellor Rumyantsev, had from the first protested against the breach with France and the ' moral ' motive that underlay it. Under these circumstances the disastrous rout of Friedland, and the politic generosity of Napoleon at Tilsit, were enough to turn Alexander's mind from his dream of becoming the arbiter of the peace of Europe to that other dream—which the unhappy Paul I had already cherished —of dividing with Napoleon the empire of the world. A vision so dazzling awakened in him the purely personal ambition, latent in his very blood, of which he had hitherto been unconscious. In the contemplation of his new greatness the interests of Europe were forgotten. ' What is Europe ? ' he said to Savary, the French ambassador ; ' what is it, if it be not you and we ? ' [2]

It is not necessary for our purpose to say more than a few words about the eventful history of the five following years, culminating in Napoleon's invasion of Russia in 1812. After 1807 Czartoryski was no longer Minister of Foreign Affairs ; and though he retained Alexander's friendship, there was little use in reminding a sovereign who—as Bismarck said later of the Emperor William I —had ' acquired a taste for conquest ' by the annexation of Finland, of his European mission or of the claim of oppressed nationalities to his protection. In his relations with Napoleon, Alexander learnt the truth of the proverb that ' who sups with the devil needs a

[2] Savary to Napoleon, November 18, 1807. In Tatishchev, *Alexandre Ier et Napoléon*, p. 239.

long spoon ' ; but it was not—to use his own phrase—
till his soul had found illumination by the burning of
Moscow that he realized the full enormity of his back-
sliding in entering into this unholy alliance with the
' Demon of Revolution.' Who shall gauge, in that
medley of motives which at this supreme crisis determined Alexander's attitude, the exact force of each ?
To Alexander himself, when he made the confession to
Bishop Eylert which I have just quoted, the religious
motive seemed uppermost ; amid the horrors of the
war the call of God had been plain, bidding him
assume once more the trust to which he had been false
—that of using his power to establish the empire of
peace. But how far was this an afterthought ?—the
outcome of hours of morbid brooding over the Bible,
night by night, during the pursuit of the broken army
of France over the pitiless snows ? There was no hint
of Christian charity in his attitude when first he realized
the desperate plight of the Grand Army : nothing but
a sense of the outrage to Holy Russia and the insult
to himself, which called for vengeance. Napoleon, in
his desperation, had stooped to write a letter in which
he appealed to any remnants of Alexander's former
sentiments. To these ' fanfaronnades ' he returned no
answer, and to Colonel Michaud, who brought to him
the news of the abandonment and burning of Moscow,
he declared his intention of continuing the struggle even
if his armies perished and he were forced to lead a guerilla
war of his peasants. ' Napoleon or I, I or he : we cannot longer reign together. I have learned to know him ;
he shall never deceive me again. . . .' [3]

[3] Count Michaud's letter describing the scene (dated July 1819) is
given in Shilder, iii. 509.

To the Prince Regent Alexander wrote (September 19, 1812) that he
would rather be crushed under the ruins of his empire than make
peace with this modern Attila, who, ' furious at not having found in
Moscow either the riches which he coveted or the peace which he
had hoped to dictate, had burned this fair city, reducing it to a mass
of ashes and ruins ' (Shilder, iii. 510).

The ruin of the Grand Army had in effect made Alexander the arbiter of Europe, and all Europe was watching anxiously to see what use he would make of his power. Would he use it, as his predecessors would have done, solely to his own greater glory and the aggrandizement of his Empire ? Or would he, now that he was conscious of the responsibility that rested upon him, rise to the height of his earlier professions and see his greatest glory in establishing the universal reign of liberty and justice, and the true interests of Russia in maintaining her due weight, and no more, in the balance of the nations ? The answer to these questions, never clear in the experiences of the years that followed, nor even yet in most opinions formed about the Tsar's policy, lay deep in the fundamental contradictions of Alexander's character. This it is necessary, not indeed to understand, for that would puzzle the high gods, but in some measure to mirror in our minds, if we are to follow with intelligence the debates in the inner councils of Europe during the years to come. I propose, then, to digress awhile from my main theme in order to attempt to throw some light on this.

Physically Alexander took after his mother, the beautiful Empress Maria Feodorovna ; there is not a trace in his portraits of likeness to the repulsive face and diminutive figure of his father, the ill-fated Paul I, though in certain of their mental qualities father and son were not unlike. Very interesting, too, is the comparison between the portraits of the youthful Alexander and those of the young Napoleon. The Russian Emperor's gigantic frame is surmounted by a round, almost chubby face, with kindly, dreamy eyes, and a weak, smiling, sensuous mouth—in the greatest possible contrast to the eagle-beaked hatchet face, with the fierce eyes and close-pressed lips, of the young Bonaparte as David drew him for us. If these two met, it is easy to see which would impress his personality on the other.

Alexander, in fact, was above all impressionable and receptive, and it is for this reason that a knowledge of his early environment is so important for the comprehension of his later policy ; since it is to the influences that surrounded him as a boy, as well as to his innate disposition, that his idiosyncrasies may be traced.

The education of the Grand Dukes Alexander and Constantine had been taken by the Empress Catherine II entirely out of the hands of her heir, the Grand Duke Paul.   But though the old Empress looked to her grandson Alexander to carry on her policy, and even meditated excluding Paul from the succession in his favour, she did nothing to initiate him into the conduct of practical affairs. Her choice of tutors for the lads did little to repair this omission.   Chief of them was Prince Nicholas Soltikov, a former lover of the Empress, who, though he took his charge seriously enough, was neither by character nor endowments equal to its proper discharge.   Of the others, Protosov, while his daily reports show that he followed with a conscientiousness almost pedantic the progress of his pupil, had, according to Czartoryski, no sort of influence over him, while Muraviev, though a man of excellent intentions, was too timid to impress either his personality or his ideas on the two high-spirited lads.

The only one who was in the least fitted for his place was Frédéric César de La Harpe, who had come to Russia in 1782 on the recommendation of Melchior Grimm to act as tutor to the younger brother of Lanskoy, the Empress Catherine's favourite of the moment.[4]   La Harpe, says Czartoryski, ' belonged to the generation of men nourished on the illusions of the end of the eighteenth century, who believed that their doctrine, a new philosopher's stone, a universal remedy, explained everything, and that sacramental phrases were enough to cause every kind of difficulty in practice to disappear.'[5]   He was, in short, a *philosophe* and a prig, the last person in the world

[4] La Harpe, *Le Gouverneur d'un prince*, p. 9.
[5] *Mémoires*, ii. 272.

to do anything to remedy the gaps in Alexander's education due to Catherine's jealous exclusion of him from practical affairs. But such as he was he succeeded in exercising over the imaginative boy an empire which was destined to survive the most singular vicissitudes. Even his excursions in practical Jacobinism during the Revolution in Paris and in Switzerland did not discredit him in Alexander's eyes. At the outset of Alexander's reign he appeared at the court of St. Petersburg swaggering in his uniform sash and huge sabre as a member of the Swiss Directorate, to contribute interminable dissertations to the counsels of the young Emperor's secret committee of reform ; he appeared again, to the great disconcertment of the Allies, at the Tsar's side during the advance on Paris in 1814 and at the Congress of Vienna. To the last Alexander proclaimed the obligations under which he lay to him for his influence and his teaching.[6]

This influence and teaching had been directed to turning the young Cesarevich out a very gentle, complete, and perfect Jacobin, an imperial apostle of the new gospel of humanity. ' Providence,' La Harpe wrote later, ' seemed at last to have taken compassion on the millions of people who inhabit Russia ; but a Catherine was necessary who was willing to have her grandsons brought up as men.' [7] And the education of a man meant, of course, education in the principles of Rousseau. ' It is necessary,' said La Harpe, ' for every good citizen to know these principles, but above all a prince must early be penetrated with them. He will thus learn that there *was* at least a time when all men were equal, and that if things have changed since then, this can never have been in order that the human race, bound hand and foot, should be given over to the caprice of a single man, and that there should be found absolute monarchs generous

[6] ' . . . à vous, cher ami, de qui je tiens la presque totalité des notions et des connaissances que je possède.' Letter to La Harpe. Weimar, November 23/December 5, 1818. In Grand Duke Nicholas Mikhailovich, *L'Empereur Alexandre I*[er] (1912), i. 341.

[7] *Mémoires* (ed. 1864), p. 74.

and truthful enough to proclaim publicly to their subjects : " We glory in saying that we only exist for the
good of our peoples." ' [8]

La Harpe ceased to be Alexander's tutor in the spring
of 1795, when the Cesarevich was sixteen years old, but
the seed he had scattered had fallen on receptive soil, and
produced in the course of the next few years a singular
crop of youthful ideals. In 1797 Alexander found a sym-
pathetic soul in Prince Adam Czartoryski, who, with his
brother, had been brought to the Court of Catherine II
as a hostage for the good behaviour of his family in
Poland, and has left in his ' Memoirs ' an account of the
Grand Duke's confidences, so interesting in itself, and
so valuable in the light it throws on Alexander's future
attitude, that I shall quote from it at some length.

' He told me then,' writes Czartoryski, ' that he did not
at all share the ideas and doctrines of the Cabinet and the
Court ; that he was far from approving the policy and conduct of his grandmother ; that he condemned her principles ;
that he had prayed for Poland and her glorious struggle ;
that he had deplored her fall, and that in his eyes Kosciuszko
was a man great by reason of his virtues and the cause which
he had defended, which had been that of humanity and
justice. He protested to me that he detested despotism
everywhere and in whatsoever manner it was exercised ;
that he loved liberty, which was the birthright of every man ;
that he had taken the most lively interest in the French
Revolution ; that while disapproving its excesses, he wished
success to the Republic and rejoiced in it. He spoke to me
with veneration of his tutor, M. de La Harpe . . . that he
owed to him all that was good in him, and all that he knew—
above all, those principles of truth and justice which he was
happy to carry in his heart.' [9]

We have also the independent testimony of the
young Alexander himself in a letter to La Harpe, dated
October 8, 1797, preserved in the Russian Imperial
archives.[10] This letter was carried to Switzerland by the

[8] Quoted in Shilder, i. 227, n. 51.   [9] *Mémoires*, i. 96.
[10] Shilder, *op. cit.* i. 280. Appendix XV.

Grand Duke's new-found friend and confidant Novosiltsov,
who was charged to secure La Harpe's advice and assistance on an affair of great importance—no less than a
plan to give Russia a free Constitution.   Alexander begins
by recounting all the abuses and follies of his father Paul's
fantastic tyranny.   He had thought, he said, of leaving
the country ; but this being impossible, he was devising
instead a plan by which Russia should become free, so
that she should never again become the plaything of mad-
men (*servir de jouet à des insensés*).   The best kind of
revolution directed to this end, he thought, would be
one operated by the legal power (i.e. the autocracy),
which should cease to exist as soon as the Constitution
was achieved and the country had representatives.

' I have communicated this idea to certain enlightened
persons who have long shared my views in this matter.   In all
we are but four, i.e. M. Novosiltsov, Count Strogonov, the
young Prince Czartoryski, my aide-de-camp, and I.'

' Our idea is during the present reign to have translated
into Russian as many useful books as possible, publishing
those of which the printing is allowed, and reserving the rest
for a future time, in order to begin to spread enlightenment
and educate men's minds as much as possible.   On the other
hand, when once my time comes, it will be necessary to work,
of course little by little, to establish a representation of the
nation, which under direction shall devise a free Constitution ;
after which my power shall cease absolutely and, if Providence support our work, I shall retire into some corner and
live content and happy in seeing the well-being of my country
and rejoicing in it.'

Alexander was only eighteen years old when he wrote
this, and if, when brought face to face with the hard
realities of his position, he failed to realize his early ideals,
no one with any experience of life would be disposed to
accuse him of conscious hypocrisy.   In those early days
he was, as Czartoryski said, ' under the spell of youth
as yet scarce begun, which builds projects that reach
out of sight into a future that has no end.'   Czartoryski,

who had the best reason to know, and also the best reason to resent, the failure of Alexander to fulfil his early promises, expresses no doubt of his sincerity, both then and afterwards. His views and his intentions, he says, remained precious as the purest gold, and the great qualities he displayed were all the more precious, since he developed them in spite of the education he had received and of the example of those among whom he lived.

Two other influences, of which I must speak very shortly, introduced into Alexander's complex character traits wholly contradictory to this early Utopianism. Of these one was the love of military detail and display with which he and his brother Constantine had been infected by their father, Paul I. After all, in the Empress Catherine's palace they had no importance beyond their rank, and no serious duties ; their rank in Paul's toy army at Gatchina gave them at once a sense of importance and something to do. Thus it was that Alexander, though at times he seemed to realize its absurdity, was a victim all his life to what Czartoryski calls ' paradomania, that epidemic malady of princes.' [11]

The second influence, the most fateful one in his life, was the effect produced upon him by the murder of his father. That he was privy to the plot against Paul is now established. Who can tell what arguments were brought to bear on the young idealist to induce him to clear out of his path this fantastic and ruinous obstacle to the realization of his dreams ? It would have been easy to persuade him that the deposition of Paul was necessary, not only for the safety of himself and his family, but for the very preservation of Russia.[12] He was privy,

[11] *Mémoires*, i. 109.

[12] We may again refer to the letter to La Harpe quoted above, in which he says : ' . . . The happiness of the State counts for nothing in the present régime ; there is nothing but an absolute power which acts at random. It would be impossible to enumerate all the acts of madness which have been committed ; and to these must be added a severity which knows no justice, extreme partiality, and the greatest inexperience in everything. . . . My poor country is in an indescribable state.'

then, to the plot ; but when the plot issued in murder, though this was an issue more than probable,[13] he was overwhelmed with misery and remorse. ' This inefface-able blot,' says Czartoryski, who hurried back from his mission in Naples to the side of the young Tsar, ' attached itself like a canker to his conscience, paralysing at the outset of his reign the best and fairest of his faculties, and plunged him at the end of his life into a pro-found depression and into a mysticism which at times degenerated into superstition.' [14]

This latter element in Alexander's character, which in the end dominated and obscured all the others, deserves special study, since it not only determined, in the Holy Alliance, his attitude towards the idea of a federated Europe, but in the later years of his life profoundly affected all his policy. It is true that, as Czartoryski says, the haunting horror of his father's murder, by which his soul was tormented, predisposed Alexander to emotional religion ; but in this he was by no means singular among his contemporaries, and in order to understand this development of his character we must realize something of the religious tendencies of that particular age.

It was an age of violent reaction against the shallow enlightenment of the eighteenth century ; against that ' Reason ' which had been set up on the desecrated altar of Notre Dame and was held responsible for all the woes which the Revolution had brought upon Europe. In France there was the Catholic Reaction, heralded by Chateaubriand's ' Génie du Christianisme,' one symptom of that romantic movement, with its appeal to an idealized vision of the Ages of Faith, which was so profoundly to affect the art and the thought of Europe. In Germany, tormented for a quarter of a century by so great an

[13] ' C'est difficile d'admettre qu'en disant oui, il pût s'abuser sur la nature du danger ' (The Grand Duke Nicholas Mikhailovich, *op. cit.* i. 8).
[14] *Mémoires*, i. 237.

accumulation of woes, there was, under the influence of
the Pietists, a reaction, not so much to the standpoint of
the old Protestant orthodoxy, with its dryasdust theology
and its reverence for things established, as to the Bible,
the fountain-head of Divine revelation, the infallible
oracle which it was believed would solve all mysteries
for those who had eyes to see and ears to hear.
Here men began to seek the explanation of the
portents of the times, and there were plenty of seers who,
guided by their own inner light, were willing and anxious
to interpret to seekers after truth the utterances of the
oracle.   Mysticism hung like a fog over the stricken land,
at first over the lower social levels, but rising gradually
to the most exalted heights.   Prophets and disciples
were drawn from every rank, and whatever impassable
social barriers there may have been in the life of the world,
in this strange other-world of the spirit there was a complete confusion of degrees.   Of its leaders some, like
Jung-Stilling at Karlsruhe, were writers of repute ; some,
like the Baroness von Krüdener, persons of rank ; but
sovereign princes and princesses did not disdain to listen
to the exhortations of converted cobblers and to take
comfort in the visions of inspired housemaids.   In view
of what human nature is, it is not surprising that con-
versions and visions multiplied.

This mystical spirit, long before Alexander himself
was touched by it, had invaded the most influential circles
of the Russian Church and State.   Among the servants
and intimates of the Emperor two were particularly
affected by it : Prince Alexander Golitsin and Alexander
Ivanovich Koshelev.   Golitsin, Alexander's friend from
childhood, had been appointed by the young Emperor
Procurator of the Holy Synod at the early age of thirty.
His previous life had in no way fitted him for the office ;
but responsibility sobered him, and both as Procurator
and later as Minister of Religion and Education he threw
himself zealously, in the spirit of evangelical piety, into
the work of elevating the intellectual and spiritual level

of the Church.   Koshelev, who had come under the influence of Swedenborg's teaching and long corresponded
with the mystics of many lands, in 1812 resigned his office
of Grand Marshal of the Court in order to devote himself
wholly to mystical religion.   These two men it was who
were mainly instrumental in determining Alexander's
religious development, Golitsin by introducing him to
the Bible, Koshelev by suggesting its mystical interpretation.[15]

It was in the summer of 1812, when he was on his
way to meet Bernadotte in Finland, that Alexander first
began to read the New Testament.   Golitsin, in pressing
him to do so, had very wisely recommended him to confine
himself to the Gospels and Epistles, and not to read the
Apocalypse or the Old Testament for the present.   But
Alexander's appetite once aroused was insatiable ;   the
Bible became his daily study, and the apocalyptic books
precisely those over which he brooded most.   Their
mystic language, capable of many interpretations, enabled
him to give form to his own confused and nebulous
emotions, and in their oracular utterances he sought with
child-like faith the solution of the world's problems and
his own.   Such being his actual mood, it is not difficult
to realize the effect upon him of the apocalyptic horrors
of the campaign of 1812.   The disasters of his armies
were the visible judgment of God upon him ;   the flames
of Moscow God's revelation to him of the mission to
which he was called.   All the signs of the times, as interpreted by the prophets, pointed to this.   Napoleon was
quite evidently Antichrist and the Beast ;   the ' latter
days were about to be accomplished,' and everywhere
the belief was vocal that, as Isaiah had foretold, a man
would be raised up ' from the north . . . from the rising
of the sun,' by whom Antichrist would be overthrown

[15] The Grand Duke Nicholas Mikhailovich, *op. cit.* i. 167.   The
Grand Duke comments on the absence of material for the life of
Koshelev, whose influence over Alexander he describes as profound
and abiding.

and the way prepared for the second advent of Christ
to establish his thousand years' rule upon earth. Who
could ' the Man ' be but Alexander himself ? There
were plenty of flattering voices to suggest it to him ; and
after all, King David, a meaner murderer than he, had
been the man after God's own heart.

If the burning of Moscow had seemed to Alexander
the outpouring of God's wrath upon him, the awful fate
of the Grand Army was no less a manifestation of the
Divine judgment—*adflavit Deus et dissipati sunt*. His
spirit was exalted by a victory which he ascribed to the
act of God ; and though he could not as yet find peace
for his own soul, tormented by remorse, he accepted
the Divine mission of becoming the peacemaker of the
world.   In his private letters, as in his public acts, during
the years to come it is to the overruling providence of
God that he ascribes the successes of his policy and of
his arms.   But of God working through *him*, the chosen
instrument, the dispenser of benefits from above.   For
Alexander, for all his talk of renunciation, was—as boys
always are and men not seldom—the ὄμφαλος of all the
visionary worlds he created.   ' The Emperor,' writes
Czartoryski, in a passage often quoted that must be quoted
again, ' would willingly have consented that every one
should be free, on condition that every one should do
his will alone.' [16]

Such was the complex character of the man—autocrat
and Jacobin, *philosophe* and pietist, altruist and egoist—
who on January 1, 1813, crossed the Niemen into Prussia,
proclaiming his mission as the liberator of Europe.

[16] *Mémoires*, i. 345.

II

THE GRAND ALLIANCE

Alexander's proclamation—Treaty of Kalisch—Appeal to the principle
of nationality—Renewed influence of Czartoryski—Alexander and
Poland—Partial alliances of Teplitz and Reichenbach—Capo
d'Istria—Alexander revives the idea of a Universal Union—
Questions involved in a territorial ' restoration ' : France, Germany,
Italy, Poland—Threatened disruption of the Alliance—Mission of
Castlereagh.

IT is not my purpose to deal with the stirring events of
the War of Liberation ; the national uprising of Prussia
and Germany ; the negotiations, issuing in a series of
treaties, which culminated in that coalition of the nations
by which the power of Napoleon was crushed in October
1813 on the field of Leipzig ; the long negotiations with
Napoleon during the advance of the Allies towards France,
and the discussions, revelations of divided aims, and
recriminations to which these gave rise in the councils
of the Alliance. Since, however, my object is to trace
the origins of the underlying ideas of the ' Confederation '
which succeeded to the place of Napoleon in Europe, I
shall gather from the records such material as may serve
to throw light upon these, putting for this purpose into
what to some may seem undue relief those proclamations
of the sovereigns addressed to the peoples, and those
solemn preambles to the treaties, which have usually,
and perhaps not unnaturally, been regarded as mere wind
and words, hypocritical appeals to the gallery, intended
to serve no more than a temporary purpose.

The first of these, dictated by Alexander, was pub-

lished by Marshal Kutusov when he first entered East
Prussia. ' Providence,' it ran, ' has blessed the arms
of the Emperor my master. . . . Independence and
peace will be the result. His Majesty offers his assistance
to all the peoples which, to-day forced to oppose him,
shall abandon the cause of Napoleon and henceforth
follow only their own interests.' The offer was repeated
with greater elaboration, and with a special appeal to
the peoples by name, in the proclamation issued by
Alexander himself from Warsaw on February 10th, in
which he goes so far as to call upon the peoples whose
princes should persist in ' their miserable system of submission ' to *force* these to join in the glorious cause.[17]
In the preamble to the Treaty between Russia and Prussia,
signed at Kalisch on February 28th, the principle of the
independence of the peoples is again asserted, and it is
combined with a hint of a system to be established by
which this independence is to be for ever guaranteed.

' The total destruction of the hostile forces which had
penetrated into the heart of Russia,' it runs, ' has prepared
the great epoch of independence for all the states which shall
desire to seize the occasion to throw off the French yoke which
has for so many years weighed upon them. . . . In leading
his victorious troops beyond his own borders, the first idea
of H.M. the Emperor of all the Russias was to rally to the fair
cause in which Providence has so visibly protected him his old
and most dear allies, in order with them to fulfil the destinies
on which depend the happiness and repose of the peoples
exhausted by so much unrest and so many sacrifices. The
time will come when treaties shall be more than truces, when
it will again be possible for them to be observed with that
religious faith, that sacred inviolability, on which depend the
reputation, the strength, and the preservation of empires.' [18]

The Treaty of Kalisch, so far as its public articles were
concerned, was published on March 20. Five days
later Alexander and his new ally, Frederick William III

[17] Garden, *Histoire générale des traités de paix*, xiv. 139.
[18] *Ibid.* xiv. 167.

of Prussia, issued their famous proclamation to the German people. The alliance, which deserved the enthusiastic support of all classes, aimed only at recovering for the German nation its imprescriptible rights of liberty and independence. The Confederation of the Rhine, ' the chain by which Germany had been garrotted,' must cease to be. The desire of the Russian Emperor was that Germany should be re-established ' on the ancient spirit of the German people,' and that with youth renewed, vigorous and united, it should once more take its due place among the nations of Europe.[19] ' In 1792,' comments Sorel, ' France had preached war and the cosmopolitan Revolution ; in 1813 Russia unchained the war of nationalities.'

The principle of nationality was to become, as it still is, the main obstacle to any realization of the vision of perpetual peace ; and in appealing to it Alexander without doubt had no conception of the power and tendencies of the forces he was unloosing—forces which were destined to mingle with the air his daydream of a confederated Europe, and from the insurrection of the Greeks in 1821 to the present time, to keep Europe in a state of war or ominously quiet under the oppressive shadow of the ' armed peace.' But was Alexander insincere ? Were his appeals to the nations mere loud-sounding nothings ? In the project of peace submitted by Alexander to Pitt in 1804, not only the principle of constitutional liberty, but also that of nationality, is recognized. It is there argued, perfectly justly, that in order to secure the stability of an international system, the boundaries of the nations must first be fixed, not only so as to give to each its natural frontiers—rivers or mountains or sea —but ' so as to compose the several states of homogeneous peoples, which could agree among each other and act in harmony with the government that rules them.' [20]   And

[19] Garden, *Histoire générale des traités de paix*, xiv. 180. Sorel, *op. cit.* viii. 68. It was issued by Marshal Kutusov in the name of the sovereigns.   [20] Czartoryski, *Mémoires*, ii. 36.

the prime cause of all the unrest in Europe for centuries past is stated to be that no attention had been paid to this national equilibrium.

During the alliance with Napoleon, Alexander may have forgotten this principle ; or, to put the best, and not an improbable, interpretation on his policy, he may have realized after Friedland the hopelessness of its application, and seen in an understanding with the French Emperor the only means of ensuring the general peace. This illusion shattered, he returned to his earlier plans. At Kalisch, moreover, Czartoryski was once more at his side. On December 12, 1812, he had written to Novosiltsov to say that the Tsar's victories should lead to something 'stronger and fairer' than commonplace conquests, and pointed to the restoration of Poland as a thing not only glorious in itself but required by the interests of all Europe.[21] On the 6th he had written anonymously to the Emperor Alexander in the same sense—acknowledging the authorship of the letter in another of the 15th—praying him not to treat the Poles as a conquered people, but to reconcile them to Russia by putting into execution as soon as possible the project for their national restoration which he had so long harboured. He pointed out that in this matter the Emperor was under no obligation to the other Powers, adding the significant sentence : ' It is to the general confederation that the matter will have to be addressed, and with this that it will have to be settled.'[22]

In view of the part played by Poland in the late war, this was to ask much of the Russian Emperor's generosity. Though Adam Czartoryski himself had kept as far as possible in the background, his father had presided over

[21] To Novosiltsov, Imp. Russ. Hist. Soc. ix. 431, quoted in Shilder, iii. n. 220, p. 381.

[22] The letters are printed in full in the Appendix to the Grand Duke Nicholas Mikhailovich's *L'Empereur Alexandre I*[er], vol. i. In Prince Ladislaus Czartoryski's *Alexandre I*[er] *et le Prince Czartoryski* (Paris, 1865) they are given (p. 197 *seq.* Nos. XVIII and XIX) with considerable cuts.

the Diet which, at the declaration of war, had proclaimed the kingdom of Poland and recalled all the Poles in Russian service to join the Polish contingents of Napoleon's armies. But Czartoryski well knew the character of the ruler to whom he appealed, and that in his present exalted mood he was not likely to let petty motives of resentment or narrow considerations of policy stand in the way of the realization of a long-cherished dream. Alexander's reply is dated from Leypouny on January 13, 1813. Nothing, he said, had been altered in his sentiments and intentions towards Poland. How much he would be able to do would depend on the success of his arms and on the attitude of the Poles themselves. But meanwhile he had given orders to his generals to treat them as friends and brothers. So soon as he should be in a position to do so he would realize their aspirations, on the lines of Liberalism, which were those that he himself preferred.[23] The letter is obviously sincere ; it shows also a clear perception of the obstacles to be overcome—the jealous opposition of the Powers and the resentment of the Russian people at the part played by the Polish troops in Napoleon's invasion.

During the campaign of 1813 another significant figure appeared at Alexander's side, that of the Greek Capo d'Istria. He had entered the Russian diplomatic service in 1811 as attaché to Baron Stakelberg, the ambassador in Vienna, and was now attached to the staff of General Barclay de Tolly as chief of the political division. If Czartoryski represented Polish nationalism, Capo d'Istria championed that of the Greeks. It was not this, however, which attracted Alexander's special attention to him, though it was of great importance later. The neutrality of Switzerland, which Alexander had guaranteed, had been violated at the instigation of the oligarchy of Bern, and the Emperor proposed to send a plenipotentiary to the

---

[23] *Alexandre I*er *et le Prince Czartoryski*, No. XX, p. 206.

Landamman and Diet in order to call ' ces messieurs ' to order. For this mission he chose Capo d'Istria, whom he commended to La Harpe as ' a man highly recommendable for his honesty, his tact, his enlightenment and liberal views.' ' He is from Corfu,' he added, ' and consequently a republican, and it is the knowledge of his principles that has led me to select him.' [24] These principles were to carry Capo d'Istria far into the Tsar's confidence after the signature of the first Peace of Paris. He was destined to play an influential part during the Congress of Vienna, and from 1815 to 1822, as adjunct Foreign Minister under the Chancellor Count Nesselrode, he was to be one of the main supporters of Alexander's liberalism and of his plans for a Confederation of Europe.

It is from Capo d'Istria, indeed, and in connection with his Swiss mission, that we have the next definite proof that, throughout this period, Alexander had never lost sight of his favourite plan for organizing peace on a permanent basis. On January 1, 1814, the anniversary of the passage of the Niemen, the Russian headquarters were established at Basel, Alexander himself leading his troops over the bridge across the Rhine in a storm of sleet and wind. Here, on the eve of his advance into France itself, he communicated to Capo d'Istria, before he left for Zürich, his plan for the restoration of Europe. So far the treaties which bound the Coalition together, at Kalisch, at Teplitz, and at Reichenbach, were not instruments common to all the Allies, but mere agreements between this Power and that, though all directed to a common end, namely, the overthrow of Napoleon. That end attained, the Emperor Alexander declared his plan to be ' to restore to each nation the full and entire enjoyment of its rights and of its institutions ; to place all, including ourselves, under the safeguard of a general alliance, in order to guarantee ourselves and to save them from the ambition

[24] To La Harpe, Freiburg-im-Breisgau, December 22/January 3, 1813-14.

of a conqueror : such are the bases on which we hope,
with the help of God, to establish this new system.   Providence has placed us on the path which leads directly
to this goal.   We have traversed part of it.   That which
it remains for us to do is encumbered with great
obstacles.   Our duty is to remove them.' [25]

The obstacles to be removed were indeed formidable
enough ; and the least formidable of them was Napoleon
himself, though the unexpected vitality of his brilliant
defence during the next few months more than once
threatened to dissolve the Great Alliance into its elements.   But as his power of resistance declined, with
every fresh advance of the allied arms, the sole tie which
bound the Coalition together was loosened.   Of the
spoils to be divided only a comparatively insignificant
portion had been earmarked.   What of Poland, of Italy,
of Germany, of France itself ?   Above all, for the present,
what of France ?   The Allies had loudly proclaimed
throughout that they were making war, not on France,
but on Napoleon.   But what did they mean by France ?
The France of the old régime ?   Or the France of 1792,
with its rectified frontier and the alien *enclaves* absorbed ?
Or France as Frenchmen have ever conceived it in its
perfection, with its natural frontiers of the Rhine, the
Alps and the Pyrenees ?   And in this France, however
defined, what government was to be established ?

What of Italy ?   Was Murat, ranked now with the
enemies of Napoleon, to be allowed to realize his dream
of exchanging the crown of Naples for that of Italy ?
What of Germany, which, now that Napoleon's system
was overthrown, reflected as in a convex mirror all the
intricate problems of Europe ;   where there were as
many conflicting interests and ambitions as there were
states, and everyone was clamouring for compensations,
from the rival Great Powers, Austria and Prussia, down
to the crowd of mediatized princes, who, now that the

[25] *Aperçu de ma vie,* by Count Capo d'Istria, in Imp. Arch., and
Sbornik of the Imp. Russ. Hist. Soc. iii. 178.

age of restorations had begun, petitioned insistently for the recovery of their ' liberties ' ? And last, and by no means least, what of Poland ? Would Alexander keep the engagements made at Kalisch, and subsequently twice confirmed, and partition the duchy of Warsaw with his Allies ? Or would he take advantage of his overgrown power to realize, in despite of Austria, his lifelong dream of restoring Poland, with himself as king ?

With every advance of the Allies these questions, shelved or but vaguely determined in earlier conferences, became more and more urgent ; and in December 1813 the British Government, in order to prevent the Coalition from falling to pieces, decided to send Lord Castlereagh to the headquarters of the Allies. In the councils of the Coalition the other Allies were represented by the sovereigns themselves or by their Foreign Secretaries ; it was rightly judged that the views of Great Britain would carry more weight if represented there by the Secretary of State for Foreign Affairs in person. Castlereagh's full instructions are contained in a Cabinet Memorandum of December 26, 1813.[26] He was to ascertain with precision the basis upon which it was proposed to negotiate, and to come to a clear and definite understanding with the Allies, not only on all matters of common interest, but on such points as were likely to be discussed with the enemy, so that the Allied Powers might in their negotiations with France act in perfect concert and together maintain one common interest. The interests of Great Britain in the negotiations were clearly defined. The maritime power of France must be restricted within bounds by her absolute exclusion from Antwerp and the Scheldt, Holland being guaranteed, under a prince of the house of Orange, by a barrier ; the Italian monarchies must be assured against French aggression, and likewise the Spanish peninsula.

[26] F.O. Records : Continent, France, i. Cf. *Castlereagh Corresp.*, 3rd Ser., i. 115 : ' Instructions.' These are only general, and empower him to ' negociate and conclude, on behalf of His Majesty, conventions or treaties for the restoration of peace.'

Subject to these conditions, Great Britain might be induced to apply the greater portion of her conquests to promote the general interests, to which Castlereagh was ' to evince a desire as far as possible to conform.' The memorandum, after detailing the colonial conquests which Great Britain was prepared if necessary to restore, concludes with a paragraph of great importance to our present subject. ' The Treaty of Alliance,' it runs, ' is not to terminate with the war, but is to contain defensive engagements, with mutual obligations to support the Power attacked by France with a certain extent of stipulated succours. The *casus fœderis* is to be an attack by France on the European dominions of any one of the contracting parties.'

Here we have at the very outset the European Alliance as Great Britain from first to last conceived it. In contradistinction to Alexander's unlimited union with indefinite objects, it was to be a limited union with definite objects. In taking this attitude Great Britain was doubly strong ; she was materially strong because on her financial support the whole combination depended ; she was morally strong because from the very first she clearly defined her own requirements and the limits within which she was prepared to sacrifice her own immediate profit to the ultimate good. Sorel, writing as usual from a somewhat narrow French point of view, says in his summary of Castlereagh's character and policy that ' he piqued himself on principles to which he held with an unshakable constancy, which in actual affairs could not be distinguished from obstinacy ; but these principles were in no degree abstract or speculative, but were all embraced in one alone, the supremacy of English interests ; they all proceeded from this high reason of state.' [27]

Now, even had this been entirely true, it could hardly be put to Castlereagh's discredit ; it is the duty of a statesman to consider first of all the interests of

[27] *Op. cit.* viii. 248.

his country. But it is only partly true—or rather it is a *suggestio falsi*. Castlereagh put English interests first ; but he believed firmly that these interests were not inconsistent with the general good. Years later, Canning was to declare that henceforth Great Britain was to ' revolve in her own orbit.' If Castlereagh brought her into the European system, allowing her course to be deflected by the influence of alien bodies, it was because he believed—and I think rightly—that under the circumstances of the times this was the only way to produce and preserve the general peace.' [28] ' The interests of Great Britain,' we find in a memorandum signed by the British plenipotentiaries at Langres on February 2, 1814, ' neither require to be asserted with chicane nor with dexterity—a steady and temperate application of honest principles is her best source of authority.' And these principles, as Sorel rightly says, were in no degree abstract or speculative. We may sum them up as those of *Realpolitik* tempered by altruism. They stood from first to last in contrast and opposition to the principles championed by the Emperor Alexander, which may be summed up as altruism tempered by *Realpolitik*—principles which he maintained with that invincible obstinacy which, as Caulaincourt rightly observed, in spite of an apparent pliability, due to the dissimulation almost obligatory on princes, lay at the very root of his character. [29]

[28] ' The wish of the government is to connect their interests in peace and in war with those of the Continent . . . that whilst the state of Europe afforded little hope of a better order of things, Great Britain had no other course left than to create an independent existence for herself, but that now she might look forward to a return to ancient principles, she was ready to make the necessary sacrifices on her part to reconstruct a balance in Europe ' (in Castlereagh to Liverpool, Châtillon, February 6, 1814. F.O. : Continent, France).

[29] See the interesting analyses of Alexander's character in Caulaincourt's letters of September 19 and November 10, 1810, to Champagny, published in the Grand Duke Nicholas Mikhailovich's *Relations diplomatiques de la Russie et de la France, 1808–1812*.

III

THE TREATY OF CHAUMONT

Castlereagh at Langres—The British policy defined—Contrast with Alexander's views — Divisions in the Alliance — Austria and Russia—Conferences of Châtillon—Effect of Napoleon's victories —'Criminations and recriminations'—General character of Austrian policy—Metternich—Fear of Alexander's designs on Poland—Mediation of Castlereagh—Treaty of Chaumont—Declaration of Châtillon.

CASTLEREAGH arrived at Langres, where the headquarters of the Allies were established, on January 25, 1814. He at once realized the difficulties of the task before him. The principal object of his mission was to draw closer the bonds between the Allies by substituting a general treaty for the series of dual treaties which had hitherto bound them together, in order to present a serried front to Napoleon whether for purposes of negotiation or of war. For the success of such a treaty it was necessary that the Powers should agree at least as to the main feature of the territorial settlement to be effected in the event of their ultimate victory; and it was just such a concert that it was impossible to obtain. The Emperor Alexander had hurried to Langres on the 22nd in order to urge Schwarzenberg, the Austrian commander-in-chief, to continue the advance; on the 25th Metternich had also arrived there, intent on defining the bases of the ultimate peace, as the condition indispensable to the continuation of the war. The chief obstacle to such a definition was the Emperor Alexander. As to his designs about Poland, especially, he maintained an obstinate silence, which Metternich interpreted as proof of his intention to establish a greater Poland at Austria's expense.[30] Scarcely less disconcerting was his attitude towards France. In view of the condition of the Allied Army, the insecurity of its communications, and the disastrous consequences to be expected from a possible reverse, the representatives of Austria, Prussia, and Great Britain were agreed as to the expediency of coming to terms with Napoleon. But Alexander was inexorable. He had received from La Harpe, recently arrived from Paris, accounts of the state of French opinion which confirmed him in his resolution to make no terms with him. If Austria refused to advance, he would himself join the Silesian army under Blücher and Gneisenau, whose insubordinate impetuosity, encouraged by Stein as Alexander's mouthpiece, flouted the prudent counsels of the Prussian King and his politic advisers. The crowning triumph of the occupation of Paris, Alexander determined, should be his. He himself would lead the victorious armies into the French capital, and there dictate the terms of a magnanimous peace. As for the future government of France, that should be left for the French themselves to decide, in an assembly presided over by a Russian representative, who could be none other than La Harpe.

The answer of Austria to those proposals was a threat of making a separate peace with Napoleon ; the alliance seemed on the verge of dissolution ; but, after heated debates, more prudent counsels prevailed, and it was decided to continue the Allied advance, not indeed to Paris, but as far as might be ' consistent with the dictates of military prudence.' At the same time it was agreed to invite Caulaincourt, Napoleon's representative, to Châtillon, where the peace negotiations were to be resumed on February 3. With a view to these conferences

---

[30] Were this to happen, Metternich argued, the whole settlement as projected by Great Britain would break down, as Austria would have to revive her claim to the Low Countries (Fournier, p. 61).

the representatives of the Powers agreed, on January 30,
to a formula which, though the general treaty seemed
as far off as ever, once more consecrated the principle
of common action.   As a result of the debate on the form
the negotiations should take, wrote Castlereagh to Liverpool,[31] it was decided ' that the negotiators should act
as common parties under a general instruction, and that
they should consider themselves as maintaining one and
the same interest on behalf of themselves and their Allies,
now collectively constituting, as opposed to France, the
whole of Europe with the exception of Turkey.'

The events of the war soon broke the harmony of this
concert into discord once more.   The Emperor Alexander,
leaving the sorry business of patching up the compromise
to his ministers, had left Langres on the 29th, the very
day on which the first conference opened, and hurried
to the Allied headquarters, which were now at Chaumont.
King Frederick William of Prussia was with him, and
it was believed that it was Alexander's intention to place
himself at the head of the Prussian army, and, with
the King at his side, to advance on Paris.   Blücher's
victory over Napoleon at La Rothière, on February 2,
the day on which the ministers assembled at Châtillon,
increased Alexander's determination.   To his Allies,
who argued that the victory should be used to secure
reasonable terms of peace with a now chastened Napoleon,
Alexander replied that the overthrow of Napoleon was
' an affair of morality and of justice ' which admitted
of no compromise.   On February 8 he ordered the
conferences to be suspended, and the next day he made
it clear to Metternich that he still held tenaciously to
his idea of marching on Paris and there holding an
assembly for the election of Napoleon's successor.   The
old controversy of Langres began again with greater
vehemence, Metternich once more threatening to withdraw from the Coalition if Alexander continued his
' tyranny.'   Napoleon's successive victories at Mont-

---

[31] F.O. : Continent, France. Langres, January 30, 1814.

mirail, Champaubert, and Etoges (February 8–10), by damping the Tsar's over-confident temper, enabled a compromise to be once more patched up. Alexander formally gave up his plan for a French Assembly, and, while refusing to consent to an armistice, agreed that the conferences should be resumed, with a view to establishing the bases of peace. Austria, for her part, consented to press the war, and Schwarzenberg was directed to advance to the support of the defeated Silesian army.

The harmony thus restored was not long preserved. At Mormant on the 17th, at Montereau on the 18th, and at Méry on February 21, Napoleon dealt such heavy blows at the Austrians that Schwarzenberg was forced to retreat with some precipitation to Bar-sur-Aube. The effect which this produced in the councils of the Alliance is described in a letter written by Castlereagh [32] from Chaumont to report the results of a conference held on the 25th to decide the future plan of campaign. ' I could not but perceive,' he wrote, ' the altered tone of my colleagues . . . their impressions being strongly tinctured by the demoralizing influence of a rapid transition from an advance made under very lofty pretensions, to a retreat of some embarrassment and of much disappointment and recrimination.' In another letter of the same date he wrote : ' The internal temper here is very embarrassing and alarming. The criminations and recriminations of the Austrian and Russian ministers are at their height. . . . Austria,' he continued, ' both in army and government is a timid power. Her minister is constitutionally temporizing . . . he is charged with more faults than belong to him, mixed up, however, with considerable means for carrying forward the machine—more than any other person I have met with at headquarters.'

This appreciation, excellent as far as it goes, gives the key to Metternich's policy, which for thirty years was to be that of Austria. Austria was a timid power,

[32] To Liverpool, Chaumont, February 26, 1814. F.O.: Continent, France.

as she had reason to be ; and Metternich, who lived
to be the last representative of the old *haute diplomatie,*
was an opportunist by training and by force of circumstances. For Alexander's shadowy idealism he had
neither understanding nor respect. His own mission—
as he confessed later—was to prop up the mouldering
institutions of the Habsburg Empire, which seemed
to be threatened by the Russian Emperor's Jacobin
humanitarianism, itself suspected of being no more
than a mask to disguise a very practical Russian *Welt-
politik.* It will be seen later how Metternich, aided by
circumstances, was able to turn Alexander's idealism
to the service of his own purposes, and to convert the
Holy Alliance, which was to have heralded the dawn
of a new era of liberty, into an oppressive instrument
for stereotyping old abuses. For the present Alexander
held quite other views ; and what would it profit Austria
to overthrow Napoleon, the son-in-law of the Emperor
Francis, only to see set up in his place, in a liberalized
France, another military adventurer—Bernadotte, whose
pretensions Alexander at this time favoured—and so
risk the almost certain recementing of that Franco-
Russian Alliance which was the dream of the Russian
and the nightmare of the Austrian Chancery ? Hence
the ' criminations and recriminations,' due to suspicion
of ulterior designs on the one side and of immediate
treachery on the other, which distracted the counsels
of the Allies during these fateful weeks. How em-
bittered were the relations between these brothers
in arms may be shown by a quotation from a letter
of Czartoryski, who arrived at Chaumont at the height
of the crisis produced by the impression of the retreat,
to his friend Novosiltsov.[33] ' Austria,' he wrote, ' is
with the greatest perfidy still supporting Napoleon and
his dynasty, and it was because of this that Blücher
was beaten ; the Austrians maintained an unworthy

[33] Dated Chaumont, March 2/14, 1814. In Imp. Russ. Hist.
Soc. ix. 435.

inactivity and exposed Blücher a second time to all
the forces of the French.'

Clearly, in view of dissensions such as these among
the Allies, Napoleon's cause was by no means desperate.
Under the impression of the series of sledgehammer blows
he had dealt their armies, already decimated by disease,
he could have come to terms with them, had he been
willing to risk wearing a discredited crown in a shrunken
France. It was a risk which, as Sorel has demonstrated,
he could not take. ' When a man like Napoleon falls,'
Count Nesselrode had written to his wife immediately
after Leipzig, ' he falls altogether.' [34]

On his part too, then, the negotiations opened at
Châtillon were but a device to gain time, to give an
opportunity for the rift within the alliance to develop till
he could complete the breach by some crowning victory.
To Castlereagh this plan was soon clear, and he pressed
for the conclusion of the general treaty which it had been
his main object to secure. The chastened temper of
the Allies after the disasters of February gave him his
opportunity. He had removed all suspicion of Great
Britain's own ulterior objects by the frank declaration
of her requirements made at Langres, in the conference
of January 31, and he was in the better position to
act as mediator between the conflicting interests. By
eliminating all mention of the most contentious questions
and scheduling certain others for further deliberation
and settlement, he succeeded in securing a concert.
The Emperor Alexander was content with an instrument
which embodied two of his main objects : the overthrow of Napoleon and the establishment of a balance
of the Powers under a European guarantee, from which,
however, he was careful to exclude his own Asiatic
dominions. Prussia, too, was equally agreeable ; and
Metternich, the other Powers being unanimous, had no
choice but to bring Austria into line. The result was

[34] Zeitz, October 22, 1813. *Lettres et papiers du chancelier comte
de Nesselrode*, v. 146.

the signature, on March 10, of the Treaty of Chaumont,
'perhaps the most far-reaching treaty,' Metternich
wrote, ' that has ever been signed.' [35]

Since the Treaty of Chaumont is the foundation
upon which the ' Confederation of Europe ' in all its
subsequent phases ultimately rested, it will be well to
examine its provisions in some detail. The preamble
declares its object to be ' to draw closer the ties which
unite [the Powers] for the vigorous pursuit of a war
undertaken with the salutary object of putting an end
to the misfortunes of Europe . . . of assuring the repose
of Europe by the re-establishment of a just equilibrium
. . . and of maintaining against all attacks the order
of things that shall be the happy outcome of their efforts.'
The treaty, that is to say, is directed to two ends, the
one temporary and particular, i.e. the successful prosecution of the war with France, the other permanent and
general, i.e. the collective protection or guarantee of territorial and other arrangements agreed upon as the result
of successful war. With the articles of the treaty falling
under the first of these heads we need not here concern
ourselves. Of the articles falling under the second head,
the most important are the 5th, 6th, 7th, and 16th.

Article V provides that the Allies will, without delay,
concert as to measures for preserving the peace when
established, and for mutual protection against any attack
by France. Article VI provides, in any such event,
primarily for ' amicable ' intervention ; Article VII
stipulates that, such amicable intervention having failed,
each of the contracting Powers shall place 60,000 men in
the field. To save waste of time in such an emergency,
the question of the supreme command and of the pay of the
troops is determined. Article XVI, which from our present
point of view is the most important, runs as follows :

The present Treaty of Alliance having for its object the
maintenance of the balance of Europe, to secure the repose

<hr />

[35] The treaty was antedated March 1.

and independence of the Powers, and to prevent the invasions which for so many years have devastated the world, the High Contracting Parties have agreed among themselves to extend its duration for twenty years from the date of signature, and they reserve the right of agreeing, if circumstances demand it, three years before its expiration, on its further prolongation.[36]

It is important to note, in view of later discussions, that the Treaty of Chaumont, while announcing the intention of the signatory Powers to maintain the ' order of things ' established by them against all attacks, contemplates these attacks as likely to be made only from one direction—France, against which alone its specific provisions are directed. Even the language of Article XVI, which might bear a wider interpretation, is limited in effect by the articles which give its general principles a particular application.

To this treaty the sovereigns of Spain, Portugal, and Sweden were to be invited to accede, as well as the Prince of Orange, for whom, under one of the secret articles attached, the kingdom of the Netherlands was destined. By the other secret articles it was agreed that, in the ultimate reconstruction of Europe, Germany was to be composed of sovereign princes united by a federal tie ; Switzerland was to be independent, under the guarantee of the Powers ; Italy was to consist of independent states ; and Spain was to be restored to the Bourbons. The omission of Poland may be regarded as of especially ominous significance. ' The treaty was signed,' says Sorel, ' but in spite of the solemn nature of their engagements under it, the Allies had not abjured their disagreements and their rivalries : in the background, for the general peace, the questions of Poland and of the supremacy of Russia ; in the foreground the question of peace with Napoleon or the destruction of his empire.'

The latter was, of course, the main point immediately

[36] Text in Martens, *Nouveau Recueil des traités*, etc., i. (ix.), No. 79, p. 683.

at issue. The treaty had been signed; but for some days yet the negotiations with Napoleon continued. Alexander alone was absolutely implacable in his attitude towards the French Emperor. Even Castlereagh had expressed himself in favour of ' signing a peace with Buonaparte, provided no act of the French nation speedily overthrow him.' This latter eventuality seemed about to be realized. On March 28 Castlereagh, then at Dijon, received a dispatch from Lord Bathurst expressing the impatience of the Government at the ' project of Châtillon ' having been presented, not as an ultimatum, but as a project to which the French Government presented a counter-project. Wellington had meanwhile reported the hoisting of the white flag at Bordeaux, and in these circumstances Bathurst declared that Great Britain would break off her engagements with the Allies if these did not abide by their decision not to abate the terms offered to Napoleon at Châtillon.[37] To this Castlereagh replied that there had been no intention to abate these terms, and that if the French plenipotentiary had been ' allowed, or rather required, to state his modifications in the form of a counter-project,' this was only ' because it compelled him to give an ensemble to his demands,' which enabled the Allies at once to negative the whole.[38]

On the very day on which Bathurst's letter was received was published, in the name of the Allies, the declaration which had been drawn up at the conclusion of the conferences at Châtillon and printed at Vitry on the 25th.

It is time that Princes, without alien influences, should look after the welfare of their peoples; that the nations should respect their mutual independence. . . . All Europe is united in opinion . . . the expression of the prime necessity

[37] Bathurst to Castlereagh, March 22, 1814. F.O. : Continent, France. *Castlereagh Corresp.*, 3rd Ser., i. 328; *Wellington Supp. Disp.* xiv. 444.

[38] To Bathurst, March 29. *Castlereagh Corresp.*, 3rd Ser., i. 402.

of all the peoples. . . . The progress of events during this epoch (of the war with Napoleon) has given to the Allied Courts the sentiment of all the strength of the European League . . . nothing remains to prevent their expressing the conditions necessary for the reconstruction of the social edifice. . . . England, the only Power called upon to place anything in the balance of compensation for France, has announced the sacrifices she is prepared to make for the general pacification.[39]

As for France, her hope of preserving her ' natural frontiers ' promised to her in the Declaration of Frankfort was in this new declaration, as Sorel puts it, ' buried under diplomatic slush.' A harsh sentence could not, indeed, have been more graciously passed than in the language in which the Allies condemned France to confinement within her ancient limits. ' France,' the proclamation ran, ' restored to the dimensions which centuries of glory and prosperity under the rule of her kings have assured her, should share with Europe the blessings of liberty, national independence, and peace.'

To this common proclamation the Emperor Alexander, three days later, added one of his own. ' The Allies,' he announced, ' respect the integrity of France, such as she was under her legitimate kings ; they may even do more, because they always profess the principle that for the happiness of Europe, France should be great and powerful.' Thus were foreshadowed the terms of the First Peace of Paris, which left to the restored French monarchy the conquests of the Revolution up to 1792.

[39] Enclosed in Castlereagh to Liverpool, Dijon, March 29. F.O. : Continent, France.

III

THE PREPARATION OF THE CONFEDERATION

If ever the Powers should meet again to establish a political system by which wars of conquest would be rendered impossible and the rights of all guaranteed, the Congress of Vienna, as a preparatory assembly, will not have been in vain.—GENTZ.

I

THE FIRST PEACE OF PARIS

The fall of Paris—The abdication of Napoleon—Disquieting attitude of
Alexander—Russia and the Balance of Power—Castlereagh aims at
' grouping' Alexander—Justification of the policy of maintaining
the Alliance—Question of its legitimate sphere of influence—This
to be confined to Europe—Question of Asia, the British Empire,
the United States and Latin America—Immediate questions :
Germany, Switzerland, Italy, Spain—The First Treaty of Paris—
The future Alliance ; question of its constitution—Talleyrand
urges a wider Alliance, to include France—The principle of
' legitimacy '—The Allies and the French claim—Exclusion of
France.

In the abortive programme concerted by Pitt and the
Emperor Alexander in 1805, the three great objects
of the Alliance were thus defined : (1) the overthrow
of Napoleon, and the reduction of France to her ancient
limits ; (2) the arrangement of the territories taken
from France so as to secure a ' just equilibrium ' in
Europe ; (3) the establishment of an international
system for preserving the settlement effected on the
basis of public law. Of these objects the first seemed
to have been triumphantly attained when on March 30,
1814, Paris fell, and its fall was followed by Napoleon's
abdication under the Treaty of Fontainebleau and the
signature, on May 30, of the First Treaty of Paris
between the Powers of the Great Alliance and the
legitimate monarchy of France, restored now in the
person of Louis XVIII.

Voices, indeed, were heard in criticism of the im-
politic generosity which left to Napoleon his title and

established him, with plentiful funds and the nucleus
of an army, in an independent principality close to the
coast of Italy, where Joachim Murat, King of Naples,
was playing a dubious game, and gave, moreover, to
France frontiers wider than those of 1792.

This generosity was mainly due to the attitude
of the Emperor Alexander. Two months before the
fall of Paris, Castlereagh, in a letter to Lord Liverpool
from Langres, had commented on the *chevaleresque*
spirit in which the Tsar was conducting the war. The
Emperor Alexander was opposed to any immediate
conclusion of peace, he said, because he wanted to enter
Paris at the head of his Guards, and there prove his
quality by the magnanimity of his revenge for the burning of Moscow.[1] Fortune favoured his ambition. The
Emperor of Austria was not present when the Allied
forces entered Paris ; he was spared, men commented,
the pain of witnessing his daughter's humiliation ; and,
at the head of his splendid cavalry of the Guard,
Alexander rode down the Champs Elysées, captivating
the volatile Parisians by his handsome presence and the
charm of his smiling and friendly address. Nor were
the Parisians alone in exalting him. ' It would be an
injustice not to declare,' wrote Sir Charles Stewart to
Castlereagh, ' that, if the Continent has had the curse
of all the evil arising out of the existence of Bonaparte,
it is also crowned with the blessing of possessing a legitimate Emperor, who, by a series of firm and glorious
conduct, has richly deserved the appellation of the
liberator of mankind.'[2] But the proceedings of the
' legitimate Emperor ' soon began to be almost as disconcerting as those of the rival he had overthrown.
For the moment there was no one in Paris to dispute
his supremacy, and he showed a disquieting disposition
to play the part of Providence in France, with little

[1] *Castlereagh Corresp.*, 3rd Ser., i. 212.
[2] Stewart to Castlereagh, Heights of Belleville, March 30, 1814.
Castlereagh Corresp., 3rd Ser., i. 412.

regard for the views of his Allies. He was ominously silent on the subject of the Bourbons, for whom he had often enough expressed his cordial contempt and dislike, and Sir Charles Stewart, only five days after penning the panegyric just quoted, was writing in a flutter to Lord Bathurst, lamenting the absence of Castlereagh and complaining that the Emperor, with whom lay the management of every concern, was 'coquetting with the nation' instead of 'making any public and manifest declaration of his wishes relative to Louis XVIII.'[3] In brief, there rose before the eyes of the other Allies the nightmare vision, which was not soon to fade, of another Franco-Russian Alliance more fateful than that of Tilsit, in which the visionary autocrat of All the Russias would figure as the patron of the Jacobinism of France and all Europe. Castlereagh, on his arrival in Paris, correctly diagnosed the case and suggested the remedy. 'The Emperor has the greatest merit, and must be held high,' he wrote on April 20 to Lord Liverpool, 'but he ought to be grouped, and not made the sole feature for admiration.'[4]

Here we have the key to the continental policy of the British Government, as represented by Castlereagh, during the following years. Its consistent aim was the traditional one of establishing and maintaining the balance of power. After the downfall of Napoleon this balance was seriously threatened by Russia alone, and to preserve it Great Britain—as the secret treaty of January 3, 1815, showed—would have used against Alexander the same weapons that had prevailed against Napoleon. Between Napoleon and Alexander, however, there was from the first this essential difference, namely, that Napoleon could never have been grouped, whereas Alexander could—was, indeed, an enthusiast for grouping, so long as he was allowed to pose in the centre of the picture. This is the supreme justification for the

[3] To Bathurst, Paris, April 4. *Castlereagh Corresp.*, 3rd Ser., i. 415. *Corresp.*, 3rd Ser., i. 478.

attitude of Castlereagh towards the European Alliance after its immediate object had been accomplished. The need of Europe at the moment was peace, and the best, indeed the only, way to secure this peace was to take advantage of Alexander's ideal of a confederated Europe in order to 'group' him. The immediate questions were : of whom the rest of the group was to consist, what was to be its sphere of influence, and how it was to be kept together.

In discussing these questions it will be most convenient to take first that of the sphere of influence.[5] From the earliest stages of the Alliance its primary function, in the event of its success, was to be to deal with the territories reconquered from France, which were partly to be restored to their ancient 'rights,' partly to be rearranged so as to form a barrier against further French aggression. Beyond this, however, the Alliance, after the conclusion of the general treaty, was to survive as a sort of board of trustees for Europe, to guarantee the permanence of the settlement effected and generally to look after the common interest of the European nations. The point to notice here is that, under these agreements, the sphere of influence was to be confined to Europe. In his instructions to Novosiltsov in 1804 the Emperor Alexander had given reasons why the Ottoman Empire must be excluded from any European Concert ; at Châtillon he had only consented to pledge himself to the principles of the Alliance on it being clearly understood that his own Asiatic dominions were not to be included in its sphere ; later he was to argue that even the questions of the Near East belonged properly to the 'domestic politics' of Russia. As for Great Britain, she had anticipated all question of her Empire being included in the sphere by herself defining beforehand on a generous scale the conquests which she was willing to restore in the general interests of Europe ; and as for the

---

[5] The phrase is not used here in its modern technical sense.

vexed question of the rights of neutrals at sea, she refused to allow any interference, concerted or otherwise, with the established maritime code.[6] The abolition of the Slave Trade was the chief of her interests which she was content to bring within the sphere of international regulation, and even to secure this—as was proved at Aix-la-Chapelle—she was not prepared to pool her empire of the seas. As for America, Great Britain was still engaged in a war with the United States, which had ostensibly been caused by her insistence on her own interpretation of the maritime code ; and behind the defiance of the United States loomed the larger question, raised by the revolt of the Latin American colonies, of the whole attitude of the New World as against the Old. In August 1814 negotiations for peace between Great Britain and the United States were opened at Ghent, and in connection with this Pozzo di Borgo, the Russian ambassador in Paris, in a letter to Nesselrode, foreshadowed all the later developments of the Monroe Doctrine. ' The conclusion of this important matter,' he said, ' is uncertain. The dominant party in America, which desired the war, is aiming at a complete revolution in the relations of the New World with the Old, by the destruction of all European interests

[6] It is interesting at the present moment to note that in his *Fragments upon the Balance of Power*, published in 1806, Friedrich von Gentz had taken up the cudgels against ' the uncalled-for vindicator of the liberty of the seas, as it is termed.' He denounced the venal German scribes who, in Napoleon's interests, ' entertained, even to satiety, their credulous readers upon the BRITISH COMMERCIAL TYRANNY —upon the OPPRESSION OF THE NEUTRAL NAVIGATION—upon ENGLAND'S MONOPOLY OF INDUSTRY AND TRADE—upon the fatal consequences of the EXCLUSIVE POSSESSION OF INDIA.' He pointed out that England in time of peace ' disturbs no fisher boat at sea '; that ' in time of war it acts towards neutral states in strict conformity to existing treaties, the only standard of national rights ' ; and that ' it justly resists the cancelling of these rights by violence, and the more so, because the only power which has any interest in their being cancelled is one which has sworn the destruction of England.' He enlarged on the economic benefits accruing to Europe from the British possession of India, of which, he said, ' England holds the sceptre in no other capacity than as the first agent of the whole European league ' (Introduction, p. xxxiii).

in the American continent.' ' Will the fact that Great
Britain has a free hand,' he asks, ' stop this plan ? I
said all this in England, which takes short views, but
was not believed.' [7] In the long run, as we shall see,
the ' short views ' prevailed, and, in spite of all the
efforts to bring the question of the Spanish colonies in
America within the sphere of the Alliance, it never
got beyond the preliminary stages of discussion. The
sphere of influence of the Alliance, then, was Europe
defined within somewhat narrow limits.

It remains to glance at the immediate problems,
with respect to the territorial settlement within these
limits, that called for solution. On certain of these an
agreement had been reached at Chaumont. As we have
seen, in the secret articles of the treaty of March 1 it
was stipulated that Germany was to consist of sovereign
states united by a federal tie ; that Switzerland was
to be independent under a European guarantee ; that
Italy was to be composed of independent states ;
and that Spain was to be restored to the Bourbons.
The first Treaty of Paris repeated these stipulations,
except that in regard to Spain, which was already a
fait accompli. By Article VI, moreover, it established
the new Dutch sovereignty which became the United
Kingdom of the Netherlands, and by Article VII it confirmed the possession of Malta in full sovereignty to
Great Britain. As an essay in international government, however, Article V, regulating the navigation of
the Rhine and other rivers, is perhaps the most significant.
' The future Congress,' it runs, ' with a view to facilitate
the communications between nations, and continually
to render them less strangers to one another, shall likewise examine and determine in what manner the above
provisions can be extended to other rivers which, in their
navigable course, separate or traverse different states.' [8]

[7] Pozzo di Borgo to Nesselrode, Paris, July 28/August 9, 1814.
Polovtsov, *Correspondance des Ambassadeurs*, etc. Imp. Russ. Hist.
Soc. 112, p. 60.

[8] Hertslet, *Map of Europe by Treaty*, i., No. I. Art. V was developed
into the Regulations passed by the Vienna Congress on March 11, 1815.

The Treaty of Paris, then, to which eight Powers attached their signatures, was the first formal step in the process of the reconstruction of Europe, a cautious and tentative step moreover, as is clear from its omission of all the more burning questions that threatened a division among the Powers : especially those of the fate of Poland, of Saxony, and of Murat's Neapolitan crown. These and all other questions were to be brought before the great general Congress which it was proposed to open at Vienna on August 1. In considering the problems raised in the organization of the Congress it is important to remember that, in spite of its more widely ' European ' character, this was essentially but a continuation of the conferences which preceded the signature of the Treaty of Paris, which instrument, as modified in the second treaty after Napoleon's fall, was to rank with the Final Act of the Congress of Vienna as the foundation of the public law of Europe.

This brings us to the question of the group of Powers by whom, as trustees for Europe, this public law was to be established. It will be remembered that, by the terms of the original concert between Great Britain and Russia, as suggested by Alexander in 1804, these two Powers were to form the nucleus of a wider alliance which in time was to develop into a union of all the states. But in this universal union, according to the Tsar's project, Russia and Great Britain—as the Powers most disinterested—were to retain a preponderant influence. Circumstances had since developed this nucleus into the group of the four signatory Powers of the Treaty of Chaumont, the instrument which, as we have seen, was the foundation charter of the new Concert of Europe. The first Treaty of Paris, on the other hand, was signed, in addition to the Allies of Chaumont, by four other Powers, viz. France, Spain, Portugal, and Sweden. The question was whether this instrument thus constituted, as it were, a wider concert and gave to all its signatories the right to an equal voice in the councils of Europe, or whether the four Allies alone were to have the determining voice in the coming Congress. Such a narrower concert was certainly contemplated by the Treaty of Chaumont, which was valid for twenty years and renewable at the discretion of the Allies; and especially was it laid down that France was to have no voice in the disposal of the territories ceded by her, that is to say, in the most important matters with which the Congress would be called upon to deal.

From the point of view of France, then, it became of the utmost importance to press the principle of the wider concert consecrated by the signature of the Treaty of Paris. This was the object which Talleyrand, with consummate skill, pursued during the time preceding the Congress and at the Congress itself. His diplomacy was based on the language of the Allies themselves. They had, in proclamation after proclamation, declared that their quarrel was not with France but with Napoleon ; they had posed as the liberators of the nation from an intolerable tyranny ; they had over and over again declared that their mission was to restore ancient ' rights ' and the system of public law which the Revolution had overthrown. During the final crisis of Napoleon's fall Talleyrand, to quote Gentz,[9] had become ' the political oracle of France,' and the oracle found it convenient to repeat, with a disconcerting emphasis, the lofty sentiments of the Allied Powers. He had, indeed, laboured for the restoration of the ' legitimate ' monarchy in France in order to enable him to do so [10] ; and with magnificent impudence, the man who had served in turn every ' usurping ' Government in France, now proclaimed *urbi et orbi* the sacred principle of ' legitimacy.' ' The legitimacy of kings, or rather of governments,' he said, ' is the safeguard of nations ; the legitimacy of a government is the effect of long possession, as prescription is a title to private property.' [11]

[9] To Caradja, April 14, 1814. *Oesterreichs Theilnahme an den Befreiungskriegen.*

[10] ' A Government " imposed " would be weak. With a principle we are strong. Louis XVIII is a principle. He is legitimate King of France ' (*Memoirs*, ii. 165)   [11] *Ibid.* p. 160.

In taking this line he was doing more than merely asserting the right of France to a voice in the councils of Europe ; he was opening a rift in the Alliance, and so placing France, now strengthened by the return of the troops in garrison beyond her borders, in a position to hold the balance in a divided Europe.   The principle of ' legitimacy ' in the sense proclaimed by Talleyrand, i.e. ' the effect of long possession, as prescription is a title to private property '—was that which had been consistently upheld by Great Britain as the basic principle of any European juridical system ; and clearly, if the era of conquest was to be superseded by the era of peace, it was the only possible basis.   But it was one not likely to appeal to Alexander, who had committed himself to a principle wholly inconsistent with it—that of nationality, so far at least as this could be reconciled with his maintaining his position in countries, e.g. Finland and Poland, which he held by that very ' right of might ' it was sought to discredit.   It might appeal to Austria, which, when once the traditional Habsburg inheritance was restored to it, was to seek salvation, under Metternich's inspiration, in a rigid adherence to the principle of ' stability.'   It was not likely to appeal to Prussia, which, rent and dismembered during the Revolutionary epoch, was planning to compensate herself for losses in Poland by the annexation of Saxony. It would appeal, finally—and this was the traditional statecraft of France—to those lesser German Powers which feared to be ground between the upper and nether millstone of Austria and Prussia, and to that host of German princelings whose petitions for the restoration of their ' liberties ' were flooding the chanceries of the Allies.[12]

The time of waiting between the signature of the Treaty of Paris and the opening of the Congress of

[12] Many of these documents are preserved among the F.O. Records. Their language is that of a world even then perished beyond hope of revival.   There is much allusion to traditional ' liberties,' but the word is used in the same feudal sense as in Magna Charta.

Vienna was an anxious one for France. So far as the patent provisions of the treaty were concerned, there was indeed nothing to cause her misgiving. By Article XXII it was stipulated that all the Powers engaged on one side or the other in the war were to send plenipotentiaries to Vienna to regulate in a geneial Congress the arrangements for the completion of the treaty. But an annexed secret article, embodying the principle settled at Chaumont, laid down that the disposition to be made of the territories ceded by France under Article III of the Treaty of Paris was to be regulated at the Congress on the basis agreed upon by the Allied Powers among themselves. Whether or no, as Talleyrand wrote in his ' Memoirs,' the diplomatists were a little ashamed of their weakness in signing the Treaty of Paris, he was right in suspecting that they were not disposed to admit France to the Congress on equal terms, and that the Alliance of Chaumont was still in force. The postponement from August to October of the opening of the Congress, necessitated by Castlereagh having to attend the session of Parliament and by the urgent demand for the Emperor Alexander's presence in Russia,[13] seemed to him but a ruse to extend the period of the tutelage of France ; for, pending the completion of the arrangements as to the Balance of Power, the Allies remained armed.[14] On this point he was speedily reassured ; but his suspicions reawoke when, on August 14, it was announced that Castlereagh had reached Ghent on the way to Vienna, where preliminary conferences were to be held without France being invited to participate. ' The English minister,' writes Pozzo di Borgo, ' in explaining the matter, did so in such a way as to inspire grave misgivings as to the part assigned to the French Government in future transactions.' The explanations given by Castlereagh to King Louis

[13] Nesselrode to Pozzo di Borgo, London, June 10/12, 1814. Polovtsov, *op. cit.* p. 24.
[14] Talleyrand to Noailles, July 23. *Ibid.* p. 44.

in person, he added, were more satisfactory, and these
had been conveyed through Metternich to Talleyrand.
The preliminary meetings at Vienna, Castlereagh said,
were only concerned with transactions that had previously passed between them, and were not for the
purpose of deciding, without the knowledge of France,
any questions, whether general or particular, on which
she was naturally called to give her opinion. As to
the treaties made during the war with Napoleon, these
had no application to the legitimate monarchy.[15]

There was in all this, in spite of Pozzo's opinion,
little enough to satisfy Talleyrand. The questions
on which France was not ' naturally called to give an
opinion ' had been defined at Chaumont, and they were
precisely the questions in the solution of which it was
imperative that France should have a voice, namely,
the disposal of the territories she had ceded in such a
way as to produce a ' just equilibrium.' It was in the
controversies certain to arise over the redistribution of
these territories that Talleyrand looked for the means of
breaking up an Alliance which was still pointed against
France ; and if before the opening of the Congress these
questions should have been in principle settled by the
Allies among themselves, the diplomacy of France at
Vienna would have to be directed to undoing all that
had previously been done without her. Otherwise, so
far from gaining anything by attending the Congress,
she would by her presence forfeit all right in the future
to dispute its decisions, though she had had no voice in
their formulation. If, then, Talleyrand attended the
Congress, it was with the deliberate intention of turning
the tables against the Alliance. The restored monarchy
of France was to be the spokesman of the European
idea against the partial union of the four Allies, the
raison d'être of which had ceased with the fall of Napoleon
and the dissolution of his empire. France, content

---

[15] Pozzo di Borgo to Nesselrode, August 16/28, 1814. Polovtsov,
op. cit. p. 64.

with her legitimate boundaries, would pose as the disinterested champion of legitimacy everywhere, and, herself desiring nothing, would be in all the stronger position to resist the particularist ambitions of the Powers, sowing the seeds of dissension among them, and thus recovering her own due weight in the balance of the European states.

II

THE CONGRESS OF VIENNA

Its general character—Dictatorship of the Great Powers—Talleyrand
leads the opposition of the lesser Powers—He champions ' justice
and public law ' against the particularist ambitions of the Powers
—Questions of Poland and Saxony—Attitude of Alexander and
its causes—Threatened break-up of the Alliance—Diplomacy of
Castlereagh—Talleyrand admitted to the Conferences—Secret
Treaty of January 3, 1815—Harmony restored—The Vienna Final
Act—General analysis of its provisions from the point of view of
a basis of an international system—The return of Napoleon from
Elba—Revival of the Quadruple Alliance.

As for the great Congress—with which I only propose
to deal in its broadest aspects—it was soon clear that
Talleyrand's suspicions as to its scope and objects were
abundantly justified. In its outward aspect, indeed,
it promised fulfilment of some at least of the exalted
hopes that humanity had based upon it. Never before
had the civilized world witnessed its like. ' The city
of Vienna,' wrote Gentz to the Hospodar of Wallachia
on September 27, ' presents at present an overwhelming
spectacle ; all the most illustrious personages in Europe
are represented here in the most exalted fashion.' [16]
But this brilliant assemblage, so far as international
business was concerned, was nothing but a chaotic
mass, in which no one had any defined rights or definite
functions. As to form or procedure nothing had been
fixed ; and for three months the very fundamental character of the Congress was the subject of heated debate,

[16] Prokesch-Osten, *Oesterreichs Theilnahme an den Befreiungskriegen,*
p. 443.

i.e. as to whether it was an assembly capable of
arriving at decisions—a European Parliament, as it were
—or merely a collection of negotiators. A collection of
negotiators, in effect, it was and remained, though with
spasmodic efforts at organization, as in the formation
of committees for the settlement of particular issues,
e.g. the constitutions of Germany and Switzerland ; ' for
to the last moment there was neither certainty nor
consistency.' As for the negotiators themselves, Gentz,
who was secretary to the Congress, gives us a picture
of their unequal status. There were ' sovereigns negotiating in person, some of them as though they were
their own prime ministers [17] ; presidents of cabinets
of the first rank turned into plenipotentiaries ; plenipotentiaries of the second rank ; nearly a hundred princes
and ministers of princes of every degree, each one intent
on furthering some private interest ; deputies from
every part of Germany, agitating day and night for a
federal constitution,' and, it may be added, representatives of the great European financial houses—the ' money-
changers,' as Wellington called them—and a host of
miscellaneous hangers-on and fortune-seekers. In such
an assemblage it was obvious that the stronger must
prevail and that the weak would have to seek salvation
in intrigue. The dictatorship of the Great Powers,
comments Gentz with much truth, though theoretically
an injustice, was under the circumstances a necessity ;
for the Quadruple Alliance was the only nucleus of an
organization having behind it the sanction of force.
' The key to the Congress,' said Gentz, ' is given by the
entire lack of any plan, the preponderance of the four
Powers, and the frequent misunderstandings between
them.' [18]

The formal opening of the Congress had been fixed
for October 1 ; but Gentz dates its inception from

---

[17] This was a hit at the Emperor Alexander.

[18] Gentz's ' account of the various decisions and the final results
of the Congress ' in Prokesch-Osten, *op. cit.* p. 540 *seq.*

September 10, when the ministers of the four Allied Powers—Great Britain, Austria, Prussia, and Russia—held their first meeting. At these preliminary meetings, as was natural enough, the constitution of the Congress was discussed. The first proposal was to constitute a Congress and then to propose the nomination of a committee for the purpose of preparing a project of arrangement to be laid before it. As to the question of the constitution of the Congress itself, Castlereagh wrote on September 24, to Lord Liverpool, that there was only one opinion, that the conduct of business must practically rest with the leading Powers; and it was agreed, after some debate as to the admission of Sweden, that the 'effective cabinet' should not be carried beyond the six Powers of the first order, with an auxiliary council of the five principal German states for the affairs of Germany. In making this announcement, however, Castlereagh added that, in spite of his efforts to effect 'a coincidence of sentiment' between the French and the Allied ministers, the three continental Courts, whatever their differences with each other, seem to feel equal jealousy of admitting France either to arbitrate between them or to assume any leading influence in the arrangements consequent on the Peace.[19]

The *Protocole Séparé* of the conference of September 22, enclosed in this letter, makes the attitude of the Powers abundantly clear. Its provisions were as follows :

1. The four Powers alone were to decide on the distribution of the provinces to be disposed of as the result of the late war and the Treaty of Paris, but the two other Powers were to be allowed to hand in opinions and objections afterwards.

2. The plenipotentiaries of the four Powers would not enter into conferences with those of the two Powers for this

[19] To Liverpool, September 24, 1814. F.O. : Continent, Congress, Vienna.

object until they had arrived at a complete understanding among themselves on the questions of Poland, Germany, and Italy.

3. To save time the plenipotentiaries of the four Powers would, as soon as the Congress opened, consult the two Powers on other matters.

The underlying principle, commented Castlereagh, was that the Allies should have the disposal of the results of their own work, to which, by the Treaty of Paris, France had formally assented. The practical motive was that, while it would be open to France to raise objections in her own name or that of Europe to the arrangements made by the Powers, if she were admitted to the conferences and allowed to discuss each question in detail as it arose, there would be endless opening for intrigue, especially with the small princes of Germany.

The ' general principle ' of the coming Congress, then, as accepted in these preliminary conferences, was that there was to be a ' directing committee ' representing Europe. Particular questions were to be decided by commissions of the Powers interested in them, which were to report to the directing committee, which in its turn was to place the results before those Powers which ought, in its judgment, to be consulted. The battle was to rage round the constitution of this directing committee ; but for the present it was clear that the four Allies intended to confine it, for all effective purposes, to themselves.

Such was the condition which Talleyrand found when he arrived in Vienna. He at once protested. ' A commission,' he wrote, ' can only be appointed by consent of the Congress, which if it is to accept the decisions, should also delegate the power of making them. Business will not be expedited by passing resolutions of which the legitimacy will be disputed.' The proper procedure, he added, would be to form a committee of the eight signatory Powers of the Treaty of Paris, to settle preliminaries.[20] As for what had been done between May 30, when the Congress was agreed upon, and October 1, when it was to meet, he declared that it had no existence for him [21]; and when Metternich mentioned the Alliance he roundly told him that this no longer existed. His own idea of what the Congress should be he submitted to Castlereagh in a formal project. His proposal was ' that every prince having a universally recognized sovereignty over countries engaged in the late war, which he has not ceded, and which is not recognized as belonging to any other, as well as every state which the war found free, may have plenipotentiaries at the Congress—but no others.' [22] This project, as a pencil note on the margin of the copy in the Foreign Office Records points out, ' would have excluded Naples and admitted Saxony,' and was ' considered therefore by Prussia as particularly hostile to her interests.' It was, in fact, French policy masquerading in ' European ' guise.

The disguise was easier when only generalities were involved than when these had to be translated into practical proposals. In a circular addressed on October 3 from Vienna to all the French diplomatic agents, Talleyrand declared that his instructions were to support the principles of justice and of public law, and consequently to aim at securing the rights of each in order to secure the repose of all.[23] In an interview with the Emperor Alexander he used similar language, with Poland as his *arrière-pensée*, till the irritated autocrat was goaded into exclaiming : ' Sooner war than give up what I hold.' Socially and politically boycotted by

[20] Protest of France against the mode of conducting the Congress. Vienna, October 1, 1814. In F.O. : Congress, France, M. Talleyrand, etc., Archives, June 1814–June 1815.

[21] Talleyrand to Louis XVIII, October 4, 1814. Pallain, *Correspondance*, p. 10, No. III.

[22] Enclosed in Castlereagh to Liverpool, October 9, 1814. F.O. : Archives, Congress, etc., June 1814–June 1815.

[23] Polovtsov, *op. cit.* p. 99.

the continental Great Powers, Talleyrand put forth all
his diplomatic arts to form a party among the secondary
Powers and all the mass of princelings who had been
accustomed to look to France for support against the
aggressions of Austria and Prussia.[24] The result was a
meeting of the representatives of thirteen small German
states under the presidency of Bavaria, to protest against
the 'usurpation of the Great Powers.'[25] The fate of
Saxony, in which Talleyrand was more particularly interesting himself, was after all a question that could not
but concern them ; for its projected absorption by Prussia,
in exchange for her Polish provinces ceded to Russia,
would form from their point of view an ugly precedent.
From the British point of view, on the other hand, the
fate of Saxony was in itself of little importance. For
Castlereagh the main thing to be done at the Congress,
apart from providing safeguards against any renewed
danger from revolutionary France, was to secure the
united action of the Powers against the now overgrown
might and extravagant pretensions of Russia, and he
was willing to sacrifice Saxony as the price of Prussian
co-operation. Talleyrand's 'cavilling and creating a discontented party in Germany' was therefore wholly
objectionable to him. He had need of his co-operation
in the more vital matter of Poland, and he used every
sort of pressure—including a threat to recognize Murat
as king of Naples—to prevent France making 'such a
subordinate point' a *casus belli*. 'It was not for the

[24] The agents of the Secret Police reported that his house was
perhaps the most interesting to keep under observation, as it was a
veritable *refugium peccatorum*. To the discontented and alarmed
German princes he maintained that no Congress from Westphalia
onward had been without a mediator, that a mediator was now more
necessary than ever, and that the only possible mediator was France,
which wanted nothing for herself. (Report of October 8. Fournier,
Die Geheimpolizei auf dem Wiener Kongress, p. 167.)

[25] Castlereagh to Liverpool, October 9, 1814. This was the first
of many meetings. One was held on the 14th, at which Baron Gagern
made a long speech, protesting against the intervention of foreign
Powers in Germany, and demanding the restoration of the Holy
Empire. See Fournier, p. 169.

Bourbons,' he said, ' who had been restored by the Allies, to assume a tone of reprobating or throwing odium upon the arrangements that had kept the confederacy together.'[26]

Talleyrand seemed to be impressed. ' I left him,' wrote Castlereagh, ' in a temper apparently to be of use.' But he had his own motives for continuing to pose as the defender of legitimate rights, and for choosing to apply this principle to this particular instance. The last thing he wished was to keep the confederacy together, and in the Saxon Question he saw a ready means for breaking it up and so rescuing France from her isolation. For Austria was glad enough of an opportunity of checking the expansive ambitions of Prussia, especially in the direction of her own frontiers, and in the long run Great Britain would be guided in this matter by the opinion of Austria. In view of this attitude, then, it became impossible to exclude Talleyrand from the preliminary conferences, to which he was admitted on the motion of Austria and Great Britain. As to the Congress itself, on October 8 it was decided to adjourn its formal opening to November 1, pending the settlement of the controversies among the leading Powers, and in spite of the protests of Prussia this was agreed to, Talleyrand giving the proposal his support on condition that the opening of the Congress should be carried out ' conformably to the principles of public law.' In a circular to the French diplomatic agents the Comte de Jaucourt announced this decision, which was due, he said, to the failure of the Powers to agree. ' One would have thought,' he added, ' that the Powers would have agreed to maintain the sentiments of the King of France, but instead they seem to be more disposed to follow the principles against which they took up arms ' —the principles, that is to say, of ' le droit du plus fort.' [27]

[26] Castlereagh to Liverpool, Oct. 9, 1814. *Wellington Supp. Disp.* ix. 323.
[27] Polovtsov, *op. cit.* No. 102.

The ' effective cabinet ' of the Congress — to use Castlereagh's expression—was further enlarged, on his motion, by the admission of Spain ; and finally, at the suggestion of Count Palmella, the representative of Portugal, it was decided to include in it all the eight signatory Powers of the Treaty of Paris.[28] To this committee, Talleyrand wrote, all more important points and all matters of general interest were to be submitted. Five months after the Allies had entered Paris, he added exultantly, France had regained her due place in the councils of Europe.[29] This exultation was premature. It is true, as Gentz said, that henceforth all ostensible decisions, all public and formal declarations, were made in the name of the signatory Powers of the Treaty of Paris, as though this form had received the universal sanction. The committee of eight enjoyed for a while the honour of representing the Congress, but its dominion was neither long nor brilliant. The burning questions of Saxony and Poland were still discussed ' in the recesses of the cabinets ' until, at Russia's suggestion, a committee of four, representing the Allied Powers, was appointed to consider them. Then the old debate began again with increasing heat ; until with great difficulty Castlereagh, for reasons to be explained later, succeeded in getting Talleyrand admitted into this innermost circle, which thus became a committee of five. This committee consisted of eight representatives : Metternich and Wessenberg for Austria, Rasumovsky and Capo d'Istria for Russia (Nesselrode, temporarily out of favour, being included later), Castlereagh (replaced later by Wellington, and, after the opening of the Waterloo campaign, by Clancarty) for Great Britain, and Talleyrand for France. Their main concern was with the questions

---

[28] Cf. protest of Count Palmella at the exclusion of Portugal, dated September 30. Enclosed in Castlereagh to Liverpool, October 9, 1814. F.O. : Vienna.

[29] *Mémoires*, ii. 283.

of Poland and Saxony, but after these questions were settled, the committee absorbed all important matters, and was, in Gentz's words, ' till the last moment the real and only Congress.' From January 1815 onward, the committee of eight met but rarely, only appearing conspicuously at the very end to sign the Final Act on June 9. As for the rest, the secondary and minor Powers, they were nowhere.

I have enlarged somewhat on the constitution of the Congress because it well illustrates the essential conditions of any international organization. From the ideal point of view this constitution was extremely imperfect, for in theory all sovereign States are equal and should have an equal voice in the councils of the nations. But in practice their influence always has been, and always must be, in proportion to the force behind them ; which means that, in the last resort, all important decisions will depend on an agreement between the Great Powers, with or without the consent of the lesser. The proceedings of the Congress of Vienna have also a permanent interest, from the same point of view, as showing the difficulty of arriving at such an agreement, when there is a fundamental conflict of views and interests between the Powers, and the methods by which this difficulty is overcome. The method at Vienna was, as it always must be if one Power or group of Powers is not to dominate the rest, the application of the principle of the balance of power.

This truth Castlereagh had from the first realized, and when in January 1814 he entered the councils of the Allies he announced the policy of Great Britain to be the restoration of a ' just equilibrium ' in Europe. Napoleon was now overthrown, but the equilibrium had not been thereby restored ; for his overthrow had left the immense power of Russia without an effective counterpoise on the Continent. ' The drawback to Russia as an ally,' said Moltke, ' is that she arrives on the field very late and is then too strong.' In the struggle against Napoleon Russia had arrived late, and she was now present in Northern and Central Europe in alarming force. Not only was Poland occupied by Russian troops, but the Grand Duke Constantine was already busy organizing that Polish national army which was to be his pet preoccupation till it turned against him in the insurrection of 1830. Russian troops held Saxony until, to give weight to the counsels of Alexander at Vienna, they evacuated it in favour of the Prussians. Holstein was occupied by the Russians, and to Holstein the Tsars, as representing the Gottorp line, could advance a not too shadowy claim. Finally, so late as November, 60,000 Russians under Field-Marshal Bennigsen, were still posted on the line of the Elbe. As early as August Castlereagh, in a letter to Hardenberg, had warned Prussia of the danger of having Russia on both her flanks, and bidden him watch both the Polish and Holstein frontiers. ' I have reason to believe,' he said, ' that the French Government partakes strongly of the general alarm produced by the accumulating armament on the Russian frontier, and by the organization of a purely Polish army.' [30]

Hardenberg, in reply, used language which showed that Prussia would not readily forego the support which she hoped to receive from the Emperor Alexander in the realization of her own plans. The fears as to Russian designs he declared to be exaggerated, since the Poles would not be likely ' to respond to the Emperor's ideas.' He agreed, however, that it was important that Great Britain, Austria and Prussia should act together at the Congress, and stated that one of their chief objects should be to secure the greatest possible strength for the Germanic Confederation. His ideas as to the scope of this Confederation have a special interest, as illustrating aspirations which have never been abandoned. The

[30] Castlereagh to Hardenberg, August 8, 1814. F.O.: Congress, Prussia. Archives, Hardenberg and Humboldt, August 1814–June 1815.

Netherlands, he argued, should be united to it ' by indissoluble ties '—the safest would be that they should enter
it as the Circle of Burgundy—and Switzerland should
be, if possible, attached to the same system. In view of
the separatist ambitions of Bavaria and Württemberg,
he suggested that Austria and Prussia should be established on the left bank of the Rhine. As for Saxony,
the majority of its population desired to become Prussian,
and he would never consent to any rectification of the
Austrian frontier at its expense. Prussia would also
never consent to hand over to Bavaria the key of South
Germany, the fortress of Mainz.

Castlereagh at least agreed with Hardenberg as to
the necessity for making the new German Confederation
effective. The object which he set before himself at
the Congress was to create a Central European group
of Powers strong enough to resist aggression whether
from France or Russia. The first essential was to force
Russia out of the dangerous salient of Poland. This
accomplished, the unity of Germany was to be secured
by a cordial alliance between Austria and Prussia, the
latter erected into a first-class Power able to defend
the lines both of the Vistula and the Rhine. But everything depended on Great Britain, Austria and Prussia
' hanging together ' at the Congress ; for the ultimate
decision there rested with the four Powers of the Grand
Alliance, and if these three acted in concert Russia would
be isolated and forced to come to terms.[31]

The negotiations during the latter part of the summer
had given a reasonable hope that such a concert would
be secured. But this hope was belied by the situation
which Castlereagh discovered on his arrival in Vienna :
the Emperor Alexander obstinately bent on restoring
the kingdom of Poland in personal union with Russia ;
Prussia obstinately bent on annexing the whole of
Saxony ; Austria using towards Prussia an ' extravagant

[31] Webster, *England and the Polish-Saxon Question at the Congress
of Vienna*. Trans. R. Hist. Soc., 3rd Ser., vii. 54.

tone of war,' which in Castlereagh's opinion suggested
a willingness to compromise ; Talleyrand, on the out-
skirts, denouncing in the name of ' legitimacy ' any
interference by *force majeure* with the rights of the
King of Saxony, a principle which would have made
compromise impossible. Upon Castlereagh fell the task
of untying the knot, if it could be untied ; for of all
the Powers Great Britain was the only one which
could in these questions take up an attitude wholly
disinterested and European ; as for the others, after
two months' experience of them, he was to realize how
little they were prepared to sacrifice for the common
good.[32]

In personal interviews with Alexander he did his
best to move him from his resolution. Great Britain,
he said, would favour the restoration of an independent
Poland, but this idea of a partial restoration under the
Russian sovereign was pregnant with future troubles.
For, if the Poles were content under their measure of
liberty, those under Austria and Prussia would be discontented, and Russia would then have not only the
10,000,000 Polish subjects at her back, but 5,000,000
others nominally foreign. In a weighty memorandum
he pointed out that the Emperor's project was a violation
of the treaty under which Russia held her Polish provinces ; for by a secret article of the Convention of
St. Petersburg of January 15, 1797, it was stipulated
that none of the high contracting Powers was to include
in its title the designation of kingdom of Poland, which
was to remain for ever suppressed. It was a violation
also of the Treaty of Kalisch, according to which the
duchy of Warsaw was by a friendly arrangement to
be partitioned between the three Allies, a stipulation
confirmed by the subsequent treaties of June 27 and
September 9, 1813. Moreover, he pointed out with

---

[32] ' I have witnessed every day the astonishing tenacity with which
all the Powers cling to the smallest point of separate interests ' (to
Liverpool, December 7).

prophetic insight that the system which Alexander proposed to establish would not last, but would probably ' either be deliberately destroyed or perish at the hands of his successor.' [33] A few days later he addressed a letter to the Tsar couched in language particularly calculated to appeal to him. ' It depends exclusively,' he wrote, ' upon the temper in which your Imperial Majesty shall meet the questions which more immediately concern your own Empire, whether the present Congress shall prove a blessing to mankind or only exhibit a scene of discordant intrigue and a lawless scramble for power. . . . Give to Europe that peace which it expects at your hands ! ' [34]

The Emperor, in reply, used the curious argument that the Polish kingdom, so far from proving an increase to Russian power, would create a ' balance and check ' upon it, and that when the Russian provinces were united, as he intended, under a free system and his army withdrawn beyond the Niemen, Europe would have nothing to fear. The argument, based on a plan never likely to take form save in Alexander's imagination, was probably put forward in all sincerity for reasons to be mentioned later ; but Castlereagh may be forgiven for failing to be impressed by such language in the mouth of a Russian emperor. He was the less impressed, since, as he reported home, in any case ' His Imperial Majesty insinuated that the question could only end in one way, as he was *in possession*.' [35] In vain he pointed out that Great Britain had not acted thus, but had freely surrendered her conquests in order to help in the work of European restoration. This was, of course, to assume that the Russian occupation of Poland was on the same moral level as Great Britain's colonial conquests, a

[33] To Liverpool, October 2, 1814. Compare ' A Memorandum on the Tsar's Designs in Poland,' dated October 4, in F.O. : Congress, Russia. Archives. Enclosed in Castlereagh to Liverpool. No. 6.

[34] Castlereagh to the Emperor of All the Russias, October 12, 1914. *Wellington Supp. Disp.* ix. 329.

[35] To Liverpool, October 14, 1814. F.O. : Congress, Vienna.

suggestion offensive in view of the Emperor's avowed
intention of restoring the national existence of Poland,
an exalted motive which justified him before God and
man in retaining the hold he had acquired over the
country, even though in doing so he seemed to violate
engagements entered into with his Allies.

Not that there had been, or would be, any such
violation.   In a formal memorandum the Tsar dealt
with the special charges contained in Castlereagh's
communication.   As for the accusations of breach of
faith, he regarded them with calm.   The treaty of
1797 had been 'cancelled by circumstances,' while
the stipulations of those of 1813 were 'purement
éventuelles,' and in view of the large acquisitions made
by Austria as a result of the war, no longer applied.
On November 4 Castlereagh enclosed his answer in a
letter to the Tsar.   The Russian memorandum, he said,
contained 'maxims of public law perfectly novel in
themselves and subversive of every received principle
of confidence and good faith between states.'   As
for the stipulations of the treaties cited being 'éventuelles '—' éventuelles ' upon what ?   ' Apparently upon
the extraordinary principle that, there being ample
means to satisfy the treaty, a new right accrued to Russia,
another party to the treaty, to decide according to her
pleasure whether Austria should obtain the object stipulated or accept in lieu of it what Russia deems an equivalent at the opposite extremity of her dominions.   On
what securities will treaties rest if they are thus constantly
annulled ? '   He goes on to denounce the false principle
that states have in all cases the right to compensation
by annexations for war expenses, and points out the
peril of this principle of partition and compensation
to the future of Europe.   The answer of the Emperor
Alexander to this straightforward statement was a note
to Castlereagh, dated November 9, requesting that this
' private ' correspondence should cease.

The situation created by the stubborn temper of the

Tsar had been made worse by the mutual distrust and conflicting ambitions of the two other Allies, of whom Castlereagh reported that in proportion as they were excluded from Poland they became more pressing in other directions. He himself, as already mentioned, favoured the creation of a strong Prussia, and advocated a policy ' which Mr. Pitt, in the year 1806, had strongly at heart, which was to tempt Prussia to put herself forward on the left bank of the Rhine, more in military contact with France.' ' I know,' he wrote, ' that there may be objection to this, as placing a power peculiarly military, and consequently somewhat encroaching, so extensively in contact with Holland and the Low Countries.' Point was given to this misgiving by Hardenberg's persistence in the suggestion that the Netherlands should be invited to join the German Confederation ; but Castlereagh believed that Prussian ambitions were but a ' secondary danger,' the more immediate one being ' the systematic views of France to possess herself of the Low Countries and the left bank of the Rhine, a plan which, however discountenanced by the present French Government, will infallibly revive whenever circumstances favour its execution.' [36]

To Austria and the South German States, however, the ' great appetite ' of Prussia was for the moment more alarming than any possible danger in the future from France. At Paris Hardenberg had proposed that Prussia should be placed behind the Rhine, with a *lisière* on the left bank, her flanks supported by the fortresses of Wesel and Mainz ; and he still obstinately maintained her claim to the latter place. Austria and Bavaria, on the other hand, absolutely refused to agree to the occupation of Mainz by Prussia, which would not only give her their only great river, in addition to the Rhine, the Elbe, the Oder and the Vistula, but would ' cede to Northern interests ' the only great fortress towards

[36] The plan was in fact revived, in more or less tentative fashion, both by Louis Philippe and by Napoleon III.

the south of Germany.[37] Metternich backed up his
refusal with threats. But, as Castlereagh had expected,
he soon ' descended from the tone of war to one of compromise,' and Castlereagh was able to persuade him to
agree to the Prussian demand for the whole of Saxony,
and to a compromise on the question of Mainz, on condition that Prussia should come into line with the others
in the matter of Poland.[38] On this basis Metternich
and Hardenberg arrived at an understanding, and since
Castlereagh had taken measures to prevent a *rapprochement* between the Tsar and Talleyrand,[39] it seemed as
though his policy of isolating Russia had been crowned
with success.

He had, however, left out of his calculations the
dominating influence exercised by the Russian Emperor
over the feeble Frederick William III of Prussia, who
was styled by the wits of Vienna ' the Emperor
Alexander's shadow.' The King refused to support a
policy against which, in a stormy interview, his Imperial
friend protested ; and the Prussian Ministers yielded,
not very unwillingly, to the royal will. The break-up
of the Alliance seemed now to be inevitable, and on the
eve of the formal opening of the Congress rumours were
rife in Vienna that it would meet only to disperse. ' God
grant,' wrote the Swedish plenipotentiary Loewenhielm
on October 18, 'that the members of the Congress will
not act like the Fathers of the Council of Nicæa, who
settled the question of the Trinity with their fists.' [40]
' Unless the Emperor of Russia can be brought to a
more moderate and sound course of public conduct,'

[37] Castlereagh to Wellington, October 2, 1814. *Wellington Supp.
Disp.* ix. 301.
[38] October 9, 1814. Cf. Metternich to Hardenberg, November 2.
Congress. Austria. Archives. Metternich and Baron Wessenberg.
He offered an independent Poland, or a division of Poland, on the line
of the Vistula, into two kingdoms of North and East Poland under
Prussia and South Poland under Russia.
[39] Webster, *op. cit.* pp. 57, 62.
[40] Fournier, *Geheimpolizei*, p. 227.

wrote Castlereagh on November 11, ' the Peace which we
have so dearly purchased will be of but short duration.'

It was not until the beginning of December that
Alexander at last, to quote Castlereagh, showed ' a disposition to regard the Polish Question as a subject of
negotiation with the Allies,' and when he did so it
was to make the complete cession of Saxony to Prussia
the condition *sine qua non* of some wholly inadequate
concessions in the matter of territories to be included
in his Polish kingdoms.[41]   This decided Metternich to
throw in his lot on the Saxon question with France
and the German states.   In a letter to Hardenberg he
declared that nothing would induce the Emperor Francis
to yield on this point, and he enclosed a copy of his
letter to Talleyrand.   It was, wrote Castlereagh, the
first regular overture made by Austria to France.[42]   The
British minister now demanded that France should
be admitted to the conference on the Saxon Question,
' not,' as he explained, ' to the abandonment of the
confidential discussions between the Powers that had
been allied during the war, but that she might not feel
excluded from the consideration of a question in which
she had professed to take so strong an interest.'   Moreover, he added, until France was brought in, Saxony,
which certainly ought to yield something, would not
come to terms.[43]

The reply of Prussia, which had fortified Dresden,
was to press forward her armaments and to declare that
she would consider a refusal to recognize her claim on
Saxony as tantamount to a declaration of war.   Castlereagh feared ' some sudden coup on the part of Russia
and Prussia to coerce Austria,' and he protested that,
since the Powers were no longer deliberating ' in a state
of independence,' it would be better to break up the
Congress.   The threat was explained away ; but in view

[41] To Liverpool, December 5.
[42] To Liverpool, December 18.   Webster, *op. cit.* p. 84.
[43] To Liverpool, January 2. 1815 (dated 1814).

of the fact that it had been uttered by two great Powers
in a formal conference, it appeared to the others—to
quote Castlereagh—' to call for some precautionary
correction by which the other Powers might be induced
to feel that, in the discharge of their functions in Congress
they are not exposed individually and in details to the
destructive effect of such a domineering dictation.' [44]
The ' precautionary correction ' was the defensive alliance
between Great Britain, Austria, and France, signed on
January 3, 1815. ' I flatter myself,' wrote Castlereagh,
' that the necessity will never arise of acting upon these
engagements.' [45]

He was right. On the 5th he was able to report
home that the danger of war seemed over, Hardenberg
having invited his good offices in the Saxon Question.
The Emperor Alexander, who had heard rumours of the
alliance, met Castlereagh in the most conciliatory spirit,
and a month later the whole question could be reported
as closed. Prussia had to be content with part of Saxony,
and Alexander with a kingdom of Poland which, though
it thrust itself ominously between Prussia and Austria,
was less extensive than that of his dreams.

I have dealt in some detail with this particular
question, the most critical which the Congress had to
face, because it illustrates the difficulty of working
any international system where acute differences of
opinion arise between equal Powers, more especially
where the conflict is not only one of interests but of
principles. It may be asked where, in this particular
controversy, principle was involved. To the mass of
contemporary opinion Alexander's attitude seemed to be
dictated by no higher a motive than that of keeping what
he held, an opinion to which his language, in moments
of irritation, lent weight. In fact, however, he was

[44] To Liverpool, January 1, 1815. (Most secret and confidential.)
Webster, *op. cit.* p. 88.
[45] To Liverpool, January 3, enclosing the Convention of Alliance.
The treaty is printed in Marten's *Recueil des traités, Nouveau Suppl.*
(ed. Murhard, 1889), i. 368, No. 49.

using his power to realize his favourite idea of the
regeneration of Poland, and to fulfil the oft-repeated
promises made to his friend Czartoryski.[46] His Polish
policy was certainly not inspired by consideration for
the interests of Russia. It was hated by his people and
condemned by his Russian advisers. To have consented to the creation of an independent Poland, as
Castlereagh suggested, would have cost him his throne
and his life, and he resented the importunity of the
veteran Kosciuszko, the hero of the war of 1794, who had
come to Vienna to plead a cause so dangerous to the
Imperial person and so little flattering to the Imperial
vanity. But Castlereagh was not the only one to point
out the perils of the half-measure of independence which
Alexander proposed to bestow upon Poland. In 1832,
after the Polish insurrection, Pozzo di Borgo told Baron
de Meyendorff that in a conversation with the Emperor
at Vienna he had foretold the ruin which would result
if his Polish plans were realized, and the Emperor's
reply had merely been to enlarge, ' with eyes aflame
and in the tone of one inspired, on the injustices so
long committed against this poor Poland.'[47] Clearly,
Alexander was not acting the hypocrite when he told
Castlereagh that in insisting on the restoration of Poland
he was but performing a moral duty ; for the question
was for him not one of political expediency, to be determined by the advice of his ministers, but one of lofty
principle to be decided by himself as the anointed agent
of the Divine Will. ' The Czar,' Castlereagh had written
home early in November, ' had ceased to be guided in
the question of Poland by his regular servants. It is
unfortunately his habit to be his own minister, and

[46] ' Cette guerre . . . me dégage de tous les ménagements qui j'ai
eu à garder envers la France, et me laisse la liberté de travailler à mes
idées favorites sur la régénération de votre patrie ' (Alexander to
Czartoryski, April 1, 1812. Grand Duke Nicholas Mikhailovich,
L'Empereur Alexandre Ier, i., App., 363).

[47] Unpublished papers of Baron de Meyendorff, quoted by the
Grand Duke Nicholas Mikhailovich, *ibid.* i. 149.

to select as the instrument of his immediate purpose the person who may fall in most with his views.' The person in this case was Czartoryski, by whom the Tsar's memorandum on the Polish Question had been drawn up.

There was then nothing in Alexander's attitude really inconsistent with his ' European ' ideals,[48] save perhaps in so far as it was in conflict with his championship of the ' faith of treaties.' The Europe of his dreams, as pictured in the instructions to Novosiltsov in 1804, was a confederation of constitutional states, demarcated by their national boundaries and by homogeneity of population ; and in commenting on the Tsar's reply to his second memorandum, Castlereagh notes ' the energy of the author in pleading the rights of nations.' [49] For the most part the dream was clearly unrealizable ; but so far at least as Poland was concerned, he was in a position at least partially to realize it. The whole incident is historically mainly significant as the earliest and most conspicuous illustration of a difficulty which has ever since proved insuperable : that of reconciling the effective establishment of an international system of public law with national aspirations and ambitions.

That, speaking generally, these aspirations were little regarded in the acts of the Vienna Congress is a commonplace of history. The ultimate settlement effected by it was dictated, in fact, almost wholly by the old doctrine of the balance of power, and by the policy of erecting barriers against French aggression. Into the details of the territorial settlement I do not propose to examine, since they have no bearing on my main argument. A few words may be said, however, about the question of constitutional government as dealt with by the Congress.

[48] The Grand Duke Nicholas Mikhailovich, whose whole work is a criticism of Alexander for sacrificing the interests of Russia to his cosmopolitan idealism, comments on the fact that of the Tsar's ministers and advisers at Vienna only one, Rasumovsky, was a Russian. Of the rest Nesselrode and Stein were Germans, Capo d'Istria a Greek, Pozzo di Borgo a Corsican, La Harpe a Swiss, and Czartoryski a Pole.

[49] To Liverpool, November 21, 1814.

In Alexander's ideal scheme, as we have seen, free Constitutions played an important part ; for his perfected
European Peace Confederation included not only ' the
fixing of the relations of states to each other by more
precise rules, but the attaching of the nations to their
governments by making them incapable of acting save
in the greatest interest of the peoples subject to them,'
i.e. by the grant of Constitutions.   Alexander's influence
had been used to realize this ideal in the case of France ;
through Capo d'Istria, under the inspiration of La Harpe,
he had helped to press through the reformed Constitution
of Switzerland ; finally, the kingdom of Poland, created
by the Congress, was to be a constitutional one.   Most
interesting, however, from our particular point of view,
is the Constitution of Germany under the *Bundesakt*,
which was formulated in hurried sittings during the last
ten days of the Congress.   In spite of the great pressure
brought to bear on the Emperor Francis by the German
princes, in spite of Cardinal Consalvi's protest in the
name of the Holy See against the suppression of ' the
centre of political unity,' the Holy Roman Empire was
not revived.   Germany, as stipulated at Chaumont,
became a confederation of states, sovereign, but bound
by the Treaty of Vienna to conform to public law as
far as it was formulated in this treaty ; and among the
provisions of this law was the obligation laid on each
one of them by Article XIII of the Act of Confederation to summon ' assemblies of estates.'   Germany thus
became a sort of miniature Confederation of Europe,
the *Bundestag* representing the central council of the
Powers, and its working exactly illustrates what would
have happened if Alexander had ever succeeded in
realizing his dream of a universal union :—in the struggle
between the great Powers for predominance in the central
diet, due to the fact that their voting power was
ludicrously unequal to their effective force, the uneasy
submission of the lesser Powers to the greater, and
the jealousies of the two leading Powers which, fifty

years later, led to open war between them and the break-up of greater Germany.

What then was the outcome of the Congress from which Europe had expected so much ? ' Universal expectation,' wrote Gentz in his account of the final results of the Congress, ' has perhaps never been roused to such a pitch as before the opening of this dignified assembly. Men had promised themselves an all-embracing reform of the political system of Europe, guarantees for universal peace, in one word, the return of the golden age. The Congress has resulted in nothing but restorations, which had already been effected by arms, agreements between the Great Powers of little value for the future balance and preservation of the peace of Europe, quite arbitrary alterations in the possessions of the smaller states ; but no act of a higher nature, no great measure for public order or for the general good, which might compensate humanity for its long sufferings or pacify it for the future. ' [50]

' But to be just,' he adds, ' the treaty, such as it is, has the undeniable merit of having prepared the world for a more complete political structure. If ever the Powers should meet again to establish a political system by which wars of conquest would be rendered impossible, and the rights of all guaranteed, the Congress of Vienna, as a preparatory assembly, will not have been without use. A number of vexatious details have been settled, and the ground has been prepared for building up a better social structure.' The diplomatic history of the next few years is largely that of attempts to complete the work left unfinished at Vienna and to build up this better social structure.

As for the guarantee of ' rights,' it must be noted that there was no general guarantee even of such rights as had been established at Vienna. Early in February, indeed, Castlereagh, in answer to a proposal for renewing the Alliance of Chaumont, had suggested instead

[50] Prokesch-Osten, p. 540.

a common declaration stating the determination of the Powers to maintain the settlement effected and 'to turn the general influence and if necessary the general arms against the power that shall first attempt to disturb the Continental Peace.'[51] This declaration was actually drawn up by Gentz. But it was never issued. The news of Napoleon's return from Elba intervened, and on March 25 the four Powers signed at Vienna a treaty renewing that of Chaumont.

The Final Act of the Congress of Vienna was signed on June 9, 1815, nine days before the Battle of Waterloo. On June 2 Lord Clancarty, who had succeeded Wellington as British plenipotentiary at Vienna, wrote to Castlereagh that, to avoid delay, due to multiplication of copies, the great treaty was to be ratified only by the eight Powers, possibly only by the five, and that treaties involving the rights of others, e.g. Sardinia and the Netherlands, were to be signed separately and then incorporated.[52]

The Treaty of Vienna thus formed, as it were, the nucleus of an international public code to which additions were to be made as occasion served. It established, in idea at least, a concert of the Great Powers and the right of others to be taken into counsel when their interests were involved—a right, it may be added, destined in practice to be but little recognized. But for the moment, whatever the wider concert may have been on paper, the effective concert was once more the Quadruple Alliance directed against France.

[51] Circular Dispatch of February 13, 1815. Quoted in Webster, *Some Aspects of Castlereagh's Foreign Policy*. Trans. R. Hist. Soc., 3rd Ser., vi. 71.
[52] F.O. : Congress, Vienna, Clancarty. May–July 1815.

IV

THE CONSECRATION OF THE CONFEDERATION

The sole principle of force, whether between Governments or between their subjects, shall be that of doing each other reciprocal service, and of testifying by unalterable good will the mutual affection with which they ought to be animated, to consider themselves all as members of one and the same Christian nation.—THE ACT OF THE HOLY ALLIANCE.

La morale soutenue par des bataillons !—ABBÉ DE PRADT.

I

THE CONVERSION OF ALEXANDER

The Second Restoration—Divergent views as to the fate of France—
Action of Wellington and Castlereagh—Popularity of Louis XVIII's
restoration—But weakness of the King's position—Napoleon's
troops hold out in the fortresses—Excesses of the Allies—Danger
of a disruption of the Alliance—Question of Alexander's attitude—This determined by his ' conversion '—The Baroness von
Krüdener—The interview at Heilbronn—The Imperial prayer-
meetings—Alexander arrives in Paris—The Alliance re-cemented.

THE declaration of the Allied Powers proclaiming
Napoleon Bonaparte, as the enemy and disturber of
the world's peace, outside the pale of the law was issued
at Vienna on March 13, and reached him on March 20,
the very day on which he took up his residence once
more in the Tuileries. What would have happened
had it been delayed a few days, and had Napoleon
been able to publish the secret treaty of January 3,
a copy of which had fallen into his hands, before
the Allies had bound themselves to the principle of
war à outrance against him ? Gentz, in a confidential
memorandum of April 24, deplored the hasty resolution of the Powers, which was but the result of panic,
and was founded on the belief in the stability of
Louis XVIII's throne. The proclamation, he says,
was the outcome of long and bitter debates in which
' the preponderating influence of the English ministers,
the declarations of M. de Talleyrand, the fine phrases
of the Emperor Alexander, and the ravings of Prussia
carried all before them.' It would have been better to

wait and see what success Napoleon had, and how far
his promises of a new moderation would be kept—better
certainly for Austria, for the new war could only end
in increasing the already outrageously excessive preponderance of England, in raising the dominating influence of Russia, and favouring Prussia's schemes of
conquest. ' But of course,' adds Gentz scornfully,
' the sacred bonds of the Great Alliance must not be
broken.' [1] From all this one can see how easily they
might have been broken, had Napoleon succeeded in
breaking the ' thin red line ' at Waterloo. As it was,
Gentz proved a true prophet, for the war did increase
the preponderance of England, and after Waterloo
Wellington and Castlereagh were the arbiters of the
destinies of France and of Europe.

Fortunately there was complete harmony between
them. While repudiating any idea of forcing a government upon France,[2] both desired to see the legitimate
monarchy restored, with as little damage to its prestige
as possible ; both desired to preserve the European
Concert for the purpose of maintaining it. The first,
as matters stood, presented little difficulty. Louis
XVIII had taken refuge in the Low Countries, and,
after Waterloo, he was therefore in a position, with
the good will of Wellington, to re-establish himself, or
rather to be re-established, in Paris before the Russians
and Austrians had time to arrive. Haste was essential,
for the attitude of the Emperors Alexander and
Francis was doubtful. That of Alexander especially,
whose contemptuous estimate of the Bourbons had been
to all appearance completely justified by the ignominious
collapse of the restored monarchy, inspired serious misgivings. To ' group ' him effectually once more it was
necessary to confront him on his arrival in Paris with
the *fait accompli* of the monarchy once more restored.

[1] Prokesch-Osten, *Oesterreichs Theilnahme*, etc., p. 597 *seq.*
[2] Castlereagh to Clancarty, April 8. Congress. Vienna. Drafts to
the Earl of Clancarty.

To secure this end Wellington and Castlereagh had been at pains to impress upon Louis XVIII counsels of moderation, and had persuaded him, greatly against his will, to come to terms with Fouché, the ex-Terrorist Minister of Police, who had made himself indispensable to every Government in turn. In a letter from Paris, dated July 7, Castlereagh reported the result to Lord Liverpool. 'The decision of the Duke of Wellington's march and the commanding character of his victory,' he wrote, 'have reduced the question to one of political management. After my arrival yesterday evening we had a conference at the Duke's with Talleyrand and Fouché, in which the latter undertook to arrange the retreat of the Provisional Government, and, he hoped, of the Assemblies. He appeared to me to conduct himself with fairness, and to be in earnest, which was probably not a little owing to the intimation that the King had taken him into his service.' [3]

The success of the plot was favoured by the temper displayed by the Parisians when, on the following day, Louis XVIII entered Paris. Though he did so, as the Liberal wits put it, 'in the baggage-train of the Allies,' his reception, Castlereagh reported, was no less cordial than that of the year before. This fact is vividly illustrated by a 'private and confidential' dispatch written by Castlereagh on the same date. 'The King,' he writes, 'sent for the Duke and me this evening to the Thuilleries. . . . We found him in a state of great emotion and exaltation at the reception he had met with from his subjects, which appears to have been even more animated than on his former entrance. Indeed, during the long audience to which we were admitted, it was almost impossible to converse, so loud were the shouts of the people in the Thuilleries Gardens, which were full, though it was dark. Previous to the King's dismissing us, he carried the Duke and me to an open window. Candles were brought, which enabled the

[3] F.O. : Congress, Paris, Viscount Castlereagh, July 7-20, 1815.

people to see the King with the Duke by his side. They ran from all parts of the Gardens, and formed a solid mass of an immense extent, rending the air with acclamations.' [4]

But in spite of this striking evidence of the popularity of the Restoration, the whole situation was one of extreme uncertainty. Bonaparte was still at Rochefort ; it was not until the 17th that he surrendered, and even his surrender did not stop the resistance of his troops. Day by day reports came in that the soldiers were ' restraining the enthusiasm ' of the people for the white flag ; in some of the cities the garrisons kept the tricolour flying with the support of the citizens ; while all over the country fortresses were holding out against the invader. It was not till September 20, more than three months after Waterloo, that the last of these, Longwy, surrendered, its garrison of little more than 400 men marching out with the honours of war. In the siege 20,000 Prussians had taken part, of whom 6000 had fallen.[5]

The fact that one of the first acts of Louis XVIII had been to disband the army doubtless accounted for much of the stubbornness of this resistance—Fouché, now Minister of Police, pointed out the folly of mixing 200,000 discontented fighting men with the population—but the bitterness of the resistance was most marked, and it was backed by a growing popular sympathy. This was increased by the excesses of the Allied troops, notably of the Prussians—excesses in which it is gratifying to know that the British took no part. If these outrages were not stopped, Castlereagh wrote home, they would end by uniting France and dividing the Alliance.

There was, indeed, a serious danger that the

---

[4] F.O. : Congress, Paris, Viscount Castlereagh, July 7–20, 1815.

[5] See the interesting *Bulletins de la Correspondance de l'Intérieur*, in F.O. : Congress, Paris, Castlereagh, July 7–20, and subsequent volumes. For Longwy, *Bulletin* of September 24, in No. 28.

Alliance would resolve itself into its elements. In the letter of July 8, quoted above, Castlereagh reported that attempts were being made to poison the mind of the Emperor Alexander against the measures taken by Wellington and himself ; but fortunately the Russian Ambassador, Pozzo di Borgo, who had been present during all the interviews, was going to meet him, armed with the necessary papers, in order to give him the correct view.   More immediately serious was the attitude of the Prussians, who were treating France as a conquered country and indulging in ' measures of arbitrary and unconcerted severity,' [6] natural enough, perhaps, considering the provocation they had received, but fatal to any idea of the development and maintenance of a *European* peace policy. As for Louis XVIII himself, his position, deprived as he was of any armed force save the National Guards, was one of absolute weakness, a weakness advertised to all the world by the fact that the traitors of the Hundred Days were still at large, and that no attempt was being made to arrest and punish them.

France at war with herself—white cockade against tricolour, Catholic against Protestant—overrun with foreign invaders bent on vengeance, and, as Talleyrand was to complain, making little distinction in their attacks between the white flag and the tricolour, and presided over by a King without power—such was the condition of things when, on the evening of July 10, the Emperor Alexander, accompanied by Frederick William of Prussia, made his entry into Paris. On his attitude, hitherto ambiguous, everything depended. Would he, in his contempt and dislike for the Bourbons, now doubly discredited, join hands with the Jacobins to create a liberal France in intimate league with a Russia soon to be liberalized ? Would he, remembering

---

[6] Blücher had laid on Paris a contribution of 100,000,000 livres and equipment for 100,000 men ; and he was ' at this moment mining the Pont d'Iena with a view to blowing it up.'

the secret treaty of January 3, revenge himself by listening to his Prussian allies, who were clamouring for the utter dismemberment of France? Or would he be faithful to his vision of a European Confederation, founded upon the principles of legitimate right and a just equilibrium, and assist Great Britain in establishing and maintaining the national monarchy of France in its traditional place in Europe? The answer, in the case of this incalculable autocrat, depended largely upon the mood of the moment; and Alexander's mood at this particular moment was determined by an event that had happened shortly before, namely, his conversion by the Baroness von Krüdener.

It is impossible here even to outline the singular life-story of this lady, which, apart from the powerful but temporary influence which she exercised over the Emperor Alexander, is mainly of interest as illustrating the religious sickliness of the age. Suffice it to say that she was the daughter of a wealthy Livonian noble and widow of a Russian ambassador, and that, after a youth spent in frivolity, she had in 1806 ' found salvation ' through the agency of a pious cobbler of Riga. A prophetic peasant whom she met when on a visit to Queen Louise of Prussia in 1807 had converted her to chiliastic views, and after sitting at the feet of Jung-Stilling and other leaders of mystical religion, she had herself started on the career of a prophetess, travelling hither and thither proclaiming to all and sundry the imminent approach of the ' latter days.' Her wealth, her rank, and her astonishing flow of emotional language secured her a large following; but her colossal vanity was not to be satisfied with small spiritual game, and she had long been ambitious of crowning her triumphs by the conversion of the Emperor Alexander. On the eve of the Congress of Vienna her chance seemed to have come. In September 1814 the Empress Elizabeth was at

Karlsruhe, and she and the pietistic ladies of the Court were anxious to bring the Emperor into touch with the Baroness von Krüdener, whose ardent disciples they were. To Roxandra Stourdza, who had accompanied her brother to the Congress of Vienna, the Baroness herself wrote urgent letters, full of prophetic fervour, begging her to procure an interview. 'The storm is advancing,' she wrote. 'These lilies which the Eternal had preserved, this emblem of a pure and fragile flower which broke a sceptre of iron, because such was the will of the Eternal, these lilies which should have summoned to purity, to the love of God, to repentance, have appeared but to disappear ; the lesson is given, and men, more hardened than ever, dream only of tumult.' [7]   As for the Emperor, ' I have long known,' she said, ' that the Lord will give me the joy of seeing him. . . . I have immense things to say to him . . . the Lord alone can prepare his heart to receive them.'

These letters, which were intended for Alexander's eye and were undoubtedly shown to him, produced no immediate result, for the atmosphere of the Vienna Congress was unfavourable to religious emotion. But with the news of the return of Napoleon this atmosphere changed.[8]   Roxandra Stourdza remembered the prophecy about the lilies disappearing and persuaded herself that her inspired friend had foretold the fall of the Bourbons. In answer to her questions the Baroness said that she had written these words about the lilies ' by an inspiration ' which transported her, adding that she knew all that was passing in the soul of the Emperor, and repeating that she had great things to announce to him.[9] Alexander, who had taken no notice of the prophecy until its apparent fulfilment, was troubled,

[7] To Roxandra Stourdza, October 27, 1814. In Muhlenbeck, *Les Origines de la Sainte-Alliance*, p. 209.

[8] See, e.g., Metternich's account of Alexander's reconciliation with him (*Mem.*).

[9] April 10, 1815. Muhlenbeck, p. 214.

and his curiosity piqued. Thus, when chance threw in the Baroness's way the opportunity of realizing her ambition, the ground was already prepared.

In the spring of 1815 the Baroness was established at Schlüchtern, a village belonging to Baden but *enclavé* in Württemberg,[10] where she was busy persuading the unhappy peasants to sell all and flee from the wrath to come.   Near by, at Heilbronn, the Emperor Alexander fixed his headquarters on the night of June 4.   So clear a hint on the part of Providence was not to be neglected, and that very night the Baroness sought an interview. To the Tsar, who had been reading the Bible in solitude, her sudden arrival came as an answer to his prayers. She was at once admitted, and for three hours preached her strange gospel, while the Autocrat of All the Russias sat sobbing, with his face buried in his hands. At last, alarmed at the effects of her words, she ceased, and prayed the Emperor to pardon her temerity. 'Do not be afraid,' replied Alexander ; 'all your discourse has justified itself to my heart ; you have helped me to discover in myself things which I had never yet perceived.   I thank God for it.   But I shall often have need of similar conversations, and I beg you not to leave my neighbourhood.'[11]

Next day, at the Emperor's invitation, the Baroness,

----

[10] She had been expelled from Württemberg itself.   In 1809 it had been inexpedient to allow Napoleon to be publicly described as ' the Beast,' and there were other more permanent reasons making her presence undesirable.

[11] H. L. Empeytaz, *Notice sur Alexandre, Empereur de Russie* (2nd ed., Paris, 1840).   The Baroness von Krüdener's letters to Alexander and Prince Golitsin are published in the Grand Duke Nicholas Mikhailovich's *L'Empereur Alexandre Ier*, ii. 215 *seq*.   That of June 23, 1815 (p. 221), is a farrago of mystical and emotional nonsense covering several pages of close print.   It ends with a long address to the Almighty, of which the following is an instructive sample : ' Je ne Vous demande plus : Pourquoi m'avez-Vous attaché a cet Empereur ? . . . Vous le destinez à de si grands choses et daignez me choisir pour Vous obéir dans cette éducation.   Montrez-lui donc combien je Vous dois.'   For Alexander's relations with Madame de Krüdener, see also the *Mémoires* of Countess Edling (Roxandra Stourdza).

with her disciple the Swiss evangelist Empeytaz, joined the Russian headquarters, which she accompanied to Heidelberg, and later to Paris. Here she was lodged in the Hôtel Montchenu, next door to the Elysée Palace, where Alexander was established ; a private door connected the two houses, and every evening during his residence in Paris the autocrat went to take part in the prayer-meetings conducted by the Baroness and Empeytaz.[12] Madame de Krüdener had, for the time at least, become a power to be reckoned with, and admission to her spiritual *séances* was sought by a crowd of people celebrated in the intellectual and social world. Of the effect of these mystical influences on the development of Alexander's idea of the Holy Alliance I shall speak later on ; meanwhile, the Tsar's religious exaltation reacted upon his whole policy at the time, and played a very important part in determining his attitude during the negotiations that led up to the signing of the second Treaty of Paris.

[12] ' Since he has come to Paris he has passed a part of every evening with Madame de Krudener, an old fanatic ' (Castlereagh to Liverpool, September 1815. *Wellington Supp. Disp.* xi. 175).

II

THE SECOND TREATY OF PARIS

Problems of the settlement with France—The question of dismemberment—Attitude of Castlereagh and Wellington ; of Alexander ; of
the German Powers—Compromise embodied in the second Treaty
of Paris ; the limits of 1790.

CASTLEREAGH, in announcing to Lord Liverpool the
arrival of the sovereigns, reported that Alexander was
in ' a cordial, contented, and reasonable disposition,'
and, what was considered of particularly good omen,
' disposed to keep the Jacobins at arm's length.' The
immediate effect was to re-cement the Alliance, which
had been in serious danger of breaking up. At a conference held on July 13 the principle of concerted action
was again strongly affirmed. It was declared that none
of the cabinets could or would act in isolation, and in
view of the necessity of a common military and civil
policy, it was decided that political control was to be
exercised by the ministers of the four Powers, who were
to confer on all questions with the heads of the armed
forces. As for the Prussians, who were the main source
of trouble, the Duke of Wellington declared that unless
the system pursued by them, and imitated by the
Bavarians, was effectually checked, ' the Allies would in
a short time find themselves situated in France as the
French had been in Spain.' It was decided, therefore, to
submit a special memorandum to the King of Prussia,
pointing out to him the absolute need for common
control of all actions, whether civil or military. ' For

the moment,' ran the protocol, ' the four cabinets regard themselves as a single authority. In consequence, the French Government shall be invited to address all further communications to them in common.' The ministers of the four Powers were to meet in conference at the house of the British ambassador every day regularly at 11 o'clock.[13] Thus was constituted that Committee of Ministers which represented, as it were, the European Executive, and continued to exercise a controlling influence, more or less effective, in the affairs of France until the Congress of Aix-la-Chapelle.

It is not my purpose to follow the long course of the negotiations that led up to the signature of the second Treaty of Paris on November 20, our concern being more immediately with the other treaty, signed on the same day, by which the European Alliance was renewed with certain important modifications. It is, however, important to realize what were the problems involved in this second settling of accounts with France, and the influences within the Alliance that led to their solution. The principle of concerted action had been admitted in the conference of July 12, but as to the policy to be pursued towards France there was no concert, and for the moment it almost seemed—to judge from the complaints of Talleyrand—that the sole outcome of the establishment of the principle was to throw upon the Allies as a whole the odium of the hideous outrages which continued to be perpetrated by the Prussians.[14] In a letter of July 24 Castlereagh makes a report on the views of the various Governments as regards France. In favour of dismemberment were certain Powers which desired to rectify their frontiers and increase their territory : the King of the Netherlands, the Bavarians,

---

[13] F.O. : Congress, Paris, Castlereagh.   July 7–15, 1815.   Protocol of the conference enclosed in Castlereagh to Liverpool of July 14.

[14] These apparently included outrages on women at Fontainebleau. See *Actes divers d'Administration par les Agens des Puissances Alliés*. Enclosed in Talleyrand of July 20, in Castlereagh to Liverpool, July 24.

the Württembergers, and, most insistent of all, the Prussians. Russia was inclined to protect France, being remote from danger. ' But,' adds Castlereagh, ' the Emperor's principles naturally led him to this line. He may also incline to keep up a connexion with France, and not to see her reduced too low. In conversation with His Majesty I could see that his mind was averse to any permanent abduction of the territory of France and that, as a measure of security, he looked with more favour to dismantling than to temporarily occupying certain of her fortresses. Austria, on the other hand, is nearer our mode of viewing this question, but in acting upon this principle the Austrian minister will be afraid to give Russia too much the lead in point of conciliation towards this Government, so as to produce between France and Russia too close a connexion.'

' Our mode of viewing this question ' was that of the traditional British policy, namely, that of safeguarding the Netherlands by a barrier of fortresses. For the rest, though public opinion at home, and even Liverpool and certain members of his cabinet, urged a policy of dismemberment, both Castlereagh and Wellington realized the folly of driving France to desperation or of forcing her to make sacrifices which would have rendered a renewal of the war inevitable so soon as she had regained her strength. Their policy, which in fact prevailed, was, while securing the barrier, to consolidate the power of France internally ; and this, they considered, would be effected if they ensured to the restored monarchy, under the ægis of Europe, an opportunity of persuading the nation that in the monarchy lay the best and only guarantee of its own continued existence. Talleyrand, while protesting against any cessions at all, urged the expediency of reconciling the nation to the kingship. ' All the passions, issuing in certain quarters in civil war,' he said, ' have been intensified during the Hundred Days. But the King, no longer an isolated stranger in

France, has become the rallying centre for all who want
order and peace. All will depend upon the moderation
of the Allies. If France is treated with consideration,
and the people believe that it is to the King that they
owe it, all will be well.' [15]

The exalted mood of the Emperor Alexander
inclined him to generosity, while at the same time his
anxiety to preserve the European concert led him to
go a considerable way towards meeting the views of
his allies in the matter of material guarantees. On
July 29 Castlereagh, as a result of an interview with
the Tsar, reported that in his opinion it would be
possible not only to bring him into line with British
principles, but even to prevail upon him to take the
initiative himself, so as to take off the British negotiators
the onus of curbing the ambitions of ' the limitrophe
Powers.' The Emperor's attitude was shown by a Russian
memorandum of July 28, enclosed in Castlereagh's letter.
Put briefly, it is to the effect that the episode of the
Hundred Days had made no difference in the situation
as regards Europe and France. The objects of the war,
which had been assured by the battle of Waterloo, were
to overthrow Napoleon, to replace France on the basis
of the Treaty of Paris, and to guarantee to her and to
Europe the inviolable maintenance of the transactions
based upon this treaty and completed by the Acts of the
Congress of Vienna. Since the Powers, in the declarations of March 25 and May 12, had again asserted that
they did not regard France as a hostile country, it could
not now be treated as conquered ; and, since the object
of the war was to maintain the Treaty of Paris, the end
of the war should not entail a modification of the treaty
and its consequences. To dismember France would not
only make a new process of balancing necessary, but
would proclaim the Allies' lack of confidence in their

[15] *Mémoire du Cabinet Français sur les Institutions politiques de la
France.* Addressed by Prince Talleyrand to the allied ministers. In
Castlereagh to Liverpool, July 24.

own work and make the government of their legitimate King seem to the French a calamity.

The guarantees proposed by the Tsar were both moral and real. The moral guarantee, which recalls the language of the instructions to Novosiltsov in 1804, was to be a Constitution uniting the Crown and the representatives of the nation in a sense of common interests, and supported by the Allies. The ' real ' guarantees were to be (1) a renewal of the Treaty of Chaumont against any menace from France to the peace of Europe ; (2) the occupation, with the consent of the French Government, of a part of France, so long as this should be judged necessary ; (3) the strengthening of the border states. For these purposes a considerable contribution should be levied, the Allied troops remaining in occupation until it was paid, the occupation then to be terminated by a formal treaty.

This Russian memorandum, which proposed to leave to France the frontiers of 1792, was certainly calculated to curb the ambitions of the limitrophe Powers, and was especially disconcerting to Prussia. In Germany public opinion was bent on undoing the work of Louis XIV and restoring to the Fatherland the Imperial territories in Alsace and Lorraine which had been lost in the seventeenth century, and this opinion was reflected in the Prussian army, which was reported to be in a state of revolutionary exaltation. Prussian statesmen, moreover, had other designs of their own. Castlereagh reported home, on August 24, that Prussia was now aiming at the expansion of her territory at the expense of Hanover and Liége, the former to be compensated in Luxemburg, while the King of the Netherlands, to whom the former Prince-bishopric of Liége had been assigned, was to receive an equivalent in French Flanders. ' The policy of this plan,' he added, ' is to commit the two immediate allies of Great Britain irretrievably with France, to augment their own possessions under the protection of these advanced works, and, by making the security of the whole depend exclusively upon them, not only to hold the Low Countries and Hanover in a state of constant dependence, but to secure to themselves the means of at all times dictating to all, even to Great Britain, the price at which they would continue to afford their protection.' [16]

Nothing but absolute necessity, therefore, could persuade the Prussian statesmen to abandon their policy of revenge and dismemberment. In a counter-memorandum Baron Humboldt sought to justify this attitude on the ground that the declaration of March 25 had been issued in the belief—rapidly disproved by events— that Napoleon was not supported by the French people, and that an enforced cession of territory would be less irritating to France than a prolonged occupation. ' It is a dangerous error,' he said, ' to think that we can conciliate French opinion by concessions and generosity.' Metternich, not daring to run wholly counter to German sentiment, prepared a memorandum on the Russian note which, while it embodied the principle of the substantial integrity of France, recommended the cession of the first line of offensive fortresses to form a barrier on the side of Belgium. This was also the view of Lord Liverpool and of the Government at home generally, who were inclined to go even farther in the direction of enforcing the Prussian demands. It was not at first the view either of Castlereagh or of Wellington, who realized that a generous policy was the only sound one. Wellington's opinion is given in a letter to Castlereagh, dated Paris, August 11. The Revolution and Restoration, he said, had left France too strong in relation to the other Powers ; but, in spite of Baron Humboldt, the Powers were bound by the engagements of March 25 and subsequently ' not to make any material inroad on the Treaty of Paris.' ' It is ridiculous to suppose that we could have overrun France after one battle if the people had been against us.' As for ' a great

[16] To Liverpool, August 24. F.O. : Congress, Paris, Castlereagh.

cession,' if the King were to refuse—as he possibly would
—he would rally the whole nation round him, and the
Allies would have to remain to defend their conquest ;
if he accepted, he would lose his throne.   In 1814 the
unpopularity of the restored Monarchy in the Army
was ascribed to its disinclination to go to war in
order to recover the Rhine frontier.   This being so, no
French statesman could advise his sovereign to disarm.
' Our great object is the peace of the world, and this
Revolutionary France is more likely to disturb than
France under a regular Government, however long her
frontiers.' [17]

This was substantially the view expressed in the
Russian memorandum.   The main difference between
the views of the Emperor Alexander and the British
negotiators was as to the quality and quantity of the
' material ' guarantees of good behaviour to be exacted
from France.   Though Castlereagh regarded any cession
of fortresses with some misgiving, as likely to rouse
up national sentiment in France, he recognized that
the temper of the Germans made some concessions
inevitable, more especially as Metternich, for the reasons
already stated, was proposing this course.   It became
necessary, then, to win over Alexander to the principle
of modifying the terms of the first Treaty of Paris,
if this should seem necessary in order to preserve the
concert and secure Europe from all danger of a renewed
French attack.   On August 17 he was able to announce
to Lord Liverpool that he had succeeded.   The whole
letter throws so much light on the problems to be solved
that it is worth quoting.   ' The Emperor of Russia,'
he writes, ' is in favour of restraining France within
the frontiers of 1790, and has not shown himself dis-
inclined to adopt such measures of salutary precaution
as I suggested to him. . . . I not only deprived him
of that character of being the *exclusive* protector of
the King, a relation in which, for the general politics

[17] F.O. : Continent, Congress, France, Viscount Castlereagh.

of Europe, it is of great importance that he should not be permitted to place himself, but I have gradually brought him publicly to adopt all the principles of the other Allied Powers as his own, and to push them as far as it is at all clear they can be pushed without a dangerous reaction.' [18]

Alexander, that is to say, had once more been successfully ' grouped.' The problem, however, though simplified by this fact, was still sufficiently difficult. Peace was the supreme object of Castlereagh's diplomacy, and to secure this he rightly maintained that it was essential not to force upon France terms calculated to leave a permanent sense of resentment, while at the same time, in order to maintain the ' European police ' effective for the purposes of international peace, it might be necessary to throw a sop to the Germans, who were by no means so eager for a rapid settlement as Great Britain. ' I agree with you,' Castlereagh continued, ' that our interests are with Austria and Prussia rather than with Russia. But we must be careful not to commit ourselves to a course of policy in common with them in which Great Britain has no interest. I much suspect that neither Austria, Prussia, nor the smaller Powers are anxious to end the present situation. Their armies are paid, clothed, and supported by France, and the British subsidies are free to go into their own pockets, which nothing can deprive them of previous to April 1, 1816, except the actual conclusion of a treaty with France. The Austrians have marched Bianchi's corps into Provence, in order to feed upon that poor but loyal province. The Prussians have 280,000 men in France, for whom they draw rations. The Bavarians have brought troops from Munich to the Loire in wagons at a moment when their service in the field was out of the question, the transport of these troops being, of course, at the expense of the country.' After commenting on the immense burden imposed upon

[18] *Castlereagh Corresp.*, 3rd Ser., ii. p. 484.

France by the Allied occupation and by the indemnity, he says that in the view of Great Britain the indemnity should be spent on fortresses, but that this opinion is not shared by Austria and Prussia, and that 'we shall have to contend upon grounds of remote precaution against the immediate pressure of avarice and poverty.' 'To my surprise,' he adds, 'Russia, but remotely interested, has agreed to set aside one-third for fortresses.'

As for Austria and Prussia, their politics were at the moment strongly affected by the public sentiment of Germany, which clamoured for dismemberment, since neither was willing to yield to the other the influence in Germany which belongs to what is most popular. But even were France dismembered, none of the Powers which would benefit would be in a position to maintain their military establishments, and upon Great Britain would fall the burden of the fresh war which would be sure to result. Therefore the idea of the Duke of Wellington was best, namely, not to annex, but to occupy, certain fortresses for a time, a course which the French Government itself desired and which would leave no unhealable wound.

'If we push things to extremities, we leave the King no choice but to disavow us, and when once committed against us in sentiment, he will soon be either obliged to lead the nation into war himself, or possibly be set aside to make way for some more bold and enterprising competitor. The whole of this view of the question turns upon a conviction that the King's cause in France is far from hopeless if well conducted, and that the European Alliance can be made powerfully instrumental to his support if our securities are framed in such a manner as not to be ultimately hostile to France after she shall have given protracted proofs of having ceased to be a revolutionary state.'

If Lord Liverpool thought it necessary, Castlereagh proceeds, to demand securities against which every Frenchman must protest, then his advice towards Great

Britain and the Allies would be 'to have no reserve towards France.' In such a case the Prussian proposals did not go far enough, since they would leave France nearly intact, while depriving her of precisely those objects which would revive in every Frenchman, whatever his principles, a desire for war at the first favourable moment. No doubt the acquisition of one or two famous fortresses would be most popular in England, 'but it is not our business to collect trophies, but to try and bring back the world to peaceful habits. I do not believe this to be compatible with any attempt now materially and permanently to affect the territorial character of France as settled by the Peace of Paris, neither do I think it a clear case (if we can, by imposing a strait-waistcoat upon that Power for a number of years, restore her ordinary habits), and weighing the astonishing growth of other states in latter times, and especially of Russia, that France, even with her existing dimensions, may not be found a useful, rather than a dangerous, member of the European system.' [19]

The British proposal, then, was for (1) a large war indemnity, to be spent on fortresses along the French frontier; (2) a temporary occupation of certain French fortresses; (3) an army of occupation of 100,000 men. A Prussian counter-memorandum of August 28 put forward the view of 'the limitrophe Powers.' The army of occupation was to number not 100,000 but 240,000 (60,000 of each of the four Powers). France was to cede the fortresses of Condé, Valenciennes, Maubeuge, Philippeville, Charlemont, and Givet to the Netherlands; Sarrelouis and Thionville to Prussia, which was also to receive Luxemburg; Bitsch, Landau, Fort Vauban and Huningue (Hüningen) to South Germany; Forts Joux and L'Écluse to Switzerland and Savoy. The fortifications of Quesnay, Mézières, Sédan, Montmédy, and Longwy (which had not yet fallen) were to be

[19] To Liverpool, Paris, August 17, 1815. *Castlereagh Corresp.*, 3rd Ser., ii. 484.

razed. Strassburg might be erected into a Free City of
the Empire.

'It is curious to observe,' wrote Castlereagh to
Clancarty on September 4, 'the insatiable spirit of
getting something without a thought of how it is
to be preserved. There is not a Power, however
feeble, that borders France from the Channel to the
Mediterranean that is not pushing some acquisition
under the plea of security and rectification of frontier.
They seem to have no dread of a kick from the Lion
when his toils are removed, and are foolish enough to
suppose that the Great Powers of Europe are to be in
readiness to protect them in the enjoyment of these
petty spoils. In truth, their whole conception is so
unstatesmanlike that they look not beyond their sop ;
compared with this, the keeping together an European
force has little importance in their eyes.' [20]

In dealing with 'this petty spirit of German
intrigue' Castlereagh had now the invaluable aid of
Alexander, who, under the influence of the religious
atmosphere of the Hôtel Montchenu, was aglow with
love for humanity in general and France in particular.
There can be no doubt that the high tone taken by
Louis XVIII and his ministers was inspired by confidence
in the Tsar's support. In answer to the proposals of
the Allies, the French Government protested against
Louis XVIII being made responsible for the crimes of a
usurper, and while admitting the principle of the cession
of recent acquisitions, refused to agree to any curtailment
of the ancient frontiers of France.[21] This was followed
on the 23rd by autograph letters—said to have been
drafted by Stourdza, the Tsar's Roumanian secretary—
addressed by Louis XVIII to the Emperors Alexander
and Francis, in which he declared his intention of
resigning his crown rather than yield a foot of the soil

[20] F.O. : Congress, Paris, Castlereagh.   No. 51.
[21] In F.O. : Congress, Paris, Castlereagh.   September 21/October 4.
No. 28.

inherited from his ancestors.[22] The situation had meanwhile been modified by a crisis in the French cabinet ;
for on the day following the writing of the King's letter
it was announced that Talleyrand and Fouché had
resigned and that their resignations had been accepted.
In his letter of the 25th announcing this fact, Castlereagh
complained of the duplicity of French ministers in ad-
vising the answer to the propositions of the Allies when
they were actually out of office, and of the weakness of
the King, who had not only yielded to the pressure of
the Court party in making the position of Talleyrand
and Fouché impossible, but had allowed them to retire
covered with the glory of having taken ' high ground,
which their successors must occupy without credit or
retire from with disadvantage.'

The proposals of the Allies referred to were of
the nature of a compromise between the views of
Castlereagh and those of Prussia. On September 14
the Allies had come to an agreement on the question of indemnities, except Prussia, which held out
for an indemnity of 1,200,000,000 francs instead of
600,000,000. On the 21st Castlereagh wrote to Liverpool
that, desiring to arrange the terms of peace before the
meeting of the Chambers on the following Monday,
he had agreed to the principle of Prussia receiving
Luxemburg and Sarrelouis,[23] with the subsidiary compensations to others, on condition of Prussia's accepting
the indemnity of 600,000,000 francs. This was the
basis of the proposals which the French cabinet had
rejected. The new minister, the Duc de Richelieu,
was, as Castlereagh expected, as loth as Talleyrand

---

[22] Paris, September 11/23, 1815. *Ibid.*

[23] Sarrelouis was demanded by Prussia on the ground that it was
a fortress necessary for her defence. It is now known, however, that
the true reason was that an industrial magnate named Böcking had
pointed out to the Prussian plenipotentiaries, on their way to Paris
in July 1815, the enormous economic importance of the Sarre coal-
fields, especially if Prussia could also acquire Sarrebruck with its
steel-works. See P. Vidal de la Blache, *La France de l'Est*, pp. 219 *seq.*

had been to accept them. The King would consent to cede the *enclavés* fortresses of Landau, Philippeville, and Marienburg ; not even an offer to reduce the indemnity could induce him to yield on the point of the cession of Condé and Givet as compensation to the Netherlands for Luxemburg. To have persisted, Castlereagh wrote on October 1, ' might have driven the King and his minister to some ostensible act of despair, and might have created disunion among the Allies.' [24] It was then agreed to accept the French offer, Prussia being compensated by the right to garrison Luxemburg, of which the sovereignty was left to the King of the Netherlands. Accordingly, at a conference of ministers on October 2, the basis was agreed upon of the terms embodied in the second Treaty of Paris, signed on November 20, namely, the limits of France in 1790, subject to certain modifications and rectifications necessitated by mutual convenience and interests, such as the abolition of *enclavés*.

Under the terms of the treaty France was to remain under the tutelage of the Alliance. Pending the paying off of the indemnity her territory was to be occupied by an Allied army under the Duke of Wellington, and, though this was not mentioned in the treaty, the Council of Ministers of the Powers continued its sessions in Paris, keeping in close touch with Wellington on the one hand and the French cabinet on the other. Not till, after a period of this strait-waistcoat, she had given proof of having been cured of her revolutionary madness, would France be restored into the bosom of the family of nations.

[24] Castlereagh to Liverpool. Nos. 68, 69.

III

THE HOLY ALLIANCE

Question of the future of the Alliance—Proclamation of the Holy
Alliance—A revival of the idea of a universal union—Comparison
with the ' instructions ' of 1804—Renewal of the Treaty of Chaumont agreed upon—Differences as to necessary modifications—
The Russian project—Castlereagh's counter-project—The Treaty
of Alliance of November 20, 1815—Analysis of this—Article VI
the basis of the future Concert of Europe.

THE bases of the treaty settled, the Allies had time
to consider what form the future relations of the
European family should take, and the discussions
revealed interesting differences of opinion. The first
symptom of these differences was a project of which
the intention was certainly not to introduce discord
into the Concert. It was on September 26 that the
Emperor Alexander, at a great review of the Allied
troops held on the plain of Vertus near Châlons,
proclaimed in his own name and that of his brother
sovereigns of Prussia and Austria the conclusion of
the Holy Alliance,[25] which all the Christian sovereigns
of Europe were to be invited to join. The solemn
instrument in which this idea was embodied, which
Alexander presented for signature to his astonished Allies,
had been drawn up under the evangelical influences of
the Imperial prayer-meetings ; but though the Baroness
von Krüdener claimed the merit of being its inspirer,
if not its author, it was but an effort to embody an

[25] Signed on September 14.

idea which had been for years in Alexander's mind, and, as he himself declared later,[26] would have been put forward by him at the close of the Congress of Vienna, but for the return of Napoleon from Elba : the idea, that is to say, of that great republic of Christian States which he had foreshadowed in his instructions to Novosiltsov in 1804.

There was nothing in the conception to deserve the sinister connotation which the name of the Holy Alliance from the first carried with it in the public mind. In general, it merely stated the intention of the signatory sovereigns to govern henceforth in accordance with the principles of the Gospel of Christ ; to regard each other as brothers and their subjects as their children. It was most certainly not consciously a conspiracy against popular liberty. Part of the scheme outlined in the instructions to Novosiltsov had been to attach the nations to their Governments by setting up Constitutions based on ' the rights of humanity ' ; the Constitutions granted to France and about to be granted to Poland proved that the Tsar was not yet converted from his Jacobinism ; and Alexander was for years to come to disconcert his autocratic allies by insisting that the granting of Liberal Constitutions was the logical outcome of the sacred principles to which they had subscribed.[27] Nor was there anything in the view, which gained a wide currency, that the exclusion of Turkey from the Holy Alliance meant that Alexander was meditating a concerted attack on the Ottoman Empire. It was the prevalence of this opinion, especially in England, that led Alexander, in March 1816, to

[26] Alexander to Golitsin, Laibach, February 8–15, 1821. In the Grand Duke Nicholas Mikhailovich's *L'Empereur Alexandre Ier*, i. 221.

[27] In a letter to Castlereagh of March 21, 1816, given by Martens in his *Recueil des traités conclus par la Russie*, Alexander uses the following remarkable language : ' There are countries where the attempt is now being obstinately made to revive institutions which have perished of old age. The new spirit of the peoples is too little consulted,' etc.

publish the text of the Holy Alliance. On this occasion, in a letter to Count Lieven, his ambassador at the Court of St. James's, he explained its meaning : ' The sole and exclusive object of the Alliance,' he wrote, ' can only be the maintenance of peace and the union of all the moral interests of the peoples which Divine Providence has been pleased to unite under the banner of the cross. An act of this character could not contain any design hostile to the peoples who have not the happiness to be Christians. Its only aim is to favour the internal prosperity of each state and the general welfare of all, which ought to be the outcome of the friendship between their sovereigns, made all the more indissoluble by the fact that it is independent of accidental causes.' To make this quite clear, the Emperor added that he had instructed his envoy to address to the Sublime Porte a declaration in the same sense and calculated to dissipate all misgivings.[28]

In its origin and idea, then, the Holy Alliance was not a conspiracy of tyrants ; it was not a Christian league against Turkey ; nor was it altogether the ' piece of sublime mysticism and nonsense ' that Castlereagh judged it to be. Its political significance did not lie on the surface, but it was none the less there. It was that, in contradistinction to the treaties on which the Grand Alliance was based, it had been signed by all the sovereigns of Europe except the Prince Regent of Great Britain, the Pope, and the Sultan. It represented, that is to say, a revival by the Emperor Alexander of that idea of a ' Universal Union ' or ' Confederation of Europe ' which he had propounded to Pitt in 1804. It is clear, as we shall see when we come to deal with the debates at the Congress of Aix-la-Chapelle, that this is what Alexander had in his mind, and also that he believed that, in securing their signatures to

[28] Shilder, *Imperator Aleksander*, iii. 552. The Emperor Alexander to Count Lieven, St. Petersburg, March 18, 1816. Also in the Grand Duke Nicholas Mikhailovich's *L'Empereur Alexandre Ier*, i. 171.

the act of the Holy Alliance, he had committed the sovereigns to the principle of an all-embracing international system.

It will be remembered that in 1804 the Tsar had written in the instructions to Novosiltsov : ' It is no question of realizing the dream of perpetual peace, but one could attain at least to some of its results if, at the conclusion of the general war, one could establish on clear, precise principles the prescriptions of the rights of nations. . . . On principles such as these one could proceed to a general pacification, and give birth to a league of which the stipulations would form, so to speak, a new code of the law of nations which, sanctioned by the greater part of the nations of Europe, would without difficulty become the immutable rule of the cabinets, while those who should try to infringe it would risk bringing upon themselves the forces of the new union.' Clearly, if the ' universal union ' thus conceived and symbolized by the Holy Alliance were to be made effective, it would need what the Napoleonic idea had provided : a central legislative authority, a central executive, and a common armament to enforce its decrees. But even in matters of purely external policy this would be to endanger the sovereign independence of the nations ; and if, as was inevitable, it should become difficult to draw a sharp dividing line between external affairs and internal affairs having an external effect, what would become of national liberties ? Great Britain at least, who had strained her resources to the uttermost in the successful effort to save the principle of national independence by destroying the Napoleonic system, was not likely to consent to see it replaced by one equally obnoxious and probably far less effective. Pitt, as we have seen, had been willing to assist in establishing at the restoration of peace a convention and guarantee for the mutual protection and security of the different Powers, and a general system of public law in Europe ;

and Castlereagh had proposed such a system of mutual guarantee at Vienna. But both Pitt and Castlereagh had in their minds a very definite idea of the object and scope of the concert, which was to be directed solely to guaranteeing rights defined by treaty. As for a union with vague and indefinite ends, Castlereagh from the first realized the danger involved in any interference of such a body, in the supposed general interests of Europe, with the liberties of the nations. He was a firm supporter of the Grand Alliance, with its clearly defined aims; from first to last he set his face against the vague and dangerous underlying principles of the Holy Alliance.

The difference of opinion was revealed in the discussions at Paris as to the future constitution of the Alliance. It was unanimously agreed to renew, simultaneously with the signature of the Treaty of Peace, the Treaty of Alliance concluded at Chaumont and renewed at Vienna, with such modifications as had become necessary owing to the restoration of the legitimate dynasty in France. It was as to the character of these modifications that differences arose. The original draft of the treaty, drawn up by the Emperor Alexander, asserted in every line the right of united Europe to watch over the internal affairs of the country, provision being made for armed intervention in case of 'revolutionary madness,' etc. The fourth article provided that the Powers would renew among themselves, after the expiration of the temporary occupation of France, the treaties of reciprocal guarantee of their respective possessions as well as for the general peace and repose. The sixth article, which appeared in a significantly modified form in the actual treaty, ran as follows:

In order to facilitate the execution of the present treaty, and in order to give the necessary effect to the system of reciprocal guarantees, the High Contracting Powers have agreed to renew at fixed periods, either under their own

immediate auspices or by their respective ministers, conferences of which the results shall afford constant proofs of the
permanence and intimacy of their union.[29]

This draft was subjected by Castlereagh to a searching
criticism. It was, he said, not sufficiently definite in
the scope and nature of its stipulations. It bore upon
the face of it too strong and undisguised a complexion of interference on the part of the Allied
sovereigns in the internal affairs of France, without
sufficiently connecting such interference with the policy
which a due attention to the immediate security of
their own dominions prescribed ; and it appeared to
make the Allies too much the umpire in all the
constitutional struggles of France. Finally, it presented but an indistinct view of the extent of the means
with which the Allies were prepared to support their
engagements, as well as of the particular objects to which
those means were to be directed.[30]

In his counter-project Castlereagh, to use his own
language, ' endeavoured to keep the internal affairs of
France in the background, and to make the colour of
the contingent interference as European as possible ' ; to
make it clear, that is to say, that the Allies would only
intervene in the event of revolutionary troubles breaking
out which should be an active menace to the general
peace. In the preamble, as drafted by him, it is no
longer stated that the object of the Powers is ' to
establish royalty in France,' but that the Sovereigns,

in order that the general peace, the object of the prayers of
humanity, and the constant goal of their efforts, should not
be troubled anew, desire to draw closer the ties that unite
them for the common interests of their peoples, have resolved
to give to the principles consecrated by the Treaties of
Chaumont and Vienna the application best adapted to the
actual conditions of public affairs, and to fix in advance by a

[29] F.O. : Congress, Paris, Castlereagh. *Projet de Traité.* Enclosed
in Castlereagh to Liverpool, Paris, October 15, 1815, No. 80.
[30] To Liverpool, Paris, October 15, 1815. *Loc. cit.* No. 80.

solemn treaty the line of conduct which they propose to follow in order to guarantee Europe against the dangers that might yet threaten her.

By Article I the Powers bind themselves to carry out the second Treaty of Paris, and see it carried out. By Article II they renew the engagements entered into at Chaumont, and in the event of revolutionary troubles are to concert among themselves and with Louis XVIII and his successors the measures they shall think necessary for the safety of their states and the general peace of Europe. The third and fourth articles define the contingents to be provided by each Power in the event of armed intervention. Article V provides that the ' defensive engagements ' of Chaumont shall remain in force after the temporary occupation of France. Article VI, based on the sixth article of the Russian draft above quoted, but with significant alterations, runs as follows :

In order to consolidate the intimate tie which unites the four sovereigns for the happiness of the world, the High Contracting Powers have agreed to renew at fixed intervals, either under their own auspices or by their representative ministers, meetings consecrated to great common objects and the examination of such measures as at each one of these epochs shall be judged most salutary for the peace and prosperity of the nations and for the maintenance of the peace of Europe.

This counter-project of Castlereagh's, with certain modifications, was embodied in the Treaty of Alliance signed on November 20, 1815, which was to form during the following years the basis of the European Concert.[31] This represented a triumph of British *Realpolitik* over Alexander's dangerous idealism. None the less, the sixth article was so far a compromise with the Emperor's ideas that it was capable of being strained in their support. It is true that, when we compare it with the equivalent article in the Russian project, we find that the mutual

[31] Text in Hertslet, *Map of Europe by Treaty*, i. 374, No. 44.

guarantee of possessions has disappeared ; and though periodic meetings of the Allies consecrated to great common objects are provided for, the language of the rest of the sentence, when compared with that of the sixth article of the Russian draft, suggests that these meetings were not to be considered as part of a permanent system, but were merely a convenient diplomatic expedient for facilitating the common action of the Allies on any question as it should arise.   This certainly was the view held from the first by British ministers.   But the terms of any compromise are apt to be ambiguous ; and, as we shall see when we come to deal with the proceedings at Aix-la-Chapelle, this was not the view held by the Emperor Alexander.

V

THE CULMINATION OF THE CONFEDERATION

The last attempt to provide the transparent soul of the Holy Alliance with a body.—
GENTZ.

THE CONFERENCE OF AIX-LA-CHAPELLE

Unsettled questions—The reaction in Europe—Ambiguous attitude of the Emperor Alexander—Metternich suggests an Austro-British Alliance—Refusal of Castlereagh—Conditions in France—Rumoured Franco-Russian Alliance—Conference of Aix-la-Chapelle—Evacuation of France concerted—The future of the Alliance—Question of the admission of France to the Alliance—This opens the question of the future form of the European Concert—Alexander revives the idea of a Universal Union—Attitude of Austria and Prussia—Opposition of Great Britain—The principle of non-intervention—Outcome of the negotiations—Fresh proposals for a treaty of guarantee defeated by Great Britain—General character of the Conference—Its proceedings illustrate the difficulty of an international system.

NEARLY three years passed between the signature of the Treaty of Alliance of November 20, 1815, and the meeting of the Conference of Aix-la-Chapelle, the first occasion on which the sixth article was put into operation, the supernational authority being represented meanwhile by the Council of Ambassadors in Paris, whose primary duty was to advise and watch over the French Government, but who dealt also with such general questions as were referred to them. These three years were a period of great anxiety for those who had the peace of the world at heart. The Vienna settlement had not embraced questions which, precisely during these years, were becoming every day an increasing menace. The proposal to settle the matters at issue between Russia and Turkey, arising from the non-fulfilment by the latter of the terms of the Treaty of Bucharest, and to include the Ottoman Empire under the universal guarantee, had been dropped during the hurry and confusion which followed the return of Napoleon from

Elba, and the unsolved Eastern Question thus remained outside the recognized sphere of the Grand Alliance, into the councils of which it none the less penetrated as a disturbing and disruptive influence. Equally if not more dangerous was the situation created by the successful revolt of the Spanish American colonies against the mother country, complicated by the aggression of the Portuguese in the territories of the River Plate, which threatened to transfer the war to Europe, and raised a whole host of questions of which no cognizance had been taken at Vienna. With these questions, lying outside the treaties, I shall deal separately later on.

Meanwhile, in that narrower Europe which lay under the covenanted supervision of the Allied Powers there was cause enough for anxiety. It must be remembered that the views of the sovereigns and statesmen of the Alliance, though conservative, were not wholly reactionary. They had fought the principles of the Revolution because they believed them to be subversive of all established order and of the world's peace, but they watched with disapproval and misgiving the practical working out of the principles which they had set up in their place. The diplomatic correspondence of the time reveals with what genuine disgust they watched the proceedings of some of the rulers they had helped to restore. They had no sympathy with Pius VII, one of whose first acts on re-entering Rome was to reconstitute the Society of Jesus ; or with the unspeakable Ferdinand VII of Spain, who, to the wrath and alarm of his Bourbon brother of France, had set up the Inquisition once more and was busy conducting a war of extermination against all that savoured of Liberalism ; or with Victor Emmanuel I of Sardinia, obstinately bent on restoring everything in Piedmont to the exact form it had possessed before the Revolution ; or with such petty malignants as the Elector of Hesse, who returned to rule his subjects by divine right in the spirit of a usurer put in possession. All this, as the Powers were well aware, could not in the long run fail to breed revolution. And even had all the restored sovereigns been as wise as Nestor, there were, owing to the very imperfect and tentative nature of the arrangements made at Paris and Vienna, a mass of problems awaiting solution, of which some at least were pregnant with future trouble. In Germany, for instance, the ambiguities and incompleteness of the Act of Confederation gave infinite scope for intrigue and the development of particularist ambitions. Article XIII, which decreed that there were to be assemblies of Estates in all the constituent states of the *Bund*, was interpreted by each sovereign in accordance with his prejudices or his policy. Some, like Austria—which carried Prussia in its wake—insisted on its literal interpretation, in the sense of the traditional provincial assemblies of the Estates of nobles, burgesses, and peasants. Others, like the 'Middle States,' Bavaria and Württemberg, made it the excuse for granting representative institutions on the revolutionary model, in order to win popular sympathy with their struggle against the preponderance of the Great Powers ; and their liberalizing policy to the alarm and disgust of Metternich, was encouraged by the Emperor Alexander, who had not yet had time to experience the practical inconveniences of the Constitution he had granted to Poland in 1815, and whose Jacobin sympathies with the aspirations of German Liberals had not as yet been alienated by the crime of Karl Sand.

It was, indeed, the enigmatic attitude of the Russian Emperor that caused the most heart-felt alarms. In spite of his ostentatious pose of the world's peace-maker, his huge armies remained in being, while his agents in the various European Courts indulged in intrigues and used a language little consistent with loyalty to the common cause. The very confusion of principles revealed in these intrigues and this language— loud patronage of Liberalism in Germany, equally loud patronage of reaction in Spain—which doubtless reflected accurately enough the contradictory influences in the Emperor's own mind, increased the suspicion aroused, since the only rational explanation seemed to be that it was no question of principles at all, but merely of Machiavellian expedients. To the apprehensive mind of Metternich at least this seemed to be clear, and equally clear that it was against Austria that these expedients were mainly directed. Alexander's patronage of the liberalizing princes in Germany he interpreted as aimed against Austrian influence in the Confederation. His patronage of the Bourbon states, and notably the naval assistance given by him to Spain against the revolted colonies, argued an intention to establish his power and influence in the Mediterranean, preparatory to a renewed attack upon Turkey. The Austrian estimate of Alexander's policy is clearly stated in a memorandum drawn up by Baron Vincent at Paris when the question of the impending withdrawal of the Allied forces from France was under discussion. ' One can believe,' he wrote, ' that the Cabinet of St. Petersburg has anticipated this moment, and has prepared the means for drawing France into the system destined to establish the political preponderance which it seeks to attain by affecting the language of moderation, by veiling the preparation of a great permanent military force under a display of evangelical abnegation, and by employing in turn the language of mysticism and of inspiration for the support of its maxims of government.' [1]

That the Alliance was kept together during these critical years was mainly due to the good sense and straightforward diplomacy of Castlereagh.[2] He acted throughout in the closest harmony with Metternich, not because he shared all his views or was blind to the defects of his character, but because Austria and Great Britain

[1] Memorandum of Baron Vincent, June 10, 1818.   *Wellington Supp. Disp.* xii. 653.

[2] See C. K. Webster, *Some Aspects of Castlereagh's Foreign Policy*, ii Castlereagh and Metternich, 1815–1817.

were equally interested in maintaining peace on the basis of the established order, while the fact that their interests in the Eastern Question were identical, and nowhere seriously clashed, made it possible for them to work together for this purpose. Metternich, indeed, in his terror of Russian designs, early proposed to convert this cordial understanding into a definite alliance on the model of that of January 3, 1815. But Castlereagh kept his head, although the reports which reached him from almost every quarter were filled with accounts of the almost openly hostile attitude of the Russian diplomatic agents towards Great Britain. To Metternich's reiterated proposals for a separate alliance he finally replied, in May 1817, in a characteristic dispatch, in which he gave his reasons for refusing to agree to such a policy.[3] It was to the general interest, he argued, that the existing system should be preserved as long as possible, and he was opposed to taking any 'measures of precautionary policy on speculative grounds' by which the harmony of the Powers might be prematurely broken up; it would be time enough to act when the mysterious activities of Russia should have taken shape in some 'real and obvious danger.'

The best way to counteract the possibility of such a danger was, he still believed, to keep the Emperor Alexander 'grouped' by flattering his vanity. 'To counteract the party in his Councils that may be labouring to exasperate him against the Turks,' he wrote to the British Ambassador in Berlin, 'we must all, as far as possible, never suffer His Imperial Majesty to forget what he has accomplished for Europe during the last four years, how much this may now be endangered and his fame impaired by now measuring himself with such a Power, that the principle of acquisition once acted upon may loosen existing ties, and open interminable questions.'[4] By using such language, 'held in the spirit

[3] Castlereagh to Stewart, May 24, 1817. Webster, *loc. cit.* p. 84.
[4] To Rose, April 4, 1817. Webster, *loc. cit.* p. 87.

of confidence rather than distrust in the Emperor's intentions,' Castlereagh did in fact succeed in keeping on friendly terms with the Tsar. Russian ministers continued to pursue a policy hostile to British views and interests ; but Alexander never allowed them to go far enough to endanger the Alliance which he believed to be essential in order to guard against the danger which might at any moment arise from France.

France had, indeed, during these years been the chief source of anxiety for the Allies. At the outset this anxiety had been aroused, not by any revolutionary movements but by the conduct of the violent reactionary party, nicknamed by Fouché ' ultra-royalist.' For the tragic mistake of the execution of Marshal Ney the Allies, and notably Great Britain, were primarily responsible [5] ; but they had no sympathy with the White Terror of the South or with the blood-lust of the Court party, as reflected in the clamour for proscription and more proscription of the first Chamber elected after Waterloo. The international Council of Ministers, backed by Wellington, supported the moderate policy of Richelieu and Decazes ; for they knew well that the violence of the *Chambre introuvable* would end in a Jacobin reaction. But it was not till the King had summoned up courage to dissolve the Chamber and, by altering the electoral law, to secure another composed of more moderate elements that the Allies began to listen to the urgent remonstrances of the Duc de Richelieu against the continued occupation of French soil. The elections, he argued, sufficiently proved that France desired the monarchy ; but the monarchy would never be really strong so long as it seemed to rest upon foreign bayonets. As for the payment of the indemnity, which was the excuse for maintaining the Allied army of occupation,

---

[5] Louis XVIII was anxious for him to escape, and heard of his capture with unfeigned regret. ' By letting himself be caught,' he said, ' he has done us more harm than he did on March 13 ' (Daudet, *Louis XVIII et le duc Decazes*, p. 74).

France would not become a fraudulent bankrupt merely because this was withdrawn.[6]

These arguments carried weight. But the clinching argument which determined the Allies in favour of evacuation was the opinion of the Duke of Wellington that to continue the occupation would defeat the very ends at which it aimed. He had been strongly opposed to any gradual diminution of the Allied forces in proportion to the payments of instalments of the indemnity. But in 1818 he reported that such was the bitterness of public feeling that, in the event of the occupation being continued another two years, with the enormous additional burden this would impose on France, he would be compelled to draw in the scattered line of his troops and concentrate them between the Scheldt and the Meuse.[7] This had its weight with the British Government, which as late as April had insisted that a complete settlement of all matters was the only ground on which Richelieu could expect the withdrawal of the troops to be favourably entertained.[8] Something, too, was perhaps due to persistent rumours, emanating from St. Petersburg, that the Emperor Alexander, weary of the dilatory processes of the Alliance, was meditating a union of Russia and France.[9] If this were so, it was obviously necessary, if Alexander was to be kept properly 'grouped,' to reconcile France to the Alliance. It was then decided, after negotiations into which we need not enter, to summon a conference of the Powers, under Article VI of the Treaty of November 20, for the autumn of 1818.

[6] Wellington to Castlereagh, Paris, July 21, 1817. ' Upon this point he (Richelieu) went a good deal into the federal system which must grow out of the existing state of things, to which France must be a party, and which he said must always give the Allies the power to force France to be just in case she should be disposed to be unjust.'

[7] Draft Memorandum laid before the Cabinet. F.O. : Congress, Continent, Aix-la-Chapelle, September–December 1818.

[8] Castlereagh to Wellington, April 24, 1818. F.O. : Continent, Congress, Paris.

[9] Wellington to Castlereagh, August 24, 1818. *Wellington Supp. Disp.* xii. 655.

The meeting-place chosen was Aix-la-Chapelle, the old capital of the Holy Empire.

The Conference of Aix-la-Chapelle, of which the first session was held on September 30, was attended by the Emperor Alexander of Russia, the Emperor Francis of Austria, and King Frederick William of Prussia in person, while Great Britain was represented by Wellington and Castlereagh. The ministers of the other Powers were Capo d'Istria and Nesselrode for Russia, Metternich for Austria, Hardenberg and Bernstorff for Prussia. Richelieu, though not admitted to the conferences, was present on behalf of France. The first question discussed was that of the withdrawal of the Allied army of occupation, and on this there was complete unanimity. At the second session, on October 1, the four Powers signed a protocol agreeing to the principle of the evacuation of France at the end of the third year, or earlier if possible, subject to satisfactory arrangements being made for the payment of the instalments of the indemnity still due, which amounted to 265,000,000 francs. In regard to this latter, Wellington had been empowered to make an arrangement with the financial houses of Hope, of Amsterdam, and Baring, by which these agreed to take over the debt on certain terms, thus converting it into an ordinary public obligation, which, to use the language of a draft memorandum laid before the Cabinet, could not be repudiated by the French Government without an act of violent bankruptcy. The details of the negotiation outstanding on September 30 were soon settled, and on October 9 a treaty was signed by which the Allies ageed to withdraw their troops from French soil by November 30. As for the debt, 165,000,000 francs were to be paid by the French Government in nine monthly payments in bills drawn on Messrs. Baring, Hope and others, and regularly accepted by them. With regard to the other 100,000,000 francs, the Allies agieed to receive these in the form of Government stock at the price of the day the financial houses agreeing to take this stock at the same price as that at which the Allies received it from France and to pay the 100,000,000 francs in the same manner as the 165,000,000, receiving 1½ per cent. for their trouble and risk in realizing.[10] They bought the debt of 100,000,000 francs, that is to say, for 89,500,000.

In coming to this decision there was complete harmony among the Powers ; there was, however, no such harmony on the question of what further consequences were to follow on it. The Duc de Richelieu argued that the same reasoning which had induced the Powers to put an end to the armed occupation should lead them, as a logical consequence, to admit France to the Alliance on equal terms. This was, however, far from representing the mind of the Allies, whose policy of evacuation had not been inspired by any confidence in the improved temper of the French people. The autocratic Powers especially were seriously alarmed by what they considered the weak attitude of the French Government towards the Liberal revival, to which recent elections had borne disquieting evidence. Alexander I, whose Jacobinism, though by no means extinct, was already fading, declared roundly that nine-tenths of the French people were corrupted by bad principles and violent party sentiments, and that the rest were incapable of working a Constitution ; and when Richelieu pressed him to agree to the inclusion of France in the Alliance, he asked him how he could propose such a thing after admitting that the internal state of France was precarious,[11] and characterized the request in conversation with Metternich as a rank piece of stupidity.[12]

Metternich himself, as was his way, disguised a policy inspired by very practical alarms under a cloak of lofty sentiment. The Quadruple Alliance, he argued, had its

[10] Castlereagh to Bathurst. F.O. : Continent, Aix, Castlereagh, 1–13, No. 9.

[11] Castlereagh to Bathurst, Aix, October 3, 1818, Nos. 2 and 4.

[12] Interview with Metternich, September 29. F.O. : Continent, Aix, Castlereagh, 1–13.

origin in the Treaty of Teplitz, of September 9, 1813, which followed the traditional diplomatic forms ; but it had received a wholly new development in the Treaty of Chaumont, for which there was no precedent. In the ' sacramental words ' of Article XIV, which provided for the duration of the Alliance for twenty years and its eventual renewal, lay the origin of the true moral force of the Alliance. The treaty also contained temporary expedients, but its ' true spirit ' lay in the words of Article XIV, as reinforced by the preamble to the Treaty of Alliance of November 20, 1815. The Treaty of Chaumont, in short, in its essence was based on eternal principles of political morality of which the special application was directed against France. If, then, France were admitted to it, this would undermine its very foundations by mixing the conservative principle with that of innovation, the remedy with the very evil it was designed to cure, stability with movement, and security with risk. It would be better to preserve the Treaty of Chaumont and to come to some other arrangement with France. After all, in addition to the Treaty of Chaumont, there existed the Holy Alliance as its complement, and one that sufficiently advertised the lofty intentions of the Powers. If this were not judged sufficient, France might become party to a Declaration, couched in general terms, reiterating these intentions.[13]

On the question of admitting France to the Alliance on the basis of the Treaty of Chaumont the British Cabinet was at one with the other Allies, for Castlereagh and his colleagues had a strong sense of the precarious tenure of the restored monarchy in France, and believed that the maintenance of the Quadruple Alliance was essential to the peace of Europe ; they realized, too, the paradox involved in making France a party to a treaty which was primarily directed against herself. On the other hand, were she to be altogether excluded, she would

[13] Memorandum of Metternich on the Treaty of Chaumont, October 7, 1818. F.O. : Continent, Aix, Castlereagh, in No. 13.

inevitably become the nucleus of a separate alliance, and everything that had been gained by the European Concert would be placed in jeopardy. As for a new treaty, in addition to that of Chaumont, which should include France, in the actual temper of the House of Commons this could never be sanctioned. The same Cabinet memorandum (September 4) in which these difficulties were pointed out contained an ingenious suggestion of a method by which they could be overcome. This was to introduce France, not on the basis of Chaumont, but on that of Article VI of the Treaty of Alliance of November 20, 1815, which was in addition to the provisions of the earlier treaty : the article which established ' a deliberative system for the purpose of consulting at fixed periods and upon common interests, and for the consideration of such measures as may be deemed most salutary for the repose and prosperity of the nations and for the maintenance of the peace of Europe.' True, in view of the fundamental objections of the British Government to anything in the nature of a universal union, this might be held to establish an awkward precedent. But as the treaty primarily concerned France only, it would not be necessary to invite other Powers to join, and in any case it would obviate the risk of so great a Power remaining outside and perhaps forming another combination as a counterpoise to this alliance.[14]

The problem of the future relation of France to the Alliance thus opened up at Aix-la-Chapelle the whole broader question of the future form of the ' Confederation of Europe.' As to this, much of course depended upon the attitude of the Emperor Alexander. His first care on arriving at Aix had been to place beyond doubt his own absolute loyalty to the European Alliance. In an interview with Metternich on September 29 he indignantly repudiated the truth of the rumours that

[14] Cabinet memorandum on the approaching Conferences, September 4, 1818. F.O. : Continent, Congress, Aix, No. 34.

he had been meditating a breach with the Alliance and a separate understanding with France. ' It will suffice,' he said, ' to explain my principles, in order to dispense with the necessity of replying in detail to false reports which have gained only too much currency. I seek the welfare of the world in peace, and I cannot find peace except in the attitude we have adopted during the last five years, and in the maintenance of this attitude. I should regard as a felon whichever one of us should think fit to establish a tie foreign to that which unites us, and as a crime any change, whatever it may be, in our relations. . . . I will admit that proposals for an alliance have been addressed to me. I will leave it to you yourself to dictate the reply which I made to such proposals. . . . You know that I am scrupulous in everything. I am equally so in politics. My conscience will always prevent my committing voluntary errors. My army, as well as myself, is at the disposal of Europe.' [15]

In subsequent interviews with Wellington and Castlereagh he used the same language, insisting that his army was the army of Europe, and that he could not admit that it would be otherwise employed than with Europe, to repress any attempt that might be made to shake the system of which his empire formed only a part.[16] In reporting this interview Castlereagh commented on the ' cordiality and earnestness of Alexander, together with an exaltation of mind which perhaps hurried him into touching upon measures from which, he trusted, his views might be brought to subside.' [17]

What these measures were was not as yet quite clear ; for in the same letter Castlereagh mentions that Capo d'Istria and Nesselrode were at work on the future colour to be given to the Alliance, but had reached no satisfactory result, while Alexander had not yet

[15] F.O. : Continent, Aix, Castlereagh, 1–13, in Castlereagh to Bathurst, No. 2.

[16] Castlereagh to Bathurst, October 3, No. 2.

[17] No. 4, same date.

made up his mind. Meanwhile, Castlereagh had laid before the Powers the proposal of the British Government to which I have already referred, which represented a compromise (a ' middle term ' Castlereagh called it) of which Metternich at once approved, while Hardenberg and Bernstorff gave it a friendly but more reserved reception. This formed the basis of the negotiations that followed, and in a couple of days Castlereagh reported home that the probable result of the Conference would be (1) to adhere strictly to the treaties, especially those of Chaumont and Paris, which constituted the Quadruple Alliance ; (2) not to admit France to them, nor to replace them by a Quintuple Alliance ; (3) to invite France to join in the deliberations of the Powers under Article VI of the Treaty of Alliance of November 20, which, as this article is the only one that survived the war or that would be operative so long as France kept quiet, would in effect place her in a line with the other Powers so long as the state of peace subsisted ; (4) in order to calm the alarm of the other Powers, to issue a declaration to the effect that, by these regular assemblies the Powers had no intention of arrogating to themselves any supremacy, or of interfering in the politics of other states in any way not warranted by the law of nations. In concluding his statement, Castlereagh enlarged on the benefit derived from the cabinets acting side by side in this matter, which had obviated a host of delays and misconceptions which would have arisen had the negotiations been conducted through the ordinary diplomatic channels.[18]

These proposals, however, did not go far enough for the Emperor Alexander. On the one hand, he was eager to publish to all the world the renewal of the disciplinary Alliance of Chaumont, which the others were anxious to keep effective, but in the background. On the other hand, he was bent on using this opportunity of realizing his political ideal

[18] To Bathurst, No. 10.

of a confederated Europe. ' It is impossible,' wrote
Castlereagh, ' to doubt the Emperor's sincerity in his
views, which he dilates upon with a religious rhapsody.
Either he is sincere, or hypocrisy certainly assumes a
more abominable garb than she ever yet was clothed
in,' and he goes on to describe how Alexander, placing
his hand on his heart and looking up to heaven, declared
that, actuated, as he trusted, by a religious and conscientious feeling, he had that secret sentiment within
him which would render it impossible for him to be
inequitable or unjust.[19]

The outcome of this religious fervour was the
presentation to the other Allies on October 8 of
a confidential memorandum of the Russian cabinet,
drafted by Pozzo di Borgo, stating the Tsar's views
on the measures to be adopted in order to preserve
Europe from a return of revolutions and of the
principle that might is right (*le droit du plus fort*).
Europe, it said, had been restored in 1815 and preserved till now by the Alliance of the great states, unalterable in principle, but extending its sphere according
to circumstances, and becoming thus the Alliance of
all the states. The results thus far achieved had been
due, less to the uncertain combinations of men than
to that Supreme Intelligence to which the sovereigns
had done homage by the act of September 26, 1815.
The woes of humanity had been caused by egoism and
partial combinations in politics, and the proof of this
was the good derived from the empire of Christian
morality and of the Rights of Man which had given
Europe peace. The system of Europe was a general
association which had for *foundation* the Treaties of
Vienna and Paris, for *conservative principle* the fraternal
union of the Allied Powers, for *aim* the guarantee of all
recognized rights. This system, which guaranteed the
best interests of the great European family, was the work
not of any man but of Providence. Its moral support

[19] To Bathurst, October 16.

lay in the Quadruple Alliance and the Holy Alliance, its material support in the armed occupation of France. Since this had now come to an end, more moral support was needed. This was not to be sought in the renewal of engagements already taken ; for to swear too much weakens the force of oaths. It must be sought in the elements constituting the actual European system, and in a combination which in the eyes of all the world would make the cohesion of the system evident, necessary, and indissoluble. These elements were the Quadruple Alliance and the General Alliance, considered, in reference to the case under discussion, the first as a principle and the second as its consequence. The compact which consecrated and defined the first was the treaty of November 20, 1815. The General Alliance was to be sought in the Final Act of Vienna and the subsequent acts signed at Paris in 1815.

The Emperor then proposed that the Quadruple Alliance should be preserved as against danger from France, and that a general Alliance should be formed, consisting of all the signatories of the Treaties of Vienna, having as its object the guarantee of the state of territorial possession and of sovereignty *ab antiquo*.

The first of these objects was to be secured by a protocol defining the *casus fœderis* and the military measures to be taken should this arise, and arranging for future meetings. The second was to be accomplished by a declaration of the Great Powers announcing to Europe the results of their deliberations at Aix, to which declaration, since the Quadruple Alliance was not a partial combination but the basis of the General Alliance, all the states which had signed the acts of 1815 should be invited to subscribe. The Quadruple Alliance, the memorandum explained, was held together as yet only by the sentiment of the parties to it ; but if it formed part of a wide European association no Power could break away from it without being at once isolated. The Quadruple and General Alliance would be proclaimed

as a single and indivisible system by the signatures of
the Powers to the declaration. Such a system would
guarantee the security of Governments by putting the
rights of nations under a guarantee analogous to that
which protects individuals. The Governments, for their
parts, being relieved from fear of revolutions, could
offer to their peoples Constitutions of a similar type
(*semblables*) ; so that the liberties of peoples, wisely
regulated, would arise without effort from this state
of affairs once recognized and publicly avowed.[20]

The language of this memorandum recalls that of
the instructions to Novosiltsov in 1804. Both in its
principles and in its proposals for their practical
application it is all but identical with the scheme submitted by Alexander to Pitt. The only important
difference is that for the Dual Alliance of Russia and
Great Britain which, under the original scheme, was to
be maintained as a sort of directorate of the European
Concert, has been substituted the Quadruple Alliance.

The proposals of the Russian memorandum met with
a somewhat mixed reception. Metternich, who was
still noting with terror the activities of Russian agents
everywhere, and especially in Italy, had begun to
recognize in the 'loud-sounding nothing' of the Holy
Alliance an excellent instrument for curbing and guiding
the Tsar's erratic ambitions, and he therefore hailed
the memorandum with diplomatic unction. 'The order
established,' he wrote to Nesselrode, after reading the
memorandum, 'needs not to be proved ; it exists ; it
is recognized ; it governs the world. "To change this
order of things would be a crime "—worthy words pronounced by your august master ! ' [21] To the Prussians,
who were in a highly nervous state about their new
acquisitions on the Rhine, the principle of a universal
guarantee was equally welcome. The British Government,

[20] Mémoire confidentielle du Cabinet russe. September 26
(October 8). Enclosed in Castlereagh to Bathurst, October 19, No. 13.
[21] To Nesselrode, October 7, in Castlereagh's of October 19, No. 13.

on the other hand, could not but view with serious misgiving these iterated efforts to revive a plan against
which it had always protested.   Public opinion in England
was increasingly opposed to a system which not only
threatened the liberties of others but might at some
future time be applied to curtail the liberties of Great
Britain itself.   Moreover, as Castlereagh pointed out
to the Emperor Alexander, ' the British cabinet had
now to deal with a new Parliament and a new people,
intensely bent on peace and economy,' and to initiate
a fresh policy of ' eventual exertion' would be to
jeopardize the sanction already obtained from Parliament for their continental engagements.   In the cabinet
memorandum already referred to it had been laid down
that the treaty between the Powers must rest ' upon
the sanction received in the address of both Houses,
of May, 1816 ' ; that its provisions ' hardly admitted
of being reinforced ' ;   and that any attempt to renew
them ' would lead to serious difference of opinion.'   So
far, indeed, from undertaking further obligations, the
cabinet was rather in a mood for withdrawing from
some of those already entered into.   In reply to
Castlereagh's letter announcing the probable outcome
of the negotiations, dispatched before the presentation
of the Russian memorandum, Bathurst wrote a long
letter, dated October 20, in which he expressed great
doubts as to whether it would be in any way advisable
to proclaim to Europe, by any new act, that it was the
intention of the Powers to hold continued meetings
at stipulated periods.   ' We admit,' he wrote, ' that
Article VI of the Treaty of Alliance contemplated such
meetings, and we are satisfied that under the circumstances as they now exist, when the Allied troops are
to be withdrawn from France, it may be of the utmost
importance to make the people of that country feel
that they are still under a sort of surveillance.   We
are therefore of opinion that the Allied Powers should
fix a period at which to hold another meeting.   This

would not be liable to the objections which we think would result from a succession of such meetings being now proclaimed as part of a permanent system. . . . When the French Government has proved that it can maintain the peace, there will be no further need of them ; and though the mind might anticipate further circumstances under which such meetings might be productive of many advantages, one may likewise contemplate those under which they might be likely to lead to great embarrassment. Article VI could hardly have been accepted under present circumstances. We do not wish to abrogate it ; but we do not think it would be politic to reinforce it by any new declaration of a general nature.' [22]

I have quoted this letter at some length in order to show the somewhat nervous temper of the British Government, not for any practical effect it produced ; for, as a matter of fact, the whole question had been settled before it was received. That it was so settled was due to Castlereagh's clever, but at the same time perfectly straightforward diplomacy. As for the Russian memorandum, ' when the Duke of Wellington and I came to consider the paper together,' he wrote, ' though abounding in the principles of unity and peace, we felt some dismay in observing the abstractions and sweeping generalities in which it was conceived. It appeared to us that, whilst we could by no means subscribe to its doctrine in the extent to which it was pushed, it would be hazardous to attempt a written answer to it, and we therefore invited discussion and had a series of conversations on this very complicated subject.' The object of these conversations was to find out how far Alexander's intention of publicly proclaiming the continued existence of the Quadruple Alliance could be reconciled with a self-respecting entry of France into the Concert, to devise means for making the future,

[22] Bathurst to Castlereagh, October 20, 1818. F.O. : Continent, September to December 1818.

conferences as little offensive as possible to the Powers not in the Alliance, and in general to compel Alexander and his ministers to ' descend from their abstractions ' so as to prepare the Conference for some practical conclusions. In this delicate task Castlereagh was helped and not hindered by the temper of Parliament, on which he was able to throw the onus of obstructing the realization of Alexander's dream in its completeness. In effect, he succeeded almost at once in inducing the Tsar to agree to something like the ' middle term ' proposed by the British Government. Alexander declared that he wished to hold close to the Quadruple Alliance— ' our sheet-anchor '—but that he had no objection to admitting France under the limitations named ; that such admission, however, must be accompanied by a declaration publicly proclaiming that the Alliance remained unbroken, and also by ' a digested plan of military concert, to be at once acted upon in case of necessity.' In order to help Great Britain out of any parliamentary difficulty, he would not ask for a new treaty, but would make a protocol or a declaration sufficient.[23]

The British Cabinet, as we have seen, objected to the issue of any declaration ; but Castlereagh had not received Bathurst's letter in which the objection was formulated, and in any case he realized that if the Alliance was to be maintained, some sort of concession must be made to Alexander's views. But if there was to be a declaration, he was determined that it should not be of a character to commit Great Britain to a policy of which it disapproved, and he at once commissioned Gentz to draw up one ' in the spirit of our own view of the question.' This, of course, was not Alexander's. In his opinion the Act of the Holy Alliance had never ceased to be in operation, or at least *in esse*, and Castlereagh reported that both the Emperor and Count Capo d'Istria ' were, in conversation, disposed to push their ideas very far indeed, in the sense of all the Powers

[23] To Liverpool, October 19, 1818, No. 13.

of Europe being bound together in a common league,
guaranteeing to each other the existing order of things,
in thrones as well as in territories, all being bound to
march, if requisite, against the first Power that offended,
either by her ambition or by her revolutionary trans-
gressions.' [24] It is not surprising that to Castlereagh
even the blessing of perpetual peace would seem too
dearly bought at the price of subjugating Europe to an
international police of which the undiminished armies
of Russia would form the most powerful element. As
Castlereagh wrote later (November 9), when the proposal for a ' universal guarantee ' had re-emerged in
another form, ' it was opening up to such a Power as
Russia . . . an almost irresistible claim to march through
the territories of all the Confederate States to the most
distant points of Europe to fulfil her guarantee,' a claim,
it may be added, which Alexander actually did make
in connection with the revolutionary troubles in Spain
in 1820.

Yet the Russian Emperor, in pressing his scheme, was
not unreasonable in believing that he was but carrying
to their logical conclusion principles to which the British
Government already stood committed. British ministers
rightly held that under the actual conditions of Europe
the maintenance of the Alliance was essential ; they had
committed themselves by Article VI of the Treaty of
November 20, 1815, to the principle of holding ' at
fixed intervals ' meetings ' consecrated to great common
objects ' ; they had even allowed the Prince Regent to
express his pious assent to the lofty doctrine of the Holy
Alliance ; they were vividly conscious of the necessity
for ' calming the alarm of the other Powers,' to which
the Kings of Sweden and Württemberg gave vigorous
expression during the sitting of this very Conference.
The formation of a universal union, as foreshadowed by
the Holy Alliance, would at once give to the periodic
meetings greater weight, and disarm all opposition by

[24] To Liverpool, October 19, 1818, No. 13.

giving to all states, great and small, a share in them ; peace, the object of the Quadruple Alliance, would be secured by making it impossible for any Power to break it, since any attempt to do so would bring down upon it the armed forces of all the rest. Castlereagh, however, was less impressed by the excellence of Alexander's logic than by the danger of applying its conclusions. A limited Alliance, for certain defined purposes, was one thing ; a universal union, committed to common action under circumstances that could not be foreseen, was quite another. The admission into the councils of Europe of a number of small states would, moreover, open the door to intrigues, the perils of which were minimized in the narrower Alliance. The difficulty of duly distributing the weight of the constituent members of such an assembly had already been illustrated by the constitution of the Federal Diet, in which the disproportionately small voting power given to Austria and Prussia had early led to a rivalry between them to gain the rest. So far from such a league leading to disarmament, the decisive voice in it would be that of the master of the biggest battalions. It was feared, in short, that the Emperor Alexander was disguising even from himself, ' under the language of evangelical abnegation,' the ambition of usurping in the new Confederation of Europe the preponderant position which Austria had already obtained in the new Confederation of Germany.

This being so, it was all the more essential to keep the Emperor ' grouped ' ; and to accomplish this it was necessary to humour him, or, as Castlereagh put it, ' to hold the Emperor's mind within the principles that could be maintained in Parliament,' and for this purpose ' to present something that would at once be in our line, and at the same time present the subject somewhat in the tone of his own ideas.' [25] This was done in the memorandum in reply to that of the Russian cabinet

[25] To Liverpool, October 19, 1818, No. 13.

which Castlereagh handed in, after preparing the ground in personal interviews.

The opening paragraph defines the British attitude towards the Holy Alliance in language which has more than a touch of irony. ' The benign principles of the Alliance of September 26th, 1815,' it runs, ' may be considered as constituting the European system in the matter of political conscience. It would, however, be derogatory to this solemn act of the sovereigns to mix its discussion with the ordinary diplomatic obligations which bind state to state, and which are to be looked for alone in the treaties which have been concluded in the accustomed form.' These treaties were of two classes : (1) those which bind the states collectively ; (2) those peculiar to particular states. To the first class belonged the two Treaties of Paris and the Treaty of Vienna, which together constituted the Great Charter of the restored territorial system of Europe. Their provisions were, however, almost exclusively territorial, and they contained in no case engagements capable of being pushed beyond the immediate objects which were regulated in the treaties themselves. There was no express guarantee by which the observance of the engagements contracted was to be enforced ; and, though breaches of these engagements might be resented collectively or separately, there was no *obligation* on the signatory Powers to do so.[26] It was not clear how ' the Confederacy ' could, without the utmost inconvenience, be made to enforce their observance.

The treaties, therefore, did not form an *Alliance*, but at most a *general pact* by which the territories affected were regulated. This pact, however, gave them no special guarantee, to the exclusion of others not affected by these negotiations, but which rested for their titles on earlier treaties of equal authority.

[26] This seems to represent a retreat from the standpoint of Great Britain at Vienna. See Castlereagh's proposal for a common Declaration at the close of the Congress, p. 114 *supra.*

To the second class, that of particular treaties, belonged those of Chaumont and Paris of November 20. These were treaties of alliance in the strictest sense of the word. Their avowed object was the restoration of Europe and the prevention of renewed danger from France ; but they did not contemplate the possibility that a mere change in the government of France itself, whether effected legally or brought about by indirect means, would constitute a *casus fœderis*, unless by such change the peace of the Allies were threatened. The latter contingency was the only one contemplated by Article V of the Treaty of Paris, and it could not for a moment be maintained that states have a right to intervene in the internal affairs of other states to prevent change whether legal or illegal, for how can foreign states be left safely to judge of what is ' legal ' in another state ?

The only safe principle was that of the law of nations— that no state has a right to endanger its neighbours by its internal proceedings, and that if it does, provided they use a sound discretion, their right to interference is clear. This was the right upon which eventual interference in France was contemplated under the Treaty of Paris (Art. III). The Allies were presumed to have a common interest in judging this question soundly whenever it should arise ; but until the case arose none of the contracting parties were engaged for more than an eventual concert and decision.

The memorandum goes on to discuss the Emperor's idea of a universal union. I quote it *verbatim*, with only insignificant omissions. ' The problem of a Universal Alliance for the peace and happiness of the world,' it runs, ' has always been one of speculation and hope, but it has never yet been reduced to practice, and if an opinion may be hazarded from its difficulty, it never can. But you may in practice approach towards it, and perhaps the design has never been so far realized as in the last four years. During that eventful period the Quadruple Alliance, formed upon principles altogether limited, has had, from the presence of the sovereigns and the unparalleled unity of design with which the cabinets have acted, the power of travelling so far out of the sphere of their immediate and primitive obligations, without at the same time transgressing any of the laws of nations or failing in the delicacy which they owe to the rights of other states, as to form more extended alliances . . . to interpose their good offices for the settlement of differences between other states, to take the initiative in watching over the peace of Europe, and finally in securing the execution of its treaties.'

'The idea of an Alliance Solidaire, by which each state shall be bound to support the state of succession, government, and possession within all other states from violence and attack, upon condition of receiving for itself a similar guarantee, must be understood as morally implying the previous establishment of such a system of general government as may secure and enforce upon all kings and nations an internal system of peace and justice. Till the mode of constructing such a system shall be devised, the consequence is inadmissible, as nothing would be more immoral or more prejudicial to the character of government generally, than the idea that their force was collectively to be prostituted to the support of established power, without any consideration of the extent to which it was abused. Till a system of administering Europe by a general alliance of all its states can be reduced to some practical form, all notions of a general and unqualified guarantee must be abandoned, and the states must be left to rely for their security upon the justice and wisdom of their respective systems and the aid of other states according to the law of nations.' As for the actual Alliance, the beneficial effect of the four Powers consulting and mediating would be much increased by adding France, which would not render it too numerous for effective concert and would add to it immense moral weight.[27]

[27] Memorandum of Lord Castlereagh, *loc. cit.*, enclosed in No. 13.

This uncompromising statement of Great Britain's attitude had its effect, and on October 20 Castlereagh was able to report home that the Powers had agreed upon a basis of arrangement practically representing the British ' middle term.' There were to be two protocols, of which the first would merely proclaim that the eventual obligations of the Treaty of Chaumont still subsisted, though its clauses, so far as they were directed against France, would be in abeyance. As this protocol would be merely explanatory of principles already approved by Parliament, there would be no necessity for laying it upon the table of the House. In addition to this secret protocol, there was to be another, publicly concluded with the co-operation of Richelieu, by which France was to be admitted to the Alliance under Article VI of the treaty of November 20. The Quintuple Alliance thus formed was to have for its ostensible object the inviolable maintenance of the Treaties of Paris and Vienna.

As to the form this protocol should take there were still, however, significant differences of opinion. Alexander objected to a phrase conceding to France the *right* to a place in the European system, an objection significantly anticipating the principle of the protocol of Troppau. Castlereagh objected to the ' threatened return of revolutionary crises ' being mentioned as a *casus fœderis*, and refused to endorse an article which described the union as having become stronger and more indissoluble by the bonds of Christian brotherhood between the sovereigns and the accession of all the European states to the act (of the Holy Alliance) which had consecrated these bonds. This latter objection Alexander admitted, professing himself, in order ' not to cause parliamentary inconvenience,' quite content with the autograph letter in which the Prince Regent had given his moral approval to the lofty principle of the Holy Alliance. The discussion having thus been brought down to the plane of practical politics, the details were soon settled, and on November 5 Castlereagh, who had meanwhile received the letter from Bathurst which I quoted earlier, was in a position to say, in answer to it, that all the objections contained in it had been met. The concert with France was brought within the limits of the most restricted interpretation that could be given to Article VI of the treaty of November 1815, i.e. was confined to the maintenance of the peace as established by the treaties therein enumerated. The eventual reunions were to be strictly limited to those interests which grew out of the transactions in question ; moreover, they were not to be held at fixed periods, but, as occasion might arise, by agreement between the five Courts, and no Power could be held as pledged, *a priori*, to any meeting whatever.[28]

In one respect only was there a further concession. It had been proposed not to publish the protocol, but merely to announce the adhesion of France to the Alliance by a circular note. To this procedure Alexander objected as not being sufficiently solemn, and as liable to lead other Powers to suspect some hidden menace which in fact did not exist. It was therefore after all agreed, Castlereagh announced, to issue a declaration, but one quite innocuous.

Everything seemed to be thus, from the point of view of the British Government, in satisfactory order, when on November 9 Castlereagh reported that the whole question of the universal guarantee had been reopened, not this time by Russia, but by Prussia, with the support of Austria. Prussia, he said, was in a state of extreme nervousness about her Rhine frontier, owing to the discontent in her new provinces and the fact that her fortresses were unfinished ; she had actually asked Alexander to leave Russian garrisons in the barrier fortresses. The question had been raised, he thought, because of his insistence on the fact that no such guarantee had been established at Vienna. Limited to a territorial

[28] To Bathurst, November 5, No. 25.

guarantee, the scheme proposed was less obviously a nullity than Alexander's universal union ; but from the British point of view the objection was that it would commit Great Britain to obligations for which, as an insular Power, she would obtain no equivalent. Metternich urged that she might give her moral support only, and reduced the mutual guarantee to one between the signatory Powers of the Treaties of Paris and Vienna only, the German Confederation to count for this purpose as a single whole. Thus modified, Castlereagh for a moment thought the scheme might be worth considering, since it would bind Great Britain to nothing and might be a guarantee against Russia should she attempt an attack on Turkey. With reflection, however, the objections to the idea grew, and Wellington and he were able to persuade the Prussian and Austrian ministers to shelve the question. On the 12th Castlereagh reported that while Alexander was still anxious to give the guarantee a permanent basis, the general feeling was that the system already arranged would be safe during the lifetime of the actual sovereigns. A project, also suggested by Prussia, for establishing a miniature European force at Brussels [29] was defeated by the opposition of Wellington himself, together with that of Castlereagh, who believed that it would be better, at whatever risk, at least to affect complete confidence in France than to court trouble by an ' intermediate system ' which by irritating the French would only create the evils against which it was intended to guard.[30]

So far as the European Concert was concerned, then, the outcome of the Conference of Aix-la-Chapelle was a compromise, embodied in two instruments signed on November 15. The first, in the form of a secret protocol, renewed the Quadruple Alliance for the purpose of watching over France in case of fresh revolutionary outbreaks menacing the peace of Europe ; this was

[29] *Wellington Supp. Disp.* xii. 809.
[30] To Bathurst, November 19, No. 37.

communicated in confidence to Richelieu.[31]   The second,
to which France was invited to adhere, was a declaration,
which ran as follows :

The Convention of October 9, 1818, which definitively
regulated the execution of the engagements agreed to in the
Treaty of Peace of November 20, 1815, is considered by the
sovereigns who concurred therein as the accomplishment of
the work of peace, and as the completion of the political
system destined to secure its solidity.

The intimate union established among the monarchs, who
are joint-parties to this system, by their own principles, no
less than by the interests of their people, offers to Europe
the most sacred pledge of its future tranquillity.

The object of the union is as simple as it is great and
salutary.   It does not tend to any new political combination—
to any change in the relations sanctioned by existing treaties ;
calm and consistent in its proceedings, it has no other object
than the maintenance of peace, and the guarantee of those
transactions on which the peace was founded and consolidated.

The sovereigns, in forming this august union, have regarded
as its fundamental basis their invariable resolution never
to depart, either among themselves or in their relations
with other states, from the strictest observation of the principles of the law of nations : principles, which, in their application to a state of permanent peace, can alone effectually
guarantee the independence of each Government, and the
stability of the general association.

Faithful to these principles, the sovereigns will maintain
them equally in those meetings at which they may be
personally present, or in those which shall take place among
their ministers ; whether they be for the purpose of discussing
in common their own interests, or whether they shall relate
to questions in which other Governments shall formally claim
their interference.   The same spirit which will direct their
councils and reign in their diplomatic communications will
preside also at these meetings ; and the repose of the world
will be constantly their motive and their end.

It is with these sentiments that the sovereigns have
consummated the work to which they were called.   They will

[31] Text in *Wellington Supp. Disp.* xii. 835.

not cease to labour for its confirmation and perfection. They solemnly acknowledge that their duties towards God and the people whom they govern make it peremptory on them to give to the world, as far as it is in their power,[32] an example of justice, of concord, and of moderation ; happy in the power of consecrating, from henceforth, all their efforts to protect the arts of peace, to increase the internal prosperity of their states, and to awaken those sentiments of religion and morality [33] whose influence has been but too much enfeebled by the misfortunes of the times.[34]

An analysis of the language of this declaration shows that it was a compromise. It was intended to conciliate Alexander by ' presenting the subject somewhat in the tone of his own ideas,' while making it clear that the foundation of the European system was the treaties and the treaties alone. It was not, however, so unambiguous as to deprive Alexander of all chance of again bringing forward his grand design, and the growing unrest in regenerated Europe was soon to give him an excuse for doing so.

I have followed in some detail the debates at Aix-la-Chapelle arising out of the question of the future form to be given to the European Alliance, because they still have a very practical value. These debates, how-ever, by no means occupied the whole time of the Con-ference. It had been decided to use the occasion of its meeting to attempt the settlement of a number of questions of common interest, the most important of which were defined in the memorandum of the British Cabinet already quoted. These were : (1) The effective suppression of the Slave Trade, which had been abolished in principle at Vienna ; (2) the suppression of the Barbary pirates ; (3) the refusal of the King of Sweden to carry

[32] In the original draft was added ' and in proportion to the means at their disposal.'

[33] The words ' among their subjects,' in the original draft, are omitted.

[34] Hertslet, *Map of Europe by Treaty*, i. 573, No. 88.

out the provisions of the Treaty of Kiel; and (4)—the most fateful of all—the proposed general mediation between Spain and her revolted American colonies.

It is clear that at this period the Alliance was looked upon even by British statesmen as something more than a mere union of the Great Powers for preserving peace on the basis of the treaties; and in effect, during its short session the Conference acted, not only as a European representative body, but as a sort of European Supreme Court, which heard appeals and received petitions of all kinds from sovereigns and their subjects alike. The German mediatized princes invoked the aid of the Powers against the tyranny of their new overlords, and received satisfaction. The Elector of Hesse begged to be allowed to exchange his now meaningless title for that of king, a request which was refused because it was judged inexpedient to make the royal style too common. The mother of Napoleon, in a pathetic letter, petitioned for the release of her son, pleading that he was now too ill ever again to be a menace to Europe, a petition refused on the ostensible ground that there was proof that the letter was a political move and had been concocted under Napoleon's own direction. The people of Monaco presented a list of grievances against their prince. Questions as various as the settlement of the ranks of diplomatic agents, the rival claims of Bavaria and the Hochberg line to the succession in Baden, a quarrel between the Duke of Oldenburg and Count Bentinck about the lordship of Kniphaussen, the situation of the Jews in Austria and Prussia, were brought under discussion, settled or postponed. In general, on these minor matters it was possible to come to an agreement. It is, however, significant that on the greater issues discussed there was no such edifying harmony. The Powers had already agreed in principle to the suppression of the Slave Trade; jealousy of British sea-power prevented their accepting that mutual ' right of search ' by which alone it could have been suppressed. The

Barbary pirates were the scourge of the whole continental sea-board ; they held up trading vessels at the mouth of the Elbe, and in the Mediterranean no ship was safe that did not sail under the British or the Ottoman flag ; yet it was found impossible to concert measures against them because of British jealousy of Russian intervention in the Mediterranean. The struggle between Spain and her colonies was regarded as a serious menace to the peace of Europe ; the Powers were agreed as to the principle of mediation, but could not agree as to its form. They did agree in calling the King of Sweden to order. He obeyed, but at the same time protested against the ' dictatorship ' arrogated to themselves by the Great Powers, a protest reinforced by an indignant letter from the King of Württemberg.

Of the more important questions thus discussed and left unsettled at Aix-la-Chapelle, the most interesting, from our present point of view, was that of the Spanish colonies, the debates on which opened up the whole question of the relations of the Old World and the New, and even foreshadowed the idea of a world-alliance. This question, however, I reserve for separate treatment in connection with the Congress of Verona and the origins of the Monroe Doctrine.

VI

THE BREAK-UP OF THE CON-FEDERATION

Things are getting back to a wholesome state again. Every nation for itself, and God for us all! Only bid your Emperor be quiet, for the time of Areopagus and the like of that is gone by.—CANNING.

I

REVOLUTION AND REACTION

The Treaty of Frankfort—Alexander and Liberalism—The Constitution of Poland—Enigmatic attitude of Alexander—Russian propaganda in Italy—Metternich and the Tsar's Jacobinism—Liberal reaction in France—Attitude of the Powers—Murder of Kotzebue—The Carlsbad Decrees—Alexander champions German Liberalism—Change in his views—Revolution in Spain—Murder of the Duc de Berri—Alexander suggests intervention in Spain—Opposition of Austria and Great Britain—Revolution in Naples—Metternich and Alexander—The idea of the Universal Union revived—Question of intervention—Attitude of Great Britain—Castlereagh and Metternich on intervention.

THE public acts of the Conference of Aix-la-Chapelle advertised the completion of the work to which the Allies had solemnly dedicated themselves by the Treaty of Chaumont. The Quadruple Alliance, indeed, survived, a rod in pickle for a France but doubtfully disciplined. The rod, however, was not to be flourished ; and, France having been solemnly restored to the bosom of the European family, the international committee of ministers in Paris suspended their irritating tutorship. Certain important details of the European settlement had been left uncompleted at Aix, and these, reserved for a conference of ministers to be summoned to Frankfort in the following year, were finally adjusted by a treaty signed on June 20, 1819. The bulk of this treaty was concerned with matters inside the German Confederation, the outstanding questions between Bavaria and Austria, and between Bavaria and Baden ; but it also arranged the cession of the border fortresses of Marienbourg and

Philippeville to the Netherlands, defined the limits of Savoy, and determined the question of the reversion of the Italian duchies. The Frankfort Final Act thus takes its place with those of Paris and Vienna as part of the Great Charter of reconstituted Europe.[1] With the break-up of the Conference at Frankfort, Europe was left for the time without any central representation, nor had any date been fixed for another meeting of the Powers.

The Emperor Alexander, however, in spite of the discouraging experience of Aix-la-Chapelle, had by no means given up the idea of materializing the Holy Alliance; and everything in the course of the two years succeeding the Conference strengthened his determination to persevere. His theoretical belief in liberty, indeed, persisted in spite of his growing uneasiness at the increasing signs of revolutionary unrest in nearly every country in Europe ; as late as the autumn of 1819, when Metternich published the Carlsbad Decrees, which formulated the plans of the German Powers for the suppression of all Liberal movements within the Confederation, he associated himself with Castlereagh's protest against a policy calculated to range the governments against the peoples, allowed Capo d'Istria to issue in his name a manifesto in which he refused to support a league of which the sole object was to enforce ' the absurd pretensions of absolute power,' and declared his belief in liberty, though liberty ' limited by the principles of order.'

His conception of liberty thus limited was luminously shown by his treatment of Poland. In November 1815 he had granted to the new kingdom a Constitution on the approved Liberal lines : biennial parliaments, responsibility of ministers, freedom of speech and of the press, securities against arbitrary arrest. But the

[1] ' The Frankfort Final Act is considered as giving additional strength to those fundamental acts upon which the European system now happily rests ' (Castlereagh to Clancarty, July 21, 1819. F.O. : Germany, Frankfort. Drafts to Lord Clancarty).

first signs of an independent spirit in the representative body he had created awoke his suspicious fears. In spite of Czartoryski's remonstrances he had left his brother, the Grand Duke Constantine, an ignorant, narrow martinet of the old Russian type, in command of the Polish army, and General Zaïonczek,[2] the titular viceroy, was his obedient tool. Constantine thus became the real ruler of the country,[3] and he governed it as might have been expected, with every abuse of the Russian system and an all but entire disregard of the Constitution and the limitations it imposed upon arbitrary power. In vain Czartoryski, using the privilege of old friendship, appealed to the Tsar's higher nature and besought him to intervene to save from ruin his own favourite creation. The kindly personal feeling between the friends remained ; but the Tsar, restored to the atmosphere of St. Petersburg, listened to his Russian advisers and chose to regard the natural resentment of the Poles as only a proof of the folly of expecting gratitude from people possessed by the revolutionary spirit.

Alexander's whole attitude during this transition period was, indeed, so enigmatic as to awaken the liveliest misgivings. By Metternich especially his Liberalism, like his evangelical professions, was regarded merely as a mask to disguise his perfidious plans of attack on Austria. In Italy Russian activities continued to be especially disconcerting. Capo d'Istria, who after the close of the Conference at Aix had made a tour in Italy, had appalled the Neapolitan ministers by his revolutionary language, and had incidentally been ' highly abusive of the Austrian Government,' [4] while a little later La Harpe was reported as travelling about

---

[2] Zaïonczek had commanded the Polish contingent in Napoleon's Grand Army.

[3] He sat in the Diet as member for a division of Warsaw.

[4] Gordon to Castlereagh, Florence, March 24, 1819. F.O. : Austria, Gordon, January–December 1819.

Italy preaching revolution and even presiding over meetings of Carbonari. Metternich saw in all this a deliberate plan to expel Austria from the peninsula and revive the idea of a united Italian kingdom under Russian patronage.

Sir Robert Gordon, the British representative at the Court of Tuscany, who was at this time in close touch with Metternich, then on a visit to Italy, and on the whole in sympathy with his views, found his fears both of Russian designs and revolutionary dangers exaggerated. ' Prince Metternich,' he wrote on April 22, 1819, from Rome, ' discovers the existence of Russian agency and intervention in every quarter and every passing event in Europe,' and in an interesting letter from Florence of July 12 he gives his own impressions of the condition of Italy and of the Russian propagandists there. After saying that he himself has seen more to inspire confidence than alarm, he adds that the discontent of the people is largely due to the distrust exhibited by the Austrians—a distrust embodied in that elaborate secret service system which was by no means confined to Italy. As for the travellers and agents of Russia, Gordon, it is true, reports that they held ' very improper language,' the conduct of M. de La Harpe being ' beyond all palliation.' But, he adds, all this perhaps depends ' more upon the character of the nation than a duty imposed upon them by the Russian Government. Magnanimity is a Russian thesis, and on his travels each Russian composes a theme of his own upon it. For this exercise of his genius he naturally attracts to his person the unfortunate and discontented . . . who may build groundless hopes upon high-sounding words. The Emperor Alexander himself has ever protected the unfortunate and preached a magnanimous doctrine. His disciples in Italy, with less wit, have thought to ingratiate themselves more by going beyond their master.'

This is a common-sense view, and perhaps gives

the key to the puzzle of which he had spoken in an
earlier letter—that of the different language of different
Russian agents. ' Decazes,' he wrote, ' complains that
Pozzo does not express the sentiments of the Tsar ;
in Germany, Kotzebue is murdered, and Stourdza nearly
so, for espousing the cause of unrestrained monarchy
and obscurantism ; while in Italy M. de La Harpe travels
up and down holding a language of the purest democracy,
not to mention that of the Russian ministers at the
different Courts of this country.' [5]   Perhaps, too, it gives
the key to the enigma of Alexander's own attitude ;
for the contradictions in the language of his agents
were but reflections of his own. As Czartoryski said,
he loved phrases for their own sake. Magnanimity
was his thesis ; the theme he had been accustomed
to compose upon it was modelled upon the philosophic
platitudes of La Harpe, and he could not get out of
the habit even when the whole trend of his practical
policy was in the diametrically opposite direction.   Yet
there is as little reason to suspect him of conscious
hypocrisy at this period of his life as earlier, when his
idealism had not yet suffered the shocks of experience.
The truth is that suspicion was in his very blood ; he
could trust neither his own servants nor the peoples
for whose abstract liberty he laboured.   So it came that
he treated his ministers as clerks, and the peoples whom
he believed himself to have enfranchised as children
who had indeed certain rights, and were entitled to
certain liberties, but ought to be grateful for such
measure of these rights and liberties as paternal
governments might choose to concede and not be
guilty of the impiety of clamorously asking for more.
In such circumstances it was the duty of the Powers,
who under the terms of the solemn covenant of the

[5] Compare Metternich to Gentz (April 9, 1819). ' Pendant qu'en
Allemagne on assassine les agents russes propter obscurationem,
d'autres agents russes président en Italie les clubs de carbonari '
(Pierre Rain, *Alexander I*, d. 391).

Holy Alliance had undertaken to treat their subjects as their children, not to spare the rod.

From his point of view the children of the European family were behaving very badly. Long before the meeting at Aix-la-Chapelle he had watched with alarm the effects of the Liberal Constitution which he had himself been instrumental in obtaining for France ; and the alarm had been increased by the discovery of a ridiculous plot to kidnap him on the way to the Conference and force him to proclaim Napoleon or his son Emperor of the French.[6] Nor was he alone in his misgivings. Castlereagh watched with uneasiness the reorganization of the French army by Marshal Gouvion St. Cyr [7] ; and Metternich shared his alarms, citing the ' seditious language ' of Baron Louis and Gouvion St. Cyr and expressing the conviction that a revolution was no longer to be avoided.[8] He was confirmed in this view by all the reports he received from Paris.[9] As for the King, Baron Lebzeltern, the Austrian ambassador, reported that he was superior to Louis XVI only ' in knowing his Horace and Virgil by heart,' and inferior to him in not being able to exist without a favourite. The favourite of the moment—Decazes—was ' piqued against the nobility, and drawn into the Liberal Party by his principles, by necessity, by the seduction of his father-in-law, further than perhaps he himself desired.' With such elements what hope was there for peace and order in France ? ' When Capo d'Istria advised a Liberal

[6] Castlereagh to Bathurst, November 12, 1818 (unnumbered). F.O. : Continent, Aix, Castlereagh. Also No. 33, containing the report of the Procureur-Général of November 6.

[7] To Gordon, January 19, 1819. F.O. : Austria, Gordon, January to December 1819.

[8] Gordon to Castlereagh, February 11, 1819, No. 10.

[9] Gordon wrote that he was uncertain how far to trust Metternich's correspondents in France. ' It is certain that of his numerous correspondents not one has chosen bright colours for his picture ; and I fear Metternich's canvas takes the dark ones too kindly.' The absurd rumour of a plot to make Bernadotte king was a ' sample of the stuff that composes his bales of correspondence.' To Castlereagh, Vienna, February 11, 1819. F.O. : Austria, Gordon, January to December 1819.

policy, when he undertook to govern France from the banks of the Neva, did he realize the harm that Russia would do ? When he spoke of a Constitution and Liberal representation for this country, did he realize the fresh horrors to which they would lead ? ' [10] To Metternich it was clear where the fault lay, and, in a dispatch on the actual state of France, he cleverly contrived to throw all the blame for it upon Russia, sarcastically congratulating Pozzo di Borgo on the effects of his policy.[11]

The worst misgivings seemed to be justified when, in May, the Abbé Gregoire, ex - Conventional and Constitutional bishop, was returned to the Chambers. Even to Pozzo the situation seemed critical ; he advised that the Alliance should intervene to persuade Louis XVIII to dismiss Gouvion St. Cyr ; and, upon a report presented by Count Golovkin, the Russian cabinet recommended that Metternich's proposal to revive the international Conference of Ministers at Paris should be accepted.[12] The proposal, formally circulated, met, however, with little encouragement. Castlereagh, who believed that any threat of intervention would only strengthen the military party, declared that it was no part of the functions of the Quadruple Alliance to attempt to correct the ' internal eccentricities ' of France, and that, as for any danger of these developing into external aggression, the Alliance was, in his opinion, most effective when operating by the ' silent force of its inactivity.' [13] As for Metternich, though he thought it a pity that the Conference had ever been suspended, he denied that he had ever proposed its resumption.[14] He held,

[10] Lebzeltern to Metternich, Paris, January 27, 1819. F.O. : Austria, Gordon, January–December 1819.

[11] Gordon to Castlereagh, February 15, 1819. *Ibid.* No. 9.

[12] *Idem* to *idem*, May 26, 1819. *Ibid.* No. 17.

[13] Memorandum of September on the Russian proposal of intervention in France. F.O. : Drafts to Lord Stewart, May–December 1919.

[14] Gordon to Castlereagh, Naples, May 26, 1819. F.O. : Austria, Gordon, January–December 1819, No. 17.

or affected to hold, the Emperor Alexander personally responsible for the system of ' falsehood and intrigue ' which was the cause of all the unrest in Europe ; he declared that his vaunted loyalty to the European Alliance was but a mark of the deepest finesse, intended to cajole and win the suffrages of those Powers which would have dreaded and objected to any separate Alliance [15] ; and he was therefore the less anxious to see Alexander again playing Providence in France in the name of Europe. He therefore agreed with Castlereagh that any intervention of the Alliance would only ' drive the evil forward,' [16] and under these circumstances the Russian proposal, after a correspondence extending over months, was dropped.

Metternich, divided between fear of revolutions and fear of Russia, was not without hope of winning over Alexander to ' good principles,' and so making the Alliance effective for his own conservative policy. A senseless crime came to his assistance. On March 23, 1819, August von Kotzebue, dramatist and Russian agent, was murdered by the *Bursche* Karl Sand at Mannheim. Metternich was at Rome when the news reached him. He at once wrote to Count Nesselrode, calling on the Emperor Alexander to co-operate in the measures necessary to suppress the anti-social propaganda illustrated by Sand's crime.[17] Clearly, whatever the condition of France might be, that of Germany was no better. To intervene in France would be dangerous ; but in view of the universal unrest, the Grand Alliance should ' knit for itself a closer texture ' [18] ; and to this end international Conferences should be established permanently, not in Paris, but in Vienna or London.[19]

[15] Gordon to Castlereagh, Vienna, February 11, 1819. F.O. : Austria, Gordon, No. 5.

[16] *Idem* to *idem*, Rome, April 22, 1819. *Ibid.* No. 14.

[17] To Nesselrode, Rome, April 23, 1819. F.O. : Austria, Domestic, April–December 1819.

[18] Gordon to Castlereagh, Rome, April 22. *Loc. cit.* No. 14.

[19] *Idem* to *idem*, Naples, May 26. *Loc. cit.* No. 17.

As for the state of Germany, ' his brilliant imagination,'
to quote Sir Robert Gordon,[20] ' immediately conceived
a remedy,' which was that policy of using the machinery
of the Federal Diet for the purpose of suppressing the
Liberal propaganda in the Universities which in the
following October was embodied in the Carlsbad decrees—
or more properly resolutions—the principles of which
were given effect to in the Vienna Final Act of May 15,
1820. From our present point of view, the most interesting thing about these acts was that they represented an attempt to realize within the group of sovereign
states forming the German Confederation the principles
of mutual guarantee and supervision which it was sought
to apply to Europe as a whole.

It was precisely this fact that made them unacceptable
to the British Government.   Metternich had been careful
to point out in his presidential address to the Conference
at Vienna that the German Confederation was an integral
part of the European states system as established by
the Vienna Final Act of 1815, and that therefore not
only the rights of the Confederation as a whole, but also
those of its constituent states, depended on the guarantee
of the treaties.[21] It followed that a principle once
admitted as applicable to a part might be logically
extended so as to embrace the whole ; and the Carlsbad
decrees were therefore rightly feared and denounced as
a menace to the liberties of all Europe. Castlereagh
saw the danger and, true to the British principle of non-
intervention, protested against the decrees as an unjustifiable interference with the rights of sovereign and
independent states, while to Count Lieven, the Russian
ambassador in London, he pointed out the folly of
producing the impression that the Governments were
contracting an alliance against the peoples. Capo
d'Istria's objections were equally emphatic [22]; but the

[20] Gordon to Castlereagh, *loc. cit.*, No. 14.

[21] In F.O. : Austria, Domestic, January–August 1820.

[22] Stewart to Castlereagh, Vienna, November 1, 1819.   F.O. :
Austria, Stewart, May–October 1819.

attitude of the Emperor Alexander, whom Metternich plied with interminable memoirs, was more equivocal. In private he admitted to Baron Lebzeltern, the Austrian ambassador, that in his opinion, so far as his knowledge went, the Carlsbad measures were necessary, and justified in view of ‘ the spirit of corruption and immorality ’ in Germany.[23] Yet he allowed Capo d’Istria to draw up and circulate a memorandum in his name, in which the decrees were denounced as an attempt to enforce ‘ the absurd pretensions of absolute power ’ and he was made to reiterate his belief in liberty, though in liberty ‘ limited by the principles of order.’ It is not surprising if Metternich saw in this only another piece of hypocrisy, an attempt to prevent the consolidation of Germany by the ostentatious support of those lesser states which, like Württemberg, had set up Liberal Constitutions and protested against the Carlsbad policy.

To those who came in closest contact with Alexander at this time it was clear that his Liberalism was waning. Two events strengthened this tendency : the military revolt under Riego in Spain, which in January, 1820 forced Ferdinand VII to accept the egregious Constitution of 1812 ; and the murder, on February 13, of the Duc de Berri, heir-presumptive to the French crown.[24] The latter, especially, produced upon Alexander a profound impression. The influence of Capo d’Istria was shaken, and the way was opened for that *rapprochement* between Austria and Russia which was consummated in the meeting of Metternich and Alexander at Troppau.

As early as November 1819 a dispatch of Lord Stewart from Vienna had foreshadowed a change in

[23] Stewart to Castlereagh. *Ibid.* During the same conversation Alexander said that the revolution could only be combated by drawing the union of the sovereigns daily closer, and described Decazes as ‘ un fourbe et un mauvais homme.’

[24] Metternich to Esterhazy, March 23, 1820, enclosing an extract of a report of Lebzeltern at St. Petersburg on the effect of the assassination.

Metternich's attitude. Metternich, he reported, was inclined to withdraw from his support of the British policy of non-intervention in France, which was ' no longer the France of Aix-la-Chapelle.' Castlereagh having ' closed the door of precautionary diplomacy towards France,' Metternich had opened ' a more anxious and flattering diplomacy towards Russia, and while seeking to expose their unjustifiable views, ' or the falseness of their proceedings,' aimed at preserving the most perfect understanding with the Russian cabinet.[25] The assassination of the Duc de Berri, by driving the Russian Government in the direction of reaction, certainly contributed to this understanding. But the time was not yet ripe for its consummation ; the suspicion of Russia's ulterior aims remained, and was certainly not lessened by her proposed action in the affair of Spain.

On April 19, 1820, the Russian Government sent to the Powers of the Quintuple Alliance a circular note, the outcome of a note on Spanish affairs presented to the Tsar by the Chevalier de Zea de Bermudez, envoy of King Ferdinand VII. This document is interesting for more than one reason. In the first place it shows that Alexander realized something of the vastness of the issues involved, which were not merely those of the particular form of government to be maintained in Spain. ' The Spanish Revolution,' says the circular, ' fixes the attention of two worlds ; the interests to be decided are those of the universe . . . and involve the future perhaps of all civilized peoples.' The idea of the Confederation of Europe, that is to say, is growing in Alexander's mind into that of a World Union. Secondly, the circular defines the Tsar's attitude towards constitutional liberty in words similar to those which he

[25] To Castlereagh, Vienna, November 1, 1819. F.O. : Austria, Stewart, November–December 1819, No. 20. ' This cabinet will always be endeavouring to create diplomacy. It is a food largely devoured and greatly sought after.'

had used when condemning the Carlsbad decrees :
' The Allies have recognized that institutions cannot
be means of peace and happiness, if, instead of being
the voluntary concession of benevolence, they are the
last means of salvation for weakness.' He is, that is
to say, still in favour—theoretically at least—of Constitutions *octroyées* from above. Thirdly, and this is
the most important, he foreshadows the policy which
two years later, at Verona, led to the definitive breach
of Great Britain with the Alliance, by suggesting that
the ministers of the five Courts should hold a common
language at Madrid, the preliminary to a concerted,
or at least to an authorized, intervention.

The circular met with a very unsympathetic reception.
The British Government was little likely to abandon
its settled policy of non-intervention, in order to assist
in riveting on the necks of the Spanish people a yoke
universally recognized as intolerable. As for Metternich,
Austria was but little concerned with the troubles of
royalty beyond the Pyrenees, while European intervention, as conceived by the Emperor Alexander, would
have meant the advance of a huge Russian army across
her territories for the purpose of acting as ' European
police ' in the South. To Metternich, for all the Tsar's
professions of disinterestedness, this appeared by far
the most imminent peril, and he decided that in this
particular instance collective action must at all costs
be avoided. He extracted himself from a difficult
situation with characteristic address. He was committed deeply to the opinion that the condition of the
world demanded an organized system of international
supervision ; his task now was to prove that the case
of Spain was the exception that proved the rule. In
a series of lengthy dispatches he covered his temporary
defection from the principles of the Alliance with a cloud
of phrases. The Alliance indeed still existed and would
continue to exist, for its moral basis was unalterable
and eternal. Having the support of all honest and

enlightened men, as against ambitious swindlers, false philosophers, and sectaries, it would still be effective for the cure of the ills of Europe, which were ' moral.' But the ills of Spain were ' material.' King Ferdinand VII, moreover, had accepted the Revolution, and any interference would merely create a ferment. As for the Russian proposal of a Conference of sovereigns and cabinets, he had always been in favour of meetings every three years or so, which, as being merely part of the established system, would not have disquieted public opinion. But a meeting called specially to consider the state of Spain would only unsettle that unhappy country yet more. Besides, the meeting would have to be one, not of the four, but of the five Courts ; and it was unlikely that the British cabinet would be willing, and the French cabinet able, to combine with the three Courts which were ' more free in their actions and more independent in their choice of forms.' The four Powers, acting separately, could do all that was necessary by a firm attitude and a common language.[26]

This was Metternich's attitude in June 1820. It underwent a significant change when, in the following month, a military revolt in Naples forced the King of the Two Sicilies to accept the Spanish Constitution of 1812. From Metternich's point of view this was an event of a totally different complexion from the revolution in Spain, since it directly threatened the stability of the whole Austrian system in Italy. In a sense it was an event which, however alarming, was not without its compensating advantages for Austria. It would serve to divert attention from the delicate Spanish Question, from which the Habsburg Monarchy could reap

[26] Metternich to Lebzeltern, Prague, June 5, 1820. Annexe No. 1 à la dépêche de juin 3, 1820. F.O. : Austria, Domestic, Esterhazy, January–August 1820. There is another long dispatch, dated June 3, to Esterhazy, sketching the history of Europe since the Revolution and repeating most of No. 1, and yet another to Baron Vincent, dated June 15, repeating it all over again.

no possible advantage, to one in which, if Metternich's self-confidence was justified, the leading part would be played by Austria and not by Russia. For whatever criticism might be levelled at the claim of any Power or group of Powers to intervene in the affairs of Spain, there could be no question of the juridical basis of Austria's right to intervene in those of Naples. By the terms of the secret article of the treaty of June 12, 1815, between Austria and Naples, King Ferdinand IV had bound himself not to allow any changes in the political system of his dominions inconsistent with the ancient monarchical institutions or with the principles adopted by His Austrian Majesty for the internal administration of his Italian provinces ; and as late as the preceding November Metternich had written to Cardinal Ruffo approving the reconstitution of the ancient Sicilian parliament, but at the same time calling his attention to the secret article of 1812, by way of warning him not to try constitutional experiments in Naples. The act of King Ferdinand in taking the oath to a revolutionary Constitution was then a distinct breach of his treaty obligations to Austria ; and if Austria considered her interests imperilled by this, she had the undoubted right to safeguard them, if necessary by force. This was the view of the British Government, which was quite prepared to leave Austria a free hand ; Prussia took the same attitude ; and there was little doubt that France would follow. The doubtful factor in the situation was again the Emperor Alexander. The Neapolitan revolutionists loudly proclaimed that they had the ' moral support ' of Russia, and whatever the personal views of the Tsar might be, their claim certainly seemed to be substantiated by the language which his agents in Italy continued to employ. That this language represented Alexander's sincere aspirations Metternich did not believe ; he saw in it rather an effort to trouble the waters in order to favour his fishing at Austria's expense. In any case, it was of supreme

importance once for all to disabuse the minds of the
Italian Liberals of the idea that they could count upon
Russian patronage. In a letter to Prince Esterhazy [27]
he poured out, for the benefit of the British Government,
his grievances against the Russian cabinet. For years
past the policy of the ' pitiable creatures ' who composed
it had been directed against what they were pleased
to term ' the influence of Austria,' thus ' confusing the
solution of conservative principles with diplomatic
intrigue.' Alexander had personally recanted his evil
opinions [28] ; but words should be proved by acts, and
now that the Revolution had infected the armies he
would perhaps show more energy.

With Alexander in this mood, an ostentatious understanding between the Emperors of Austria and Russia
would best have served Metternich's purposes, and a
meeting between them was suggested. But the very
alarms which had made him a desirable ally for Austria
had redoubled in him that desire to realize his dream
of a Universal Union which had been frustrated in Aix-
la-Chapelle ; and though for a week or two his attitude
was characteristically ambiguous, he ended by refusing
to be a party to a separate agreement. Moreover, to
Metternich's intense annoyance, he refused to segregate
the Neapolitan Question, insisting on mixing it up with
that of Spain, though, as Metternich put it, ' General
Quiroga would be beaten in the person of General Pepe,
and never to speak of July 6th without dragging in
March 8th was to create difficulties which were foreign
to the matter in hand.' [29]

They were not foreign, however, to the plans of

[27] Vienna, August 8, 1820. F.O. : Austria, Domestic, September–
December 1820.

[28] In another letter of the same date to Esterhazy, Metternich
reports that Alexander on taking leave of M. de Schöler, had said,
' J'ai méconnu l'esprit public depuis de la chûte de Bonaparte, mais
les derniers événements m'ont ouvert les yeux.'

[29] To Esterhazy, Vienna, September 21, 1820. F.O. : Austria,
Domestic.

Alexander, which seemed to embrace the problems of both worlds. In the last memorandum of the Russian cabinet on the affairs of Spain the four other Courts had been mentioned as ' placed like Russia at the centre of the General Alliance,' and if there was any doubt as to the meaning of this, it was set at rest by a dispatch of Golovkin, in which he spoke of the acts of Aix-la-Chapelle as proving that the monarchs who signed them considered themselves bound by ties of general fraternity to all the Powers signatory of the Treaty of Vienna, and regretted that ' particular interests sometimes led to a divergence of views among the allied Courts as to the course which was, so to speak, forced on them when it was a question of putting into practice the theory of the Universal Union.' [30]   In short, Alexander affected to believe that the Powers at Aix-la-Chapelle had committed themselves to his dream of a general Confederation of Europe, and saw in the attitude of Great Britain ' all the egoism of an exclusive policy,' in flat contradiction to the principles of the Declaration of 1818.   As for even the Quadruple and Quintuple Alliances, Capo d'Istria, in conversation with Lebzeltern, denied their continued existence. They had been superseded, he maintained, by the Declaration of Aix-la-Chapelle, and, faithful to this, Russia would not recognize any but a ' general association.' [31]   The immediate practical outcome of these principles was that, in view of the critical state of affairs, not in Naples only, the Emperor Alexander considered that another Conference should be summoned on the model of that of 1818.   His view was supported by

[30] Report of Lebzeltern, St. Petersburg, July 25, 1820, and copy of Golovkin's dispatch, of July 15. F.O. : Austria, Domestic, September–December 1820.

[31] ' We differ,' he said, ' as to the basis of our engagements. You base them upon the alliance of four or five Powers, and in relation to France, while we see a general association which embraces all the Powers, and of which the function is to guarantee the principles of public law—that is to say, to guarantee their state of possession and the legitimacy of thrones.'

France, where the obnoxious Decazes had given place
to the Duc de Richelieu, on the ground that the revolutionary troubles in Spain and Italy were precisely the
contingencies contemplated in the agreements made at
Aix with a view to concerted action.

Metternich, however, still hoped to come to an arrangement which, by yielding somewhat to Alexander's ideas,
should give to Austrian policy in Italy the imposing
support of the Alliance without the necessity for summoning a Conference, at which other and more awkward
questions would be likely to be raised. On August 28,
accordingly, he addressed to the Courts, in reply to the
suggestion of the two Powers, a formal 'proposition'
in which he laid down the course of action which Austria
intended to pursue. Since her special right to intervene
in Naples had been generally admitted, she proposed
to concentrate in Italy a force sufficient to crush the
'factions,' to invite the Allies to unite themselves
'morally' with her, and at the same time to make
'frank overtures' to the Courts of Germany and Italy
on the unsatisfactory state of affairs and the general
attitude of Austria towards them. For the carrying
out of this plan it was not necessary to summon a formal
Conference, which would but waste time, and of which
the moral effect was liable to be spoilt owing to Great
Britain not having a 'free hand.' It would suffice if
the allied Courts refused to recognize the revolutionary
Government of Naples, declared all its acts null and
void, and through their ministers supported such coercive
measures as the Austrian Government might judge it
necessary to employ.[32] To this proposal the reply of
Russia was favourable ; so far as Naples was concerned,
the initiative was to rest with Austria, which was to
have a free hand and to be backed by the 'moral' union
of the Powers. As for Great Britain, Metternich hoped
to gain her adhesion by persuading her that the situation,

[32] Castlereagh to Stewart, September 16, 1820. F.O. : Continent,
Circular Dispatches.

dangerous alike to Austria, to Italy, and to Europe,
was clearly one to which the treaties sanctioned by
Parliament applied. Unfortunately for him, Castlereagh
did not take this view. The suggested concert, he
declared, amounted to a hostile league against Naples,
and by adhering to it Great Britain would become a
principal in the resulting war. This she had no intention
of doing, since she refused to interfere in the internal
concerns of Naples herself or to encourage others to do
so. If Austria believed her vital interests imperilled
by the revolution in Naples, Great Britain was prepared
to stand aside and let her act. In that case a Conference
of Ministers at Vienna would be useful, since it could
receive the report of Austria and see that nothing was
done ' incompatible with the present system of Europe.' [33]

In view of this unequivocal pronouncement, Metternich was thrown back upon the idea of a Congress.
Castlereagh had declared himself ready to consider
the question of a Conference as soon as the Austrian
Government had clearly defined the purposes for which
it was to be summoned [34] ; with the revolution in Naples
—a military *pronunciamiento* in ' wanton and un-
provoked ' imitation of that in Spain—he was wholly
out of sympathy ; and Metternich was therefore not
without reason for judging that, were the Conference
once assembled, the Powers might be readily induced to
place their secret differences in the background and to
give to the action of Austria in Italy the united ' moral
support ' which was all she needed. It was the more
unfortunate that the memorandum in which he stated
his views as to the attitude to be adopted by the
Conference contained statements of principle in flat
contradiction to those which inspired British policy,
and scarcely less distasteful to France than to England.
In the affair of Naples, he argued, the interests of Austria

[33] Castlereagh to Stewart, July 19, 1820. F.O. : Continent, Circular
Dispatches.

[34] Proposition addressée par l'Autriche aux Cours. F.O. : Continent,
Circular Dispatches, 1820.

were those of all Europe, since all the Powers were equally
interested in the preservation of the treaties, and therefore also in concerting measures for the suppression of
any revolutionary movements by which the system
established by the treaties might be threatened. The
business of the Conference which it was proposed to
assemble at Troppau would therefore be to define the
principles on which the Powers would intervene in Naples,
and proceed at once to their application. As to what
these principles should be, he proceeded to set out his
own views. Revolutions, he argued, were of two kinds :
legitimate when initiated from above, illegitimate when
enforced from below. In the former case intervention
from a foreign Power should not be allowed ; in the
latter case the Powers should bind themselves over never
to recognize changes brought about in this way, and
should undertake to abolish such as had taken place in
their own states.

This was in effect to take a long step in the direction
of Alexander's union of guarantee, and it was a step
that Great Britain was less than ever disposed to take.
In the refusal of Castlereagh to accept any such basis
for the deliberations of the Conference Metternich affected
to see an intention to break up the Alliance. Castlereagh,
for his part, denied that this was the wish of his Government or that it was involved in the refusal of Great Britain
to do what she was not bound to do by the treaties on
which the Alliance rested. These were those of Chaumont
and Paris, of which the terms were quite clear, and to
which the acts of Aix-la-Chapelle had added nothing.
By her treaty obligations Great Britain was prepared
to abide, and she recognized that there were innumerable subjects outside these which from time to time
might equally call for a cordial agreement among the
Powers, but without their being bound beforehand to
any particular attitude. In conversation with Prince
Esterhazy, however, he made the limits of British sympathy with the ideal of European solidarity perfectly

clear. ' If,' he said, ' it is desired to extend the Alliance so as to include all objects present and future, foreseen and unforeseen, it would change its character to such an extent and carry us so far, that we should see in it an additional motive for adhering to our course at the risk of seeing the Alliance move away from us without our having quitted it.' [35]

[35] Observations de Milord Castlereagh sur un passage d'un rapport de M. le Prince de Metternich, etc.   Report of Esterhazy, October 1820.   F.O. : Austria, Domestic, September–December 1820.

THE CONFERENCES OF TROPPAU AND LAIBACH

Alexander recants his Liberalism—Conversation with Metternich at Troppau—Mutiny of the Semyonovski regiment—The Holy Alliance becomes an instrument of reaction—Rift between the Autocratic and Constitutional Powers of the Alliance—The Troppau Protocol—Consecration of the principle of intervention—Metternich's explanations—Protest of Castlereagh—Effect on the Powers—Adjourned Conference at Laibach—Continuation of the controversy—The British objections overridden—Breach in the Alliance.

THIS was said on the eve of the Conference, which opened on October 29, 1820; and the constitution of this august assembly emphasized its moral. At all previous Congresses and Conferences, since that of Chaumont, Great Britain had been represented by her Secretary of State for Foreign Affairs; to Troppau she did not even send a plenipotentiary, Lord Stewart, the British Ambassador at Vienna, being charged to watch the proceedings on behalf of his Government. France, too, though the Conference had been her suggestion and her attitude in the Neapolitan Question was less uncompromising than that of England, did not arm her representatives, the Comte de La Ferronnays and the Marquis de Caraman, with full powers.[36] But whatever misgivings Metternich may have felt on this

[36] Richelieu's presence had been suggested; but the Emperor Alexander remonstrated against his leaving Paris and risking the possibility of Decazes using the opportunity of his absence to regain his ascendancy over the King.

account were relieved by the changed temper in which he found the Emperor Alexander. On the afternoon of October 24, he had, over a cup of tea in the inn parlour at Troppau, that famous conversation with the Tsar, in the course of which Alexander confessed that in all that he had done between 1814 and 1818 he had been grievously mistaken. ' So we are at one, Prince, and it is to you that we owe it,' he said. ' You have correctly judged the state of affairs. I deplore the waste of time, which we must try to repair. I am here without any fixed ideas ; without any plan ; but I bring you a firm and unalterable resolution. It is for your Emperor to use it as he wills. Tell me what you desire, and what you wish me to do and I will do it.' [37] Four days later the Emperor Alexander was no longer to be without fixed ideas and without a plan. The change was wrought by the news, which reached him one day before the opening of the Congress, of the mutiny at St. Petersburg of the Semyonovski regiment of his Guard. The effect upon him was instantaneous and profound ; nor is it surprising that it should have been so. This regiment, of which as Cesarevich he had been Colonel-in-Chief, had supplied the guard at the Michael Palace on the night of Paul's murder and had since been treated by Alexander with special favour. A military Power such as Russia, as the Emperor explained to Wellington, could not afford to tolerate military revolutions in other countries, the example of which might prove infectious ; and now his worst fears were realized. In vain it was pointed out to him, by all those best able to judge, that no political motives underlay the action of the soldiers, who had been goaded to revolt solely by the intolerable tyranny of their colonel, a stupid and cruel Prussian martinet.[38] Alexander insisted that

[37] Metternich to Esterhazy, Troppau, October 24, 1820. F.O. : Austria, Domestic, September–December 1820.

[38] The mutiny occurred in St. Petersburg on October 18–30, 1820. Its immediate cause was hatred of the colonel, a German named Schwartz, who in disciplining his men after the Prussian model ' did

the mutiny was the outcome of the conspiracy of the Carbonari, who had spread their network over all Europe and covered even the soil of Holy Russia. Crowning proof of his own folly ! In the person of Napoleon he had thought to overthrow the Beast ; and behold ! it was not incarnate in one man, but a ' many-headed monster thing ' of which, in his blindness, he had himself encouraged the growth. At least his eyes were opened, by the Providence of God, before it was too late, and his duty was clear. To the servants of the Evil One no mercy must be shown ; he set aside as too lenient the sentences passed by the court martial on the ringleaders of the mutiny—two corporals and five poor privates— and ordered that they should receive six thousand strokes apiece.[39] Thus in Holy Russia at least the Lord's will could be done. As for Europe at large, to Alexander God's will was now equally clear. He searched the Scriptures, and found in the most unlikely places—in the stories of Nebuchadnezzar and of Judith and Holofernes, and in the Epistles of St. Paul—Divine lessons applicable to the perils of the hour. To the principle of Evil, bastard brood of Voltairean philosophy falsely so called, must be opposed the principle of Faith, which found its supreme expression in that revelation of the Most High—the Holy Alliance.[40] Stripped of its verbiage, this meant that in Alexander's view the Alliance was henceforth to be used as a force purely conservative, if not reactionary.

not spare them any of those indignities which are as dishonouring to those who suffer as to those who inflict them ' (Report of Adjutant Buturlin, in Shilder, *op. cit.*, iv., Appendix VIII, p. 533).

[39] *I.e.*, to run the gauntlet between two lines of soldiers armed with sticks. The sentence was of course equivalent to one of death under torture.

[40] See the extraordinary letter of Alexander to Prince Golitsin, dated from Laibach, February 8–15, 1821, in Grand Duke Nicholas Mikhailovich's *L'Empereur Alexandre Ier*, i. 221. The Grand Duke thinks, not without reason, that this letter is proof that the Tsar's mind was deranged. To Castlereagh, as early as 1815, the Emperor's mind had seemed ' not completely sound.' To Liverpool, *Wellington Supp. Disp.* xi. 177.

Alexander's conversion from Jacobinism, which, as Metternich reported, was shared by Capo d'Istria, gave a wholly new merit, from the Austrian point of view, to the conception of the Holy Alliance. With the nebulous idealism which had first inspired this Metternich was wholly out of sympathy; so long as the Tsar continued to repeat the catchwords of Liberalism, its practical objects were suspect to him; but, with the Russian Emperor in this chastened mood, it could be put to the most practical uses. ' A new era is beginning,' he had written on August 22 to Esterhazy, ' and one positively contrary to the spirit of abstract analysis.' The advantage to be derived from this far outweighed, in Metternich's mind, that of obtaining on the Neapolitan Question a complete concert of the Allied Powers. The fact that Great Britain and France were represented at Troppau only by ministers empowered to report, and not to decide, was even, under the actual circumstances, to his advantage. The Emperors Alexander and Francis were present in person, and Prussia was represented by the Crown Prince, afterwards King Frederick William IV, and the chief ministers of all three Powers were also present. The inferior status of the representatives of the two Constitutional Powers, then, gave an excuse for excluding them from the innermost councils of the three Powers ' less fettered in their forms,' and made it easier for Metternich to win over the Emperor Alexander and his faithful shadow, the King of Prussia, to his views.

The result was, after negotiations carried on by the three Powers *in private*, the issue of the famous Preliminary Protocol of Troppau, which consecrated the principle of intervention in the following words :

States which have undergone a change of Government, due to revolution, the results of which threaten other states, *ipso facto* cease to be members of the European Alliance, and remain excluded from it until their situation gives guarantees for legal order and stability. If, owing to such alterations, immediate danger threatens other states, the Powers bind themselves, by peaceful means, or if need be by arms, to bring back the guilty state into the bosom of the Great Alliance.

Having secured the adhesion of the two other autocratic States to this principle, Metternich next tried to win over the ' absent Allies ' by minimizing its effects ; for any public protest on their part would have defeated its immediate object. He forwarded a copy of the Protocol to Prince Esterhazy, the Austrian ambassador in London, with a covering letter in which he explained that it was a mere assertion of principle to which any constitutional State might assent ; that the Emperor of Austria disclaimed any right to inter- fere with the internal legislation or administration of a separate State, and that the Protocol did not apply to such internal affairs of another State as exercised no external influence, but only guaranteed legitimate power, as the Alliance guaranteed territorial possession, against force.[41] In another letter of the same date he added that he wished to prove the unity of the Powers, and asked for the moral support of those who could not sign. Lord Stewart and Sir Robert Gordon had declared that the Protocol would lead to intervention in the internal concerns of other States. To this he had replied that this was not so, and that all he was aiming at was something like the guarantee of the German Confedera- tion. ' You mean then to establish a European Con- federation ? ' they asked. This he had denied, adding that there might be an analogy between a measure of general conservation and some law of an individual State, without the sum of the laws governing this State being applied to the relations of the Powers. As for his object, it was necessary to prove to the world that the Emperor of Russia was not in favour of revolutions, and to bind him to the protection of the established order. Would Great Britain join in this plan ?

[41] To Esterhazy, Troppau, November 24, 1820. F.O. : Austria, Domestic, September–December 1820.

Great Britain would not join. In a dispatch of December 4 to Lord Stewart, after defining once more the attitude of his Government in the affair of Naples as one of 'absolute neutrality,' Castlereagh turned to the Troppau Protocol and its underlying political ideas. 'As for the idea,' he wrote, 'which prevails throughout the memoranda, especially the Russian, of some general systematic and solemn declaration to be agreed upon and promulgated, this is in effect a revival of those discussions with regard to the establishment of a general system of guarantee, not merely territorial but political, which at Aix-la-Chapelle were laid aside by common consent from the extreme difficulties in which the whole subject was involved.' After referring to his own memorandum of September 15, 1818, on the subject, he proceeded to say that the British Government would dissuade the Powers 'from attempting to reduce to an abstract rule of conduct possible cases of interference in the internal affairs of independent States.' The French Revolution, he maintained, was an exception 'from its overbearing and conquering character,' and the course of policy pursued in this case could not be applied to all revolutions.[42]

This letter had its effect. The Protocol had been signed by the three Powers before it had even been submitted to the British and French ministers. The signatures were now withdrawn, and it was explained that the Protocol was to be regarded as a draft, while renewed efforts were made to persuade the dissentient Powers to agree at least to its underlying principles. Whatever hopes may have been entertained of the success of these efforts were speedily belied. On December 16 Castlereagh forwarded to Stewart a long dispatch in which not only the particular provisions of the Protocol, but its whole underlying principle, were submitted to a masterly criticism. I shall quote it at some length, since its arguments apply not only to the

[42] In F.O. : Continent, Circular Dispatches, 1821.

immediate case of the Holy Alliance, but to all similar schemes for the organization of peace.

Of what, asks Castlereagh, is the Protocol a draft ? of a reasoned basis for the interference in Naples ? or of a general treaty to which the adherence of the other Courts is to be invited ? In the latter case the question assumed a character such as must necessarily awaken the attention of all European States with regard to its principles as well as its provisions. It raised questions both as to the position of the contracting Powers towards each other and as to their relation to the independent States which were not parties to the obligations of the Alliance. It was impossible not to be alarmed by the wide and sweeping powers claimed for the Allies by the Protocol—powers which he denied to have any basis in existing treaties. The treaty of November 1815 only stipulated that, in the event of a revolutionary convulsion in France, the Powers were ' to deliberate together ' with a view to concerting measures to secure their common safety ; but the fifth article of the Protocol proceeds at once to recognize their authority to place armies of occupation in such of those States as the Alliance may deem to require such a precaution. If this could not be based upon existing treaties, was it proposed to invite all other States to accede to this league, and thus by their voluntary consent to submit themselves in such cases to the jurisdiction of the Alliance ? Could it be supposed that all the States of Europe would choose to accede to such a system, and if not, what was to be the position of the States that did not accede ? After pointing out the disastrous effect of this system on the relations between the sovereigns and their peoples, Castlereagh goes on to consider its effect on the relations of the Powers of the Alliance to each other. The rights claimed under the Protocol, he said, were presumably to be ' reciprocal between the parties.' Were, then, the great Powers of Europe prepared to admit the principle of their territories

being thrown open to each other's approach upon
cases of assumed necessity or expediency of which not
the party receiving aid, but the party administering it,
was to be the judge ?   As for Great Britain, any minister
who should recommend the King to sanction such a
principle would render himself liable to impeachment,
and the British Government not only dissented from
it but protested against any attempt to consider it, under
any conceivable circumstances, as applicable to any of
the British dominions.

' It is proposed to create a confederacy for the
exercise of a right which, though undoubtedly apper-
taining, upon the principle of self-defence, in extreme
cases, to each particular State, has never yet, as a general
measure, been made the subject of a diplomatic regulation or conjoint exercise.'   It was proposed, he said,
to assume on the part of the Alliance a sovereign power
over the other States of Europe, on the analogy of the
German Confederation.   But in the German Confederation the power was exercised, not by its most powerful
members, but by the Confederation itself, represented
in its Diet.   In the present case there was no such regulation, and sooner or later, therefore, the claims of the
Alliance would provoke counter-alliances, thus defeating
the very objects for which they were advanced.   ' There
are extreme rights to which nations as well as individuals
must have recourse for their preservation, and for the
exercise of which no legislature can provide.   The
extreme right of interference between nation and nation
can never be made a matter of written stipulation or
be assumed as the attribute of any alliance.'   To pro-
mulgate a new code in connection with the measures
which certain Powers had thought it necessary to take
in the case of Naples would only ' open an unbounded
field for agitation and controversy.'   In refusing assent
to the Protocol, Lord Stewart was to be careful to point
out that this did not depend on ' the form or phrases
of these particular instructions ' and was ' not susceptible

of being removed by any partial modification of their stipulations.' The British Government objected to the fundamental principle on which the Protocol rested, namely, that of rendering the powers either of the existing or of any other alliance applicable, under any circumstances, to the internal transactions of independent States. For this appeared to lead immediately to the creation of a species of general government in Europe, with a superintending Directory, destructive of all correct notions of internal sovereign authority ; and Great Britain could not consent to charge herself, as a member of the Alliance, with the moral responsibility of administering a general European police of this description.[43]

The Conference at Troppau had meanwhile been adjourned to Laibach, in order to give the King of Naples the opportunity of taking advantage of the invitation sent to him to attend. The adjourned Conference, it may be remarked, which met at Laibach in the second week of January 1821, had somewhat more of the character of a general Congress than that at Troppau, owing to the fact that all the Italian princes were represented at it. Its discussions, however, were practically confined to the affairs of Naples and of Italy generally. With these we are not immediately concerned, and I shall confine myself to the debates arising out of the Troppau Protocol and its underlying principle.

Castlereagh's letter of December 16 reached Lord Stewart at Vienna. In his reply, dated January 4, Stewart remarked on the great effect it had produced. All the cabinets, he said, were now expressing their disapproval of the Protocol, the Prussian minister Bernstorff being especially impressed by Castlereagh's arguments, while Capo d'Istria was asserting that the *fact* must precede the *principle*, which meant that the Neapolitan affair must be settled before the argument on general questions was reopened. It was soon clear,

[43] F.O. : Continent, Circular Dispatches, 1821, No. 32.

however, that this attitude was dictated by the hope that, if the principle of *collective* intervention were kept in the background, Great Britain could be persuaded to hold at Laibach a common language with the other Allies in the Neapolitan Question. This hope was rapidly belied.

Pending the arrival of Lord Stewart at Laibach the preliminary conferences were attended by Sir Robert Gordon, who at once defined the British position. The King of Naples had arrived, he reported, and the letters to and from him had been drawn up by Russia and approved by the Powers. Those from the Powers declared that they were determined to abolish the actual Constitution of Naples, by arms if necessary ; that of the King advised submission in view of the circumstances. When the drafts were submitted to the Conference, Gordon quietly suggested that the words ' *sovereign* Powers ' should be substituted for ' *allied* Powers,' as Great Britain was no party to the transaction. Asked, point-blank, whether he would sign the drafts, he replied that he certainly would not do so, as Great Britain was neutral and had sent no plenipotentiary to the Conference. Upon this Capo d'Istria proposed that he should be excluded from the Conference altogether. Gordon replied that Great Britain was too much interested in discussions of such importance to consent to this, and added the clinching argument that it would give that very appearance of disunion which the Allies were anxious to avoid. The French minister, M. de Blacas, was equally opposed to the drafts as they stood, as being too reminiscent of what had been done in France in 1814 ; he proposed that the views of the Powers should simply be embodied in journals, and that, for the rest, the royal letter should be reinforced by separate instructions to the representatives of the Powers at Naples. To this course Gordon equally objected ; Great Britain could not and would not hold a common language in this matter with the coercive Powers. Thereupon Capo d'Istria, giving up the hope of making Great Britain toe the line, revived the notion of a declaration deducing the whole action of the Allies from general principles and basing it on their treaty obligations. To this Gordon objected strongly, as implying that Great Britain was departing from her treaty obligations.[44]

The situation had thus been defined when Lord Stewart arrived, and from the point of view of the solidarity of the Alliance it was not improved by his arrival. The refusal of Great Britain to come into line with the other Powers on ground outside that of the Troppau Protocol, determined them to return to the principles enunciated in it, since there was apparently nothing to be gained by deserting them. At the seventh meeting of the Conference, Capo d'Istria read to the assembled Italian plenipotentiaries a recapitulation of all the Emperor Alexander's arguments and sentiments on the questions of the general guarantee and the measures adopted at Troppau. Stewart at once protested that, if the Russian ministers thought it wise to proceed to a new development of their former sentiments, he would be forced to record ' upon the face of the proceedings ' the views entertained by his Government, which made Great Britain arrive at a different conclusion. Accordingly, he annexed to the journals of the proceedings a ' declaration ' recording that Great Britain was not at one with the Allied Sovereigns in this matter.

The strong action of the British Government, he reported, had to all appearance completely stopped for the time being all questions of ' general measures,' and he hoped that, in the event of the action towards Naples being successful, the three Powers would be less anxious for the guarantee. This was, however, far from being the case. In the Conference of January 31 he found it necessary to interrupt Metternich, who was delivering an allocution to the Duke of San Gallo in the name

[44] F.O. : Austria, Stewart, January–February 1821.

of the Alliance, and to insist once more that the British attitude should be made clear by the reading of the declaration inserted in the journals.

Two days later the Emperor Alexander himself condescended to argue the matter with him. The Troppau Protocol, he said, was necessary for the safety of Europe; and f at Aix-la-Chapelle the mutual guarantee had only been suggested, as Stewart pointed out, for territorial integrity, and not against internal revolution, this was because the Powers had never dreamed of the possibility of military revolts such as had revolutionized Spain, Naples, and Portugal.[45] On the same day Metternich read a paper in which he used the phrase ' the solidarity of the Allied Powers as established by the transactions of Troppau and Laibach.' Stewart objected to the words ' solidarity ' and ' established,' and succeeded in getting the latter altered to defined.'

Stewart now read to the assembled ministers Castlereagh's circular note and dispatches condemning the Troppau Protocol and defining the British position. This caused the utmost dismay. ' It is clear,' wrote Stewart, ' that the Emperor of Russia has grounded all his doctrines of right of interference on the conservative principles of the Alliance and of existing treaties ; and H.I.M., having availed himself of this reasoning towards his subjects (who are by no means pleased at seeing him again wandering over Europe), finds at once, when he did not look for it, a complete denial on our part of assumptions which, through the directing influence of the Russian cabinet, have been fulminated through all the transactions of the Conferences of Troppau and Laibach.' The bitterness, he added, was very evident. Metternich exclaimed that the British ministers would have done better to have stayed away from the Conferences ; to which Stewart

[45] To Castlereagh, February 2, 1821.

rep!ied that they would have done so had they not been *implored* to come.[46]

It is unnecessary to pursue the quarrel further in detail. On March 20 Stewart reported to Castlereagh the character of the acts closing the Congress of Laibach. The declaration, he said, was not objectionable from the British point of view. But the three Powers—Russia, Austria, and Prussia—had in addition issued circular dispatches and instructions to their ministers in Naples, in which they recurred to a development of the Troppau Protocol in terms which they could not but know would be highly displeasing to Great Britain and France. ' In short,' said Stewart, ' there can be little doubt from the complexion of these instruments that a Triple Under-standing has been created which binds the parties to carry forward their own views in spite of any difference of opinion which may exist between them and the two great constitutional Governments.' [47] In another letter of the same date he emphasizes the practical outcome of the whole debate that had arisen out of the Troppau Protocol. ' The first acts of Troppau,' he wrote, ' framed an Alliance between the three Courts which placed them entirely in a new attitude from us, and they have now, I consider, hermetically sealed their treaty before Europe.'

Thus at Laibach, though it must be remembered that these debates were not made publ.c, we have already foreshadowed that sharp division between the three autocratic Eastern Powers—the ' Holy Alliance,' as the term came to be understood—and the two Western Liberal Powers, a division which was to determine the international relations of Europe from the revolution of 1830 till the Crimean War. That ten years passed before the schism in the Great Alliance became defined in this sense was due to the emergence of two questions

---

[46] To Castlereagh. F.O. : Austria, Stewart, February 1821, No. 19.
[47] To Castlereagh, Vienna, March 20, 1821. F.O. : Austria, Lord Stewart, March–September 1821.

which cracked it, so to speak, on different lines of cleavage. The first of these was the outbreak of the War of Greek Independence in the spring of 1821, while the Conference of Laibach was actually in session.   The second was the progress of the revolution in Spain and the determination of France to intervene on principles similar to those which had led to the Austrian intervention in Naples. The latter question, which involved that of the future relations to each other of the New World and the Old, I reserve for a separate section.   With the other, which was destined during the next few years to act as so powerful a solvent of the Alliance, I propose to deal here only in so far as it falls within the limits of the period under review and affects the development of my main theme.

III

THE EASTERN QUESTION

Alexander and the Christians in Turkey—Suggestions to Pitt—Agreement of Tilsit—Treaty of Bucharest—Turkey and the Congress of
Vienna—Exclusion of Turkey from the Holy Alliance—Effect of
the Greek insurrection—Metternich keeps Alexander ' grouped '
at Laibach—Insurrection in the Morea—Rapprochement of Great
Britain and Austria—Peril of Russian intervention—Alexander
and Capo d'Istria—The Holy Alliance *v.* Russia—Meeting of
Castlereagh and Metternich at Hanover—Alexander agrees to a
Conference—Death of Castlereagh—George Canning—No breach
in the continuity of British policy—Castlereagh's ' instructions '
as plenipotentiary at the Conference—These handed unaltered to
Wellington—Definition of the attitude of Great Britain towards
the questions to be raised—Wellington at Vienna—Dismissal of
Capo d'Istria—The Eastern Question shelved.

THE fate of Turkey and of its Christian subject populations had long exercised the mind of the Emperor
Alexander. In 1804 he had enlarged to Pitt on the
grievances of the subject races, and had suggested that
Russia and Great Britain should concert beforehand
the measures to be taken in the event of a break-up of
the Ottoman Empire. The compact of Tilsit, however,
altered his views ; the armies of Russia advanced into
the Danubian principalities ; and in 1812 the Treaty
of Bucharest, besides giving her a foothold on the Black
Sea to the south of the Caucasus, established her European
boundary with Turkey on the Pruth and consecrated
her claim to a special right of protection over the autono-
mous Balkan States. The campaign of 1812 and the
revival of Alexander's European ideals again changed

the situation. At Vienna Alexander expressed his willingness to have the integrity of Turkey placed under
the guarantee of the Alliance. The negotiations broke
down, primarily, on the obstinate refusal of Sultan
Mahmud to ratify the terms of the Treaty of Bucharest ;
for it was obviously impossible to guarantee territories
of which the boundaries were not defined.[48] Thus it
came that, neither at Vienna nor at any subsequent
meetings of the Powers, had any attempt been made
to settle the ' Eastern Question '—as it was soon to
be called—while the exclusion of Turkey from the
territorial settlement effected by ' the Treaties ' and of
the Sultan from the Holy Alliance gave plentiful scope
for those sinister rumours as to his intentions against
which Alexander thought it necessary to issue his
solemn protest.

The sudden emergence, then, of the Eastern Question
in an acute form was a serious danger to the harmony
of the European Concert. The Emperor Alexander
might protest that he had never had any intention of
attacking Turkey ; but, rightly or wrongly, his reputation
for truthfulness was not of the highest, and appearances
were against him. The Greek Capo d'Istria, committed
as a member of the *Hetairia Philike* to the dream of
Hellenic independence, was still at his elbow. Alexander
Ypsilanti, the leader of the northern revolt, was a
Russian general and a *protégé* of the Tsar ; he had
crossed the Pruth in company with other Greeks in
Russian service ; and, above all, he had issued a proclamation stating that he was supported by ' a Great
Power.' The statement was a lie, the proclamation
empty bombast, characteristic of the whole conduct of
that foolish and tragic adventure. From the point of

---

[48] See for this and, generally, for the relations of Turkey and Russia
after the Treaty of Bucharest, a letter of Sir Thomas Liston, British
ambassador at Constantinople, to Wellington at Vienna, dated March 25,
1915. F.O. : Congress, Turkey. Misc. Archives, September 1814–
July 1815. The situation is well summed up in the *Encyclopædia
Britannica* (11th ed.), s.v., Turkey, xxvii. 455*d*.

view of Great Britain and Austria, however, for whom
the integrity of Turkey was a cardinal article of political
faith, it was fortunate that the news of the rising reached
Alexander at Laibach, where it was possible for Metternich
to exert all his newly acquired influence to persuade
him to look at the matter with ' European ' eyes.

Never had the Tsar's idealism led him into a more
awkward situation. The sympathies of his people were
wholly with their fellow-Christians in revolt ; his armies,
irritated by a stupid and galling discipline, were honey-
combed with disaffection,[49] for which a successful
campaign in Turkey would have been the obvious cure ;
every tradition of his house would have led him to pose
as the protector of the Orthodox Greeks against their
Mussulman oppressors, and incidentally to push forward
the frontiers of Holy Russia at the expense of the infidel.
But he had committed himself to the principle of organized
peace ; at Troppau and since he had loudly proclaimed
the duty of the Powers collectively to intervene to assist
legitimate sovereigns against their revolted subjects ;
how could he now risk a general conflagration in Europe
by marching to the assistance of subjects in revolt against
their legitimate sovereign ? The most that he could
do was to interfere neither on one side nor the other,
and to leave the revolt to burn itself out, as Metternich
put it, ' beyond the pale of civilization.' From Laibach,
accordingly, Capo d'Istria addressed at his orders the
letter to Ypsilanti which, by denouncing his action in
claiming the support of Russia, dashed whatever hope
of success the revolt in the north may have had.

The self-congratulation of Metternich upon the
success of his diplomacy was, however, premature.
The Conferences at Laibach had hardly come to an
end when, in May 1821, the far more serious insurrection
broke out in the Morea. One singular result of this,
and of the rapid success of the revolted Greeks, was to
postpone the public breach of the Alliance by making

[49] See note 38, p. 206.

the British Government realize once more that the principles proclaimed by the Emperor Alexander, however objectionable in their general application, might be made serviceable in particular cases. It was, in short, again necessary to group him ; and the best way to do this was once more to ' present something somewhat in the tone of his own ideas.' For this purpose it was not only convenient but imperative to come to an understanding with Austria, and Castlereagh decided to take advantage of the visit of King George IV to Hanover in October, in order to arrange a meeting with Metternich. He was fully aware of the interpretation which his political opponents would put upon this action. ' Had the question been of an ordinary character,' he wrote to Sir Robert Gordon, ' and involving the form of government under which any portion of Europe was to subsist (as that of Naples lately did), I should have felt as you have done about an interview with Prince Metternich, that it might lead to more noise and jealousy than was worth encountering. But the question of Turkey is of a totally different character, and one which in England we regard, not as a theoretical, but as a practical consideration of the greatest moment.' What these practical considerations were he explained in a letter to Charles Bagot. Of the Greeks, ' the descendants of those in admiration of whom we have been educated,' he speaks with a warmth of sympathy which could not have been exceeded by Canning. If a statesman were allowed to regulate his conduct by the dictates of the heart, instead of the dictates of the understanding, he sees no limits to the impulse that might be given to his conduct by this sympathy. ' But,' he adds, ' we must always recollect that his is the graver task of providing for the peace and security of those interests immediately committed to his care ; that he must not endanger the fate of the present generation in a speculative endeavour to improve the lot of that which is to come. I cannot, therefore, reconcile it to my sense of duty to embark in a scheme for new modelling the position of the Greek population in these countries at the hazard of all the destructive confusion and disunion which such an attempt may lead to, not only within Turkey, but in Europe.'

From this point of view the situation was, indeed, sufficiently critical. The Turks obstinately refused to carry out the terms of the Treaty of Bucharest; they still occupied the Danubian principalities; Greek ships, sailing under the Russian flag, had been impounded in the Straits; and, worst of all, the judicial murder of the Patriarch Gregorios was an outrage and a challenge to the whole Orthodox world, and had been followed by the withdrawal of Strogonov, the Russian ambassador, from Constantinople. The vacillating attitude of the Emperor Alexander betrayed the contradictory influences by which he was swayed. To Sir Charles Bagot he protested that the withdrawal of Strogonov made for peace, for had he remained at Constantinople he would have had to report all the outrages passing under his eyes, and the Porte, in a moment of anger, might have put him—in accordance with old tradition—in the Seven Towers.[50] A little later he was inquiring of Castlereagh what attitude Great Britain would assume in the event of war and the collapse of the Ottoman power.

This question Castlereagh refused to answer.[51] He admitted the special grievances of Russia, and, true to the principles he had consistently championed, he joined with Metternich in pressing the Porte to meet its treaty obligations and thus to deprive Russia of all valid excuse for intervention. The difficulty was to

[50] Copy of report of Lebzeltern to Metternich, St. Petersburg, September 16–24, 1821. Enclosed in Londonderry to Liverpool. F.O.: Continent, Hanover, Marquess of Londonderry. September–November 1821, No. 1. ' Ce qui preuve,' comments Lebzeltern, ' que l'Empereur ignore combien ce ministre a été prêt d'éprouver ce sort et ceux qui le savent se gardent bien de le lui revéler.'

[51] To Bagot, Hanover, October 28. *Ibid.*

persuade the Turks that concessions on their part would produce the desired effect. To the representations of Count Lützow, the Austrian internuncio, the Reis Effendi stated the willingness of his Government to evacuate the principalities if Austria would guarantee that they should not be occupied by Russia. The Austrian enlarged on the peacefu disposition of the Emperor Alexander as revealed at Laibach. 'It may be so,' replied the Turk, ' but he has 100,000 men concentrated on the frontier.'

It was the old distrust, born of the old contradiction in Alexander's character and attitude : the language of peace in his mouth and behind him the frowning menace of his armaments. For the moment this contradiction was, for Metternich, embodied in the two men in whom the direction of Russian policy lay—Alexander himself and his minister, Capo d'Istria. Capo d'Istria was bent on moulding this policy to Greek ends, disguised as those of Russia. Alexander, if for no other reason than that he was conscious of the immense risks of war under the circumstances, was inclined to look at things neither from a Greek nor a Russian, but from a European point of view.[52] Salvation lay in taking advantage of the Emperor's mood of the moment ; and Metternich plied him with arguments to prove that the unrest in Turkey did not differ essentially from that elsewhere in Europe, and that the Greek insurgents were rebels against legitimate authority like any others.

Such was the condition of things when Castlereagh (now Marquess of Londonderry) and Metternich met at Hanover. In the broad objects of their policy they

[52] ' I believe that the Emperor and his minister are farther apart than ever in their principles, their views, and their calculations. Situated in all essential respects like two hostile Powers, the only cement that binds them together is the want of energy in the character of the two men, the spirit of suppleness in the minister, and the lack of a man to take his place ' (to Esterhazy, Vienna, October 2, 1821. F.O. : Continent, Hanover, Marquess of Londonderry. September–November 1821).

were at one : they were equally agreed that, in order
to attain them, it was necessary that Alexander should
be ' grouped,' and they had, therefore, the less difficulty
in concerting the means for attaining this end.   These
were, briefly, to tie the Tsar down to a logical development of his own loudly proclaimed principles.   In a
confidential memorandum Metternich defined the attitude
of Austria.   Her aim was the maintenance of peace on
the basis of existing treaties, and she would therefore
continue to press the Porte to yield on the points at issue
with Russia under the Treaty of Bucharest.   The
question of war, on the other hand, she refused to consider.   ' There exists,' he wrote, ' an explicit engagement
on the part of Russia that on no hypothesis would the
Emperor ever separate himself from the conservative
principles of the Alliance.   It is to this declaration that
the Emperor of Austria has attached the moral guarantee
which he has been invited by his august ally to accord
him.   We believe that it would be sufficient, both in
the general and in the particular interests of the Powers,
to regard this basis as existing in fact.' [53]   The same
argument was used in the letter, already quoted, addressed
by Castlereagh to Sir Charles Bagot at St. Petersburg
on October 28.   As for the question of making war out
of sympathy for the oppressed Christian subjects of
the Porte, ' the nature of the Turkish power,' he wrote,
' was fully understood when the existing state of Europe,
including that of Turkey, was placed under the provident
care and anxious protection of the general Alliance.'

In so far as this asserted the equal sanctity of all
treaties, it was but emphasizing a principle for which
the British Government had throughout contended.   But
it went far beyond this in claiming that all territorial
treaties, and not only those executed in common, were
equally ' placed under the protection of the general

[53] *Mém. confidentiel et secret.*   Hanover, October 22, 1821.   F.O. :
Continent, Hanover, Marquess of Londonderry.   September–November 1821.

Alliance.' The language of the last sentence, indeed, seemed to endorse the principle of a universal guarantee, against which Great Britain had hitherto set her face, and to come perilously near a recognition of that idea of a universal union against which she had always protested. At whatever cost of consistency, however, it served its immediate purpose. Metternich's diplomacy, thus supported, was successful ; the Emperor Alexander, faced with the alternative of offending the sentiment of his people or of bringing down in ruin the whole edifice of his international ideal, chose the former. After much correspondence, with which it is unnecessary to concern ourselves, it was decided to summon another solemn Conference of the Allies, to which, among other outstanding questions of general interest, that of Turkey was also to be submitted. Whatever turn the debates on this subject might take, the danger of a separate intervention of Russia in the Ottoman Empire was at least postponed. The Emperor Alexander was once more ' grouped.'

The so emn Conference, which the Russian Emperor signified his intention of attending, was fixed for the end of October 1822, at Verona. A preliminary meeting of ministers was, however, to be held at Vienna in September, at which the Eastern Question (as it now began to be called) was to be the main subject of discussion. It was Castlereagh's purpose to attend an assembly fraught with such momentous issues for the peace of Europe, and all his preparations were made. Overwork and anxiety had, however, wrought upon his brain, and on August 12, in a moment of crushing depression, he put an end to his life. The wits of the Opposition found matter for jesting even in the tragic circumstances of his death ; at his funeral the mob was loud in its demonstrations of joy ; and the triumph of the political tendencies he had opposed stereotyped for three generations an estimate of his character and his aims founded upon ignorance and party spite. It has been reserved for the present age to begin to realize something of the debt of gratitude which Great Britain and Europe owe to a statesman who, if he lacked superficial brilliance, possessed in his high sense of duty, in his transparent honesty of purpose, and in his clear common sense, qualities far more valuable in a man of affairs than those which are more apt to win the admiration of the crowd.

The death of Castlereagh was, from Metternich's point of view, a supreme misfortune for Europe, an opinion strengthened by the subsequent career of that ' malevolent meteor ' George Canning, who succeeded him at the Foreign Office. In fact, however, the change produced less effect than was commonly supposed upon the attitude of Great Britain towards the Alliance, for Canning merely took up and developed the policy of Castlereagh, for which, indeed, as a member of the Cabinet, he had been equally responsible. It is true that Canning, whose knowledge of European conditions was less intimate than that of Castlereagh, had long viewed with impatience the supposed hampering of the free initiative of Great Britain by her continental ties, and he therefore regarded the possibility of a breach with the Alliance with a complacency which Castlereagh could never have felt. But the difference between the two statesmen was less in their fundamental attitude than in its expression. If Canning posed ostentatiously as the champion of a ' British ' policy, this was to do less than justice to Castlereagh, in whose mind the interests of his country had ever held the first place. If he looked forward to the gradual dissolution of the Alliance by the gradual withdrawal of England, this was but to emphasize the opinion of Castlereagh that, in certain eventualities, the Alliance would ' move away from England ' without her having quitted it. For Castlereagh, like Canning, had already made the discovery that the fundamental difficulty in any attempt to organize an international system is not so much that of holding the balance 'between conflicting nations,' though that is difficult enough, as that of holding the balance ' between conflicting principles.' Had he lived, his eventual policy would probably have differed from that of Canning only in the more conciliatory choice of its forms.

This is proved by the tenor of the memorandum, drawn up for his own use at the Conference, which was handed over unaltered to the Duke of Wellington, to whom the mission was now confided.[54] The selection of the Duke to represent Great Britain was in itself proof that there was no intention of violently reversing the continental policy with which, equally with Castlereagh, he had been throughout identified. But this made all the more significant the limitations imposed upon him by his instructions, which defined the course that, in certain eventualities, Great Britain would be forced to follow, and in doing so laid down the lines on which Canning's policy in opposition to the continental Powers was presently to develop.

The subjects which, according to the memorandum, were to come up for discussion at the Conferences sufficiently illustrate, in their complexity and the wideness of their range, the immensity of the task which the Allied Powers had undertaken in making themselves collectively responsible for the world's peace. There was the Turkish Question, including both the controversy of the Porte with Russia and the internal situation arising out of the Greek revolt ; the Spanish Question, involving the fate of the nascent republics of Latin America, and complicated now by the claim of France to intervene, as Austria had done in Naples, for the purpose of ending a revolutionary *régime* of which she feared the contagion ; there were the multiplex questions arising out of the affairs of Italy, where Austria, having

[54] The original of this memorandum is misplaced in the Foreign Office records. It will be found bound up with papers relating to the Congress of Vienna in F.O. : Continent, France, 6.

crushed the military revolts in Naples and Piedmont, still looked to the Alliance to perfect and to consecrate with its approval the edifice of her supremacy. Outside these matters of ' European ' interest there were others scheduled as more specifically British. These included the inevitable question of the suppression of the Slave Trade, which had throughout been a severe handicap on Great Britain in her negotiations, and the situation arising out of the *ukaz*, issued by the Emperor Alexander in the preceding year, excluding all but Russian ships from the Behring Sea and from the Pacific coast of the American possessions of Russia. The inclusion of the latter subject for discussion by the Allies has a special interest in view of later developments, since it directly affected the United States of America, which, equally with Great Britain, had immediately protested against the *ukaz*.

As regards the subjects of general European interest to be discussed, the memorandum defines very carefully the attitude to be adopted, from the point of view of principle, in each case. But for the extreme urgency of the Eastern Question, the precedent of Troppau and Laibach would have been followed, and Great Britain would not have been represented by a plenipotentiary. Lord Londonderry's mission was intended, as is specifically stated, ' to counteract the probable effect of the Ottoman refusal to send plenipotentiaries to the frontier,' and not as a proof that Great Britain had once more placed herself on the same platform as the other Allies. This was made especially clear in reference to the affairs of Italy—so far as England was concerned a *chose jugée*. ' With regard to the Italian States,' the memorandum ran, ' the position of the British minister must necessarily vary from that of his colleagues at Vienna, as we are no parties to the acts taken by the allied cabinets. We acquiesced in their measures, and reserved to ourselves the right to interfere when we saw occasion, but we did not agree to charge ourselves with any superintendence of the system decided on.'   As for the Greek Question, the memorandum is equally explicit as to the attitude of Great Britain towards any possible suggestion of a concerted intervention between the Porte and the insurgents ; care was to be taken not to commit her to any concert which should go beyond the limits of good offices, and engagements of the nature of a guarantee were to be considered altogether inadmissible. On the other hand, the situation had been radically altered by the collapse of the Ottoman naval power in the Levant, by the consequent total inactivity of the Turkish commanders in the Morea, and the progress made by the Greeks towards the formation of a Government. ' So long as the force of the insurgents was directed by the mere will of the leaders, the principle of neutrality led to no other consideration than that of giving an equal rule of accommodation to the parties, but by the erection of a Government admitting of formal acts being done on the part of that Government, we are more positively brought to deal with them *de facto*, upon matters of blockade and other questions dependent upon the law of nations.   Considering the course pursued by Great Britain now for so many years towards the local Governments exercising dominion in South America, and her avowed neutrality as between the Greeks and the Turks, it may be difficult for this country, if a *de facto* Government shall be actually established in the Morea and the western provinces of Turkey, to refuse it the ordinary privileges of a belligerent.'

On the question of Spain and of her colonies the language of the memorandum was equally explicit. As for Spain herself, there was to be ' a rigid abstinence from any interference in the internal affairs of that country.'   The problem of the colonies offered a wider choice of alternative action.   It was certain that, if Spain did not succeed in re-establishing her authority within a given time, other States would, sooner or later, acknowledge their separate existence ; and, this being so, it was to the interest of Spain herself to find the means of restoring an intercourse, when she could not succeed in restoring a dominion. It was impossible now to interrupt the intercourse which had grown up between Great Britain and the Spanish colonies, and the question had resolved, itself into one rather of the mode of the relations between them, than as to whether they should or should not subsist ' to the extent in matter of right as regulated by the law of nations.' Recognition might take three forms : either *de facto*, as was actually the case, or by diplomatic agents, or *de jure*, ' so as to create a certain impediment to the assertion of the rights of the former occupant.' There was as yet no fair pretence for calling upon Great Britain to recognize the Latin American republics *de jure*, but it was a question how long it would be before she would in her own interests have to recognize them by the dispatch of diplomatic agents. On this matter an attempt was to be made to obtain a concert, but in such a way as to leave Great Britain independence of action.

In the views embodied in this memorandum there is little disposition shown to subordinate the essential interests of Great Britain to those of her continental Allies, while they clearly foreshadow the later policy of Canning in the questions both of Greece and of the Latin American States. In enclosing the memorandum to the Duke of Wellington, Lord Bathurst made it clear that there was no intention of departing from the standpoint taken up in the preceding year. He pointed out that at Troppau and Laibach the position of the British minister was somewhat distinct from that of his colleagues, being limited to informing himself of what was going on and to seeing that nothing was done inconsistent with the existing system and the treaties.[55] Wellington, accordingly, was instructed to wait until the affairs of Italy had been settled before going to Verona, where

[55] Bathurst to Wellington, September 14, 1822. F.O. : Continent, Verona, Duke of Wellington. September–December 1822.

Lord Londonderry (Lord Stewart) was to attend in the same capacity as at Troppau and Laibach and with the same instructions. As to this, however, Wellington soon perceived in the course of the proceedings at Vienna that the debates at Verona would ' turn almost entirely on the affairs of Spain.' A solution, at least temporary, of the perilous Turkish Question had been reached in the preliminary conferences with surprising ease, owing mainly to the disappearance from the Tsar's side of Capo d'Istria, who, on the eve of the meeting, had passed into retirement, from which he was destined to emerge five years later as President of Greece. The removal of this implacable opponent of Austria had been due to the influence of Metternich, who now, as Wellington reported, himself became in a great degree the Russian Emperor's principal adviser and had little difficulty in impressing his views upon him. Under these circumstances the attitude of the Allied Powers towards the whole Turkish Question was settled in the sense desired by Austria, and the hopes which the Greeks had built upon the active sympathy of Russia were once more dashed. When, on October 20, the Conference was opened at Verona the only question of first-class importance raised was that of Spain, and this, with the momentous issues involved in it, occupied practically all its sessions. Before dealing with the Conference and its outcome, I shall give some account of the earlier debates in the councils of the Alliance on this question of Spain and her colonies, the immense importance of which, as involving the whole question of the relations of the New and the Old World, had from the first been recognized.

IV

THE QUESTION OF SPAIN AND HER COLONIES

The Spanish colonial system—The Latin American revolutions—
Monarchies or Republics ?—Misgivings in Europe—Conflicting
interests of the Powers—France and Great Britain—Castlereagh's
policy—Rivalry of Spain and Portugal on the River Plate threatens
a European war—Russian intrigues in Paris and Madrid—Spain
invites the intervention of the Alliance against her colonies—
Successful protest of Great Britain—Attitude of the United
States—Reasons for their delay in recognizing the independence
of the Latin American States—Question of the Spanish colonies
discussed at Aix-la-Chapelle—Proposal to invite the United
States to co-operate with the Allies—Opposition of Great Britain
to the principle of intervention—Triumph of Castlereagh's
diplomacy—French intrigue for setting up a Bourbon king in
Buenos Aires—Revolution of 1820 in Spain—Strained relations
between the Allies—Recognition of the Latin American States
by the United States—Castlereagh takes the first steps towards
recognition—The question on the eve of the Congress of Verona—
France and intervention in Spain—Wellington and the Emperor
Alexander at the preliminary conferences in Vienna.

THE revolt of the Latin American colonies had in the
first instance been directed not against the Spanish
monarchy, but against the intolerable Spanish colonial
system—the narrow trade monopoly which impoverished
the New World without enriching the Old ; the moral
and intellectual tutelage symbolized by the Inquisition
and enforced by a corrupt and extortionate administration,
in which the Creoles were not allowed to have a share ;
the narrow *conquistador* spirit which continued after
three centuries to hold the native races in slavery. The
revolution which broke out on January 1, 1809, in Buenos
Aires and, under the leadership of San Martin in the

south and of Bolivar in the north, developed into the great war of independence which lasted until in 1824 Bolivar's victories at Junin and Ayacucho completed the liberation of Latin America, was not at first a republican movement. Indeed, after Napoleon's conquest of Spain, loyalty to Ferdinand VII became the avowed motive of the insurgents, and in the earlier stages of the struggle they would have been perfectly content with practical independence under the suzerainty of the legitimate Spanish crown.[56] After the restoration of Ferdinand, however, experience of the uncompromising and blindly reactionary temper of the Court of Madrid drove them to extremes, and the war developed into a struggle for complete independence. Opinion was still divided among the Latin American leaders as to the expediency of establishing the monarchical or the republican model in the new States ; but the prevailing tendency was for them to take as their model the Constitution of the United States, of which the independence had been recognized by King Charles III in 1783. The result was that at the very time when in the Old World the Powers were engaged in curbing ' revolutionary madness ' and in setting up the principle of the prescriptive rights of legitimate sovereigns, in the New World a whole series of young republics were emerging from a chaos of revolutionary violence.

It is not surprising that this state of things should have excited the most serious misgivings in the cabinets of Europe or that, the moment they ceased to be preoccupied by the problems of the great war, their attention should have been inceasingly directed to those of the New World. It was not only that the complete triumph of democratic principles in America could not fail to exercise a profound effect, baneful from their point of view, on opinion in Europe ; the fear was already articulate that the United States, whose expansive ambitions had been illustrated by the Louisiana purchase

[56] See F. Garcia-Calderon, *Latin America*, p. 60.

in 1803 and the piecemeal annexation of West Florida from 1810 onward, would seize the opportunity to assert their hegemony over the Americas and to exclude from them all influence of the European Powers. [57] Even if this peril seemed for the time being remote, there was one more immediate in the jealousies and rival ambitions of the European Powers themselves in view of the immense possibilities opened up by the collapse of the Spanish Empire.

In France especially old dreams revived, and the ambition presently took shape of recovering for the Monarchy in the New World the prestige which it had lost in the Old. The chief obstacle in the path of this ambition was Great Britain, which had no intention of allowing a revival of the Family Compact, or of that policy of French predominance in Spain and her empire against which she had always fought. Moreover, during the war a considerable British trade—contraband from the Spanish point of view—had sprung up with the revolted colonies, and the British Government, while sincerely anxious to remain on good terms with Spain and to help her to an accommodation with her rebellious subjects, had no intention of allowing this trade to be destroyed by a restoration of the old Spanish colonial system. French statesmen, on the other hand, suspected a deliberate design on the part of Great Britain to secure

[57] See above, p. 85. As early as 1774, the Abbé Raynal had pointed out the probability of this development : ' Rompez le nœud qui lie l'ancienne Bretagne à la nouvelle ; bientôt les colonies Septentrionales auront seules plus de force, qu'elles n'en avoient dans leur union avec la métropole. Ce grand continent, affranchi de toute convention en Europe, aura la liberté de tous ses mouvemens.' The North American colonies, he added, would develop into a conquering power, and the colonies of the European absolute monarchies would either ' meet them half-way ' or follow their example in casting off their chains (*Histoire philosophique*, ed. 1774, tome xiii. L. xviii. ch. xxxiii. p. 184). In the edition of 1780, published after the Declaration of Independence, he again called attention to this danger : ' Peut-être même les possessions de nos monarchies absolues brigueroient-elles d'entrer dans la confédération des peuples libres, ou se détacheroient-elles de l'Europe pour n'appartenir qu'à elles-mêmes ' (tome x. L. xviii. ch. li. p. 371).

a monopoly of the trade with Latin America. They thus threw themselves into general opposition to British policy in the Spanish-American Question ; and in this they had the support of Russia, which hoped thereby to secure her own influence over the Bourbon States. Thus from the first the question of the Spanish-American colonies caused a rift in the Alliance, a rift which was to widen into a permanent breach at Verona in 1822.

There was nothing in the British attitude towards this question to justify the legitimate fears of the French, though it was certainly opposed to their illegitimate ambitions ; and the records of Castlereagh's diplomacy, from first to last, show that, while he was careful of British interests, he was equally careful to be loyal to the best spirit of the European Alliance. So early as 1812 he had made it clear that the British Government desired a reconciliation between the Spanish colonies and the mother country, but that it was only prepared to promote such a reconciliation on certain conditions, namely, that the grievances of the Latin Americans should be remedied by the concession to them of the full rights of Spanish subjects, and that they should have free commercial intercourse with all nations, ' Spain enjoying, as the parent State, a fair preference in this portion of her dominions.'[58] Neither at this time nor on any subsequent occasion was there any question of demanding exclusive commercial privileges for Great Britain. On the contrary, when in 1815 Spain offered such privileges in exchange for British armed mediation, Castlereagh refused the offer as invidious. But if in this matter he claimed no more than the most favoured nation treatment for Great Britain, he was determined to do his best to keep the control of the situation in his own hands, so as to safeguard British interests, and, above all, to oppose any attempt to enlist the forces of the European Alliance for the purpose of restoring the

[58] Instructions to Wellesley.   Webster, *Castlereagh and the Spanish Colonies*, i.   *English Hist. Rev.*, 1912, xxvii. 87.

authority which Spain had abused. As for mediation, he repeated over and over again that Great Britain would be prepared to mediate the moment Spain accepted the conditions which he had laid down in 1812. It was not till the eve of the Congress of Verona that the obstinacy of the Spanish Government, and the changed situation generally, compelled him to depart from the principles which he had then defined.

Meanwhile the situation was further complicated by a quarrel between Spain and Portugal, which had invaded the territories of the River Plate and occupied Monte Video ; and in the autumn of 1816 it looked as though this would lead to another Peninsular War. The firm attitude of Great Britain, backed by the authority of the Alliance, prevented this war from breaking out ; but the Spanish Government, which during this year had temporarily recovered its authority in all South America save the River Plate, refused to come to an agreement. The quarrel was one eminently suitable for arbitration, and in this case the British Government joined the other Powers in pressing Spain to submit to its settlement by the Council of Ambassadors at Paris. But the Spanish Government, as Castlereagh reported in December 1817, was as unbending as if all Europe were at its feet, and all the ministers of the Powers at Madrid failed to persuade it to send plenipotentiaries to Paris.[59] The struggle between the Spaniards and the Portuguese on the River Plate thus continued, until it was settled by British mediation in 1828.

As to the more general question, it was increasingly clear that the antithesis was between the views of Great Britain and Russia. In Paris Pozzo di Borgo was loud in his denunciation of the overbearing character of British policy. In Madrid the Russian ambassador Tatishchev was intriguing for a revival of the Bourbon alliance under Russian protection, the aim being to

[59] 'Secret and Private,' to Wellington, December 18. F.O. : Continent, Paris. Wellington, June–December 1817.

secure for Russia a preponderating influence, not in Europe only, but in the New World reduced to obedience.[60] Rumours of an alliance of Russia with Spain for this purpose were, indeed, denied by the Emperor Alexander ; but the tendency of Russian policy was revealed by the sale to Spain, very cheap, of three line-of-battle ships which, proving unseaworthy, were subsequently exchanged for three frigates. Again, it seemed, Alexander needed grouping ; but the conditions on which he was prepared to be grouped were—Castlereagh said he had reason to suspect—that terms should be offered by the Powers to the insurgents and that, in the event of their being refused, Spain should be supported by the whole force of the Alliance. The suspicion proved to be correct ; for on July 2, 1817, the Spanish minister Fernan Nuñez, strongly supported by Russia, urged on the Powers through the Conference in Paris to come to the assistance of Spain against the rebel colonies.

Castlereagh met this move with a vigorous protest, of which the language again made clear his views as to the limitations of the international system to which Great Britain was a party. ' I cannot too strongly represent to you,' he wrote to Sir Charles Stuart on August 21, 1817, ' the importance of making the Spanish and all other Governments feel that the allied ministers are limited in their functions to the execution of the late treaties and to such special duties as their courts may think fit to impose upon them, but that it neither appertains to them to originate discussions on other subjects, nor to become a channel of general reference to their courts upon subjects foreign to their immediate duties.' [61] Great Britain, he said, would be willing to take the lead in effecting a reconciliation between Spain and her colonies, on the conditions he had so often laid down, but she would never be a party to any attempt

[60] It must be remembered that until 1867 Russia was an American Power.

[61] F.O. : France, 151. Quoted by Webster, *loc. cit.* p. 87, footnote.

to dictate the terms of such a reconciliation. In this attitude Castlereagh had the support of Metternich, less interested in enforcing legitimate principles on the New World than in countering Russian influence in the Old ; and Prussia followed the lead of Austria. But Russia, though discomfited for the moment, returned to the charge in the following November, when Pozzo di Borgo presented a memorandum to the Council of Ambassadors in which an attempt was made to bring the question of colonial mediation within the sphere of the Alliance by linking it with that between Spain and Portugal, which had already been referred to the Paris Conference. The memorandum enlarged on the beneficial effect ' of these vast countries sharing in the advantages enjoyed by Europe under the stipulations of Vienna and of Paris of the year 1815 ' and suggested that, not force, but some measure of commercial coercion should be employed to bring the colonies to terms. To this pronouncement Castlereagh returned no formal answer, but contented himself to explaining to Count Lieven, the Russian ambassador in London, his fundamental objection to using force to compel a population which had become free to submit to the Government by which it had been oppressed.[62]

Castlereagh was, indeed, in a position of singular difficulty. The most certain method of defeating the Russo-Spanish intrigues would have been for Great Britain to use her overwhelming sea-power to settle the matter, either alone or in concert with the United States. But this would have meant the break-up of the European Alliance, the preservation of which he rightly believed to be indispensable for the peace of Europe. On the other hand, all Europe was awaiting with apprehension possible action on the part of the United States, which at this very time were continuing their policy of expansion by negotiating the purchase of East Florida from a reluctant Spain. The apprehension, however, was at

[62] Webster, *loc. cit.*

least premature.   It is true that, so early as the beginning
of 1817, a strong party in America, headed by Henry
Clay, was in favour of the immediate recognition of the
Latin American States ; but James Monroe, both as
Secretary of State and after his election as President
in 1816, advocated a more cautious policy ; and in this
he was supported by the weighty authority of John
Quincy Adams.   Delay, indeed, was necessary if the
negotiations with Spain for the cession of East Florida
were to be brought to a successful issue ; and, even
when the Florida Treaty was at last signed in 1819, it
was clear that the recognition of the Latin American
republics would be likely to prevent ratification.   But,
apart from this, there was little disposition on the part
of President Monroe and his advisers to challenge the
European Alliance supported, as they supposed, by
the sea-power of Great Britain, and this in the interest
of peoples in whose capacity for self-government they
had little belief.[63]

Castlereagh, for his part, was careful to foster this
cautious temper.   Apart from the chance of British
mediation being accepted by Spain on the terms he
had laid down, he early contemplated a situation arising
in which Great Britain would have to recognize the
independence of the Latin American States.   But previous recognition by the United States would have led
to the extension of American political and commercial
influence in South America at the expense of British
interests, and he therefore desired to keep the Government of Washington from taking any decisive step until
Great Britain was prepared to act, either by way of
mediation or recognition.   For this reason he long kept
the United States in the dark as to his true policy, and
it was not till the eve of his setting out for the Conference

[63] Adams, then Secretary of State, remarked in 1821 : ' I had
seen and have yet seen no prospect that they would establish free
or liberal institutions of government.'   Bushnell Hart, *Monroe Doctrine*,
p. 34.

of Aix-la-Chapelle that he communicated to Richard Rush, the American minister in London, the conditions which he had from the first laid down as essential to any participation of Great Britain in securing a settlement. He did so because the renewed clamour of the Camarilla at Madrid for armed intervention made it expedient to take a step in the direction of an understanding with the United States ; but he was careful at the same time to convey the impression that concerted European intervention was probable, and so to make it impossible for the United States to take any immediate action. It was not until the rupture between Great Britain and her Allies was proclaimed to all the world that a Monroe Doctrine was possible.[64]

That the subject of the Spanish colonies was brought up at Aix-la-Chapelle was largely due to the urgency of France. In July 1817 Richelieu had spoken strongly to Wellington of the condition of South America, which was ' becoming more and more an object of attention and of hope to the disaffected in France and to the Jacobins throughout the world,' and on the eve of the Conference he urged that Ferdinand VII should be invited to Aix-la-Chapelle, not with a view to the restoration of his authority in Latin America by arms or mediation, which he now considered impracticable, but to press upon him the policy of establishing one or more of his family as independent sovereigns in the revolted provinces.[65] On August 24 the Spanish chargé d'affaires approached Alexander on the subject of the admission of Spain, on which the Emperor said that he would consult his allies. The idea broke down owing to the opposition of Castlereagh, who gave as the ostensible reason for this his unwillingness to break the existing agreement ' by receiving one Power to the exclusion of others,' or to turn the meeting into a Congress, which

[64] Webster, *loc. cit.* p. 95.
[65] Wellington to Castlereagh, August 24 and August 28, 1818. *Wellington Supp. Disp.* xii. 655, 665.

the Allies had determined to be inexpedient, as tending
to raise dangerous expectations by throwing doubt on
the finality of the settlement of 1815.[66]

This decided the fate of the proposed mediation,
the discussion of which began at Aix-la-Chapelle on
October 23, and was concluded, so far as the formal
proceedings were concerned, on November 2.[67] The
outcome of these debates was a victory for Castlereagh's
policy.   It was decided that force was not to be used ;
that the same treatment should be meted out to the
revolted as to the loyal colonies ; and that mediation
should be offered either by a board or by one delegate,
the Duke of Wellington being suggested.   The whole
question of mediation, however, was ultimately shelved,
owing to the proud refusal of Spain to accept the results
of a Conference from which she was excluded.

Before the Conference broke up, however, the debates
took a new turn, which is of great interest in the light
of subsequent events leading up to the proclamation
of the Monroe Doctrine.   This was a proposal advanced
by France and Russia to invite the United States to
take part in a Conference of Ministers to be held at
Madrid, under the presidency of the Duke of Wellington,
on the subject of the relation between Spain and her
colonies.   It was initiated by Richelieu in a memorandum
on ' the perils of the New World ' which, in view of
what has happened since and is occurring still, is certainly
a remarkable document.   In isolation, he argued, the
United States would not constitute a danger ; but
it would be different were the Latin American States
to imitate their institutions.   ' A complete republican
world, young, full of ardour, rich in the products of all
climates and with soil of incomparable fertility, establishing itself in the presence of a Europe grown old, everywhere ruled by monarchs, overcrowded with inhabitants,

[66] F.O. : Continent, Aix, Castlereagh.   Protocol 18.   In Castlereagh to Bathurst, No. 20.
[67] To Bathurst, No. 22.

shaken by thirty years of revolutionary shocks, and scarce as yet re-established on its ancient foundations, would certainly present a spectacle worthy of the most serious reflections and a very real danger.' The United States should be invited to co-operate with the Allies, partly to gain time, partly ' in order to attach the United States to the general system of Europe and to prevent a spirit of rivalry and hatred establishing itself between the Old and the New World.' [68]

In a memorandum on the French and Russian notes Wellington pointed out that it was extremely doubtful whether Spain would accept the mediation of the five Powers in this form either, and that without such acceptance it was useless to approach the United States. But, even were Spain to agree, he very much doubted whether the United States would bring to the discussion the same desire to agree and the same views as to the preservation of the ancient monarchy of Spain as animated the other Powers. In conclusion, he objected altogether to the proposed conferences at Madrid, and gave it as his opinion that no settlement was possible which did not take into account the wishes of the colonies as well as those of Spain.[69]

The matter was finally settled in an interview between Alexander and Castlereagh. Castlereagh persisted in rejecting the principle of the use of force. The Alliance, he said, was not competent to *arbitrate* or *judge*, and was therefore not competent to enforce any such judgment directly or indirectly ; it could only mediate or facilitate, but not compel or menace. As for the commercial boycott (to use a word of later date), which had again been suggested, Great Britain could be no party to it. We

[68] F.O. : Continent, Aix, Castlereagh. November 1818. In Castlereagh to Bathurst, No. 48. The last sentence is annotated in the margin, it would seem by Canning (the next comment being dated 1824), with the remark, ' Sound enough in itself, but not in its application here.' The note is printed in *Wellington Supp. Disp.* xii. 805, under a wrong heading.

[69] F.O. : Continent, Congress, Aix. November 1818.

had had a large direct trade with France during the war, and had suffered her armies to be clothed by our manufactures ; how could we interdict commerce with South America in time of peace ? Since Russia could not fight either by arms or by an interdict on trade, it would be better to tell Spain so at once than to buoy her up by false hopes in the maintenance of a false attitude. There was, besides, the *moral responsibility* involved in forcing the colonies to submit to such a Government as that of Spain.

It was the last argument, wrote Castlereagh, which made Alexander's mind ' shrink from the subject.' He expressed his regret that he had not taken the British minister's advice before the matter had been carried so far. As it was, he at once conferred with his ministers, with the result that at the next conference their tone was so altered that Richelieu withdrew his project. Thus ended the question so far as the Conference of Aix-la-Chapelle was concerned.[70]

Castlereagh's diplomacy had completely triumphed. He had torn to shreds the whole web of intrigue which for years Pozzo di Borgo and Tatishchev had been laboriously weaving ; he had forced the Powers to accept the principles which he had maintained ever since 1812 ; and by his successful assertion in the case of the Spanish colonies of the principle of non-intervention, put forward not as a counsel of expediency, but as a fundamental principle of British policy, he had established an important precedent.[71]

The situation, none the less, remained in the highest degree complicated and critical. In the United States the agitation in favour of recognition gained in force day by day ; and in Europe, though Russia for the time being had accepted the British point of view, the temper of France was less accommodating, and the discovery

[70] Castlereagh to Bathurst, November 24, 1818, No. 48.
[71] Webster, *Castlereagh and the Spanish Colonies*, ii. *English Hist. Rev.*, 1915, xxx. 635.

in the course of 1820 of a French intrigue for setting
up a Bourbon prince as king of Buenos Aires, if necessary
by force of arms, threatened to open up at once a new
and dangerous phase in the secular rivalry of France
and England. The firm language of Castlereagh averted
this particular peril. In the general question, however,
the attitude of Great Britain was still adversely affected
by the various, and to all appearance contradictory,
influences by which it was determined. On the one
hand, she remained faithful to her traditional policy
of maintaining the strength and the independence of
the Spanish monarchy, more especially against the pretensions of France. On the other hand, the Court of
Spain, magnificently contemptuous of the law of supply
and demand, continued to see little friendliness in the
fact that British merchants were taking advantage of its
weakness to carry on a lively contraband trade with
the revolted colonies, and still less in the refusal of the
British Government to acknowledge its right to interrupt
this trade. Moreover, in spite of the treaty of neutrality,
as between Spain and her colonies, signed by Great
Britain in 1814, recruiting was actively carried on in
England by the agents of the Latin American rebel
Governments, and British adventurers had taken a
conspicuous, and sometimes a leading, part in the overthrow of the royal authority in America.[72] To meet
this grievance, which was acknowledged, the British
Government in 1819 passed the Foreign Enlistment
Act, in the teeth of a loudly expressed public opinion ;
but at the same time it pointed out, in reply to the

---

[72] The most famous of these was Lord Cochrane, afterwards Earl
of Dundonald. The names of many of the English volunteers have
been preserved among the leading families of the Republics. In
the autumn of 1912, on my journey to Lima, I had the pleasure of
making the acquaintance of Señor Don Alberto Smith, Rector of the
University of Caracas, then on a special mission from the Venezuelan
Republic to the President of Peru. He told me that his grandfather,
who had fought in Bolivar's Legion, was an English officer and had
taken part in the Battle of Waterloo.

further remonstrances of Spain, that at the time the Treaty of Neutrality was signed there was a distinct understanding that commercial intercourse between Great Britain and the Spanish colonies was not to be considered a breach of its stipulations. With this interpretation the Spanish Government obstinately refused to agree. The harbours of ' ever faithful ' Cuba swarmed with pirates, disguised as privateers, whose depredations on British commerce necessitated the despatch of British warships for its protection,[73] until by the autumn of 1822 the situation had developed into something like a formal naval war between Great Britain and Spain in the West Indies, at the very time when in Europe Canning was straining every nerve to save Spain from foreign invasion.

Meanwhile, a new situation had been created as a result of the military revolt of Riego in 1820 and the compulsory acceptance of the revolutionary Constitution of 1812 by King Ferdinand VII. Its immediate effect was once more to change the attitude of the Emperor Alexander. Of Ferdinand's appeal to him, and the Russian circular which was its outcome, I have already spoken. For various reasons the suggested intervention of Russia, under cover of the general alliance, was equally objectionable to all the other Powers, and the project dropped, the sudden emergence of the Italian crisis proving a not wholly unwelcome diversion. But the ' material ' sickness of Spain, whose life-blood was being drained by her obstinate determination to preserve her over-sea dominions, was not arrested by her isolation. The expectation that the Liberal Government would in this respect show a more practical spirit was rapidly belied, and it was now becoming evident that the American empire of Spain was being hopelessly lost to her. The vast territories of the River Plate—the later Argentine Republic—had conquered their freedom as early as

[73] A vivid account of the conditions is given in Michael Scott's *Tom Cringle's Log.*

1810 ; in 1821, the year following Riego's rebellion, Mexico and Colombia (embracing the immense jurisdiction of the viceroyalties of Quito and New Granada) proclaimed their independence ; on the whole American continent it was only in Peru that the issue of the struggle was still in doubt. The United States now, moreover, decided to take definitive action. The crisis in Spain had revealed a divergence of views in the Alliance which made it clear at last that there would be no concerted intervention in the affairs of the New World ; and, above all, the Florida treaty had in 1821 at last been ratified. Accordingly, in his annual message of December 1821 and again in a special message of March 8, 1822, President Monroe proposed the recognition of Buenos Aires, Colombia, Chile and Mexico, and Congress proceeded to pass an appropriation for such missions to the independent nations on the American continent as the President of the United States might deem proper.[74]

It was now absolutely necessary that Great Britain should take action, and public opinion in England was strongly in favour of at once following the example of the United States. Castlereagh, however, was averse from acting in too sharp an opposition to the continental Allies, whose objection to the recognition of ' revolutionary '—i.e. republican—Governments he shared ; and it was only after a vain attempt to secure a concert with France, with a view to inducing the new States to adopt monarchical forms in return for recognition and trade privileges, that he began to take certain tentative steps towards recognition by the despatch of commercial agents to the Latin American countries, and by introducing a Bill into Parliament for the alteration of the navigation laws so as to make possible a reciprocity of trading rights. That he contemplated the development of circumstances which would make complete recognition inevitable is clear from the tenor of the instructions

[74] Hart, op. cit. p. 34.

which, on the eve of his tragic death, he drew up for his own use at the conferences about to be opened at Vienna, preliminary to the Congress which was to meet in Verona in October. The memorandum containing these instructions was, as I mentioned before, handed by the new Foreign Secretary, George Canning, without alteration to the Duke of Wellington.

The approach of the Conference, indeed, and the momentous issues to be raised at it, now made it imperative that Great Britain should define her attitude; and on September 27 Canning wrote to Wellington warning him not to be a party to any declaration affirming the rights of Spain over her colonies, or to fetter in any degree the discretion of the British Government as to the time, the mode, or the degree in which it might be found expedient ' tacitly to admit, or more or less formally to recognize, the *de facto* States of the South American Continent.' ' Indeed,' he added, ' it would not be fair to withhold the expression of our opinion that, before Parliament meets, the course of events, the interests of commerce, and the state of navigation in the American seas will have obliged us to come to some understanding, more or less distinct, with some of those self-erected Governments.'[75]   If the recognition was postponed for another year or two, this was due to the necessity of keeping on as good terms as possible with Spain, in view of the attitude of France.

The Revolution in Spain, which seemed to place the Bourbon Ferdinand VII in much the same position as the French Revolution had placed Louis XVI before the overthrow of the monarchy, could not but be in the highest degree disconcerting to the Government of the Restoration; and if France opposed the idea of intervention of the Alliance, this was because, in view of

[75] Canning to Wellington, September 27, 1822.   F.O. : Continent, Verona, Duke of Wellington.   September–December 1822.   See also No. 9 of October 15 and No. 16 of November 8.

the proposals of the Emperor Alexander, such intervention would have been scarcely less of a danger
to France than the Revolution itself. A providential
outbreak of cholera in the Peninsula, however, gave
the French Government the excuse for establishing a
strong cordon of troops along the frontier, and this was
maintained, long after the danger of physical infection
was past, in order to guard against the even more dreaded
moral infection. Thus matters remained in suspense
until the resignation of Richelieu on December 12,
1820, and the accession of the Ultra-royalists to power
under the leadership of the Comte de Villèle.

It had from the first been a maxim of the extreme
partisans of the traditional monarchy in France that
the Bourbons would never be firmly established until
they should have ' mounted on horseback ' and wiped
out the memory of Napoleon's glory by fresh exploits
of their own. For such adventures the time now seemed
to them singularly opportune. The ' military preparations ' of Marshal Gouvion St. Cyr, which had early
excited the apprehensions of Castlereagh, had been
completed, and an army had been created in which
the sentiment for the tricolour flag was dead. It would
add enormously to the prestige of the monarchy if this
could be used to rescue the Bourbon King of Spain
from revolutionary duress, and so not only remove a
standing menace from the borders of France, but extend
the sphere of her influence by a revival of the ' family
compact ' established by Louis XIV. The temper of
the French people, at least as reflected in the Chambers,
favoured such a plan ; for the murder of the popular
Duc de Berri had reacted violently against the cause
it was intended to serve. The diplomatic situation
was scarcely less favourable. Of the other Powers of
the Alliance, Russia was already committed to the
principle of intervention in Spain ; Austria, in view of
her own recent action in Naples under circumstances

almost identical, could hardly fail to support the French
claim to intervene; and Prussia, however much she
might dread any renewed activity on the part of France,
could be won over by playing on her fears of revolution.
The great stumbling-block, of course, was Great Britain.
Efforts would be made to win her over by protestations
as to the purity and disinterestedness of the intentions
of France. If these efforts failed—well, Troppau and
Laibach had proved that, with the other Powers united,
the protests of Great Britain could be safely ignored.
In any case, the greatness of the prize was worth such
risk as there might be from the effects of British jealousy;
for, in the event of the success of the arms of France,
not only would she be predominant in the Peninsula,
but by aiding Spain to recover her colonies she would
be able to bargain for exceptional trade privileges
throughout the vast Spanish Empire. Of these views
the Vicomte Mathieu de Montmorency, who, as Minister of
Foreign Affairs, was to represent France at the approaching Conference, was the enthusiastic champion.

The question of intervention in Spain was not formally
raised at the preliminary meeting at Vienna; but it
was informally discussed, and the discussions showed
that the French Government would have other formidable obstacles to overcome, besides the uncompromising opposition of Great Britain, before it could
hope to obtain the sanction of the Alliance for its policy.
The chief of these obstacles was the Emperor Alexander,
whose deep-seated suspicions of the inherent revolutionary
vice of the French people survived, in spite of the present
conspicuous proofs of moral regeneration. Mindful
of the British attitude in the affair of Naples, Villèle,
in conversation with Wellington, had emphasized his
determination to keep the question of intervention in
Spain wholly ' French,' in the hope that, the principles
of Troppau being ruled out, Great Britain might allow
to France the same free hand in Spain that she had

conceded to Austria in Italy.[76] In doing so he had merely placed a new diplomatic weapon in the hands of Great Britain ; for whatever her objections were in general to the whole principle of European intervention, in the particular case of Spain it was, in consonance with her traditional policy for a century past, to the intervention of France that she objected. At Vienna, in the course of a private conversation with the Emperor Alexander, Wellington repeated the substance of Villèle's communication. The Tsar expressed his surprise at the intention of the French Government to regard as ' French ' a question of which the interest was so obviously ' European.' He was, Wellington reported, in favour of interfering in Spain, but only by means of a Russian army—of that army which, as he had made clear at Aix-la-Chapelle, he maintained solely in the interests of European peace.[77] Since Austria, now that Metternich was established as the Tsar's confidant, was interested in humouring his whims, this attitude augured ill for the success of Montmorency's activities at Verona, and Wellington, in an optimistic moment, recorded his opinion that the Conference would issue in ' an unanimous decision to leave the Spaniards to themselves.'[78]

[76] Wellington to Canning, Vienna, October 4, 1822 : ' Secret and confidential.' F.O. : Continent, Verona. From the Duke of Wellington, September–October 1822.

[77] *Ibid.*   [78] *Ibid.*

V

THE CONGRESS OF VERONA

Character of the Congress—Subjects for discussion—The Spanish colonies—The Spanish Revolution—France proposes intervention —Montmorency's questions to the Congress—Answers of the Powers—Alexander proposes concerted intervention—Attitude of Austria and Prussia—Wellington withdraws from the conferences—Attempts at compromise—The policy of identical notes —Protest of Great Britain—Open breach of the Alliance—Views of Canning on this.

THE Conference which met at Verona in October 1822 was destined to be the last of the series of solemn meetings of sovereigns and their ministers growing out of the Treaty of November 20, 1815, and, though technically no more than a Conference, its imposing character justifies the description of Congress commonly given to it. The meeting at Aix-la-Chapelle had been confined to the five Powers ; that at Troppau had been of the nature of a confidential symposium of the three autocratic Powers, to whose councils the representatives of Great Britain and France had been only intermittently and grudgingly admitted ; the Conference at Laibach had worn a more universal air, owing to the presence of the Italian princes, but had been less than European both in its composition and its immediate aims. The meeting at Verona, on the other hand, summoned to decide the fate of two worlds, recalled by the splendour of its concourse the glories of the Congress of Vienna. The Emperor Alexander was there, accompanied, as became the divinely-inspired champion of ' morality based on bayonets,' by five adjutants-general and by Prince Wolkonsky, his chief of the general staff, while his diplomatic advisers were Count Nesselrode, Secretary of State for Foreign Affairs, Count Lieven, ambassador in London, and Count Pozzo di Borgo, ambassador in Paris. The Emperor and Empress of Austria came, with a numerous suite, including Prince Metternich, with his faithful henchman Gentz, Prince Esterhazy, ambassador in London, Count Zichy, ambassador in Berlin, and Count Lebzeltern, ambassador in St. Petersburg. With King Frederick William of Prussia came Prince William—afterwards the Emperor William I —Prince Charles, Count Bernstorff, and Baron Alexander von Humboldt. The Duke of Wellington, as pleni-potentiary of Great Britain, was accompanied by Lord Clanwilliam, Lord Londonderry (Lord Stewart), Lord Strangford and Lord Burghesh. France was represented by the Vicomte de Montmorency, who had with him the two ministers present at Troppau, i.e. the Marquis de Caraman and M. de La Ferronnays, and M. de Ray-neval and the Vicomte de Chateaubriand. The Italian sovereigns were present in person; the Kings of the Two Sicilies and Sardinia, the Grand Duke of Tuscany, the Duke of Modena, and, the centre of much curiosity, the Archduchess Marie Louise, Duchess of Parma, accompanied by Count Neipperg. Chateaubriand has left us an impression of this lady. ' We found her very gay : the universe having charged itself with the care of this *souvenir* of Napoleon, she no longer had cause to think about him. I told her that I had met some of her soldiers at Piacenza, and that she formerly had more of them ; she replied : " Je ne songe plus à cela." She said some light words in passing about the King of Rome : she was *enceinte*.' [79] At Verona she was in her element ; for here were renewed the gaieties at Vienna, and from these she was no longer debarred. The Roman amphitheatre, cleared at this time of its sordid occupants

[79] *Congrès de Vérone*, i. 69.

and restored, remains as the memorial of these forgotten splendours.

At the very first 'confidential meeting' of the ministers of the five Allied Powers, on October 20, Montmorency handed in, on behalf of the French Government, a paper with three inquiries : In the event of France having to withdraw her minister from Madrid, would the other Allied Powers do the same ? In case of war, under what form and by what acts would the Powers give to France their moral support, so as to give to her action all the force of the Alliance ? What *material* aid would the Powers give, if asked by France to intervene under restrictions which she would declare and they would recognize ?[80]

The discussions that arose out of these questions at once revealed the conflict of opinion in the councils of the Alliance. The views of the French Government itself, as set forth in the questions, were not without a certain ambiguity, the outcome of conflicting counsels. By her whole attitude towards Spain since 1820 France, as Wellington pointed out, had placed herself in a position in which it was perilous to advance and impossible to withdraw with dignity. Villèle, who had succeeded Richelieu as head of the Government in the preceding December, did not share the enthusiasm for a royalist crusade in Spain of which Chateaubriand was the most eloquent advocate. He was conscious of the risks of such an adventure ; for the memory of the Peninsular War was still fresh, and Great Britain had made it abundantly clear that she would regard any attempt of Louis XVIII to subjugate Spain with no greater favour than the previous attempt made by Napoleon. The precedent of Laibach had suggested a way out of the *impasse* ; for, with the example of Naples before it, the Liberal Government of Spain would, it was thought, listen to the remonstrances of France if backed by the

[80] Précis des communications verbales faites par M. de Montmorency . . . à Vérone le 20 Octobre, 1822.   F.O. : Continent, Verona. From the Duke of Wellington, September–October 1822.

moral support of the European Powers, even though Great Britain, as at Laibach, held aloof. Hence the appeal to the European Alliance. But Villèle was determined that, in making this appeal, France should control the issue ; he instructed the French plenipotentiaries not to allow the Congress ' to prescribe the conduct of France towards Spain ' ; and the language of the questions shows how little they were dictated by any but French interests. A phrase about inspiring ' a salutary fear into the Revolutionists of all lands ' was a mere blind ; more significant was the third question, which suggested that the time and nature of any eventual intervention of the Alliance should be left to France to determine.

The Emperor Alexander was little inclined to suffer any such restrictions. For him the question was European, not French. Remote as his Empire was from the troubles beyond the Pyrenees, it was not too remote to be corrupted by the infectious example of successful military revolt ; three years before, he told Wellington, he had been compelled to give the Spanish minister at St. Petersburg his passports for tampering with the loyalty of his troops. The offence, commented the Duke, seemed somewhat old to serve as a pretext for war at the present juncture ; the real reason why the Tsar was anxious to intervene in Spain was ' because of his embarrassment with his army,' which badly needed occupation ; and how could it be more beneficently occupied than as a European police force for the upholding of ' morality ' ? He at once, then, offered to march 150,000 men through Germany into Piedmont, where they would be available for use either in Spain or, in the event of a Jacobin rising, in France. As for the intervention in the Peninsula, this should be the affair of the Alliance and based on a new treaty *ad hoc* to be signed before the break-up of the Congress.[81]

[81] Wellington to Canning, ' Secret and Confidential,' Verona, October 29, 1822. F.O. : Continent, Verona. From the Duke of Wellington, September–October 1822, No. 18.

The renewal of this disconcertingly disinterested proposal for the moment drew Great Britain and Austria together, as the similar proposal had done two years previously. Montmorency had at first approved of the Tsar's design ;[82] but Wellington and Metternich combined to impress upon him the dangers inherent in its execution, and, in the end, he told the Emperor Alexander ' in positive terms ' that any movement of troops would be injurious to France. This effectually nipped the proposal in the bud once more, but in doing so it also widened the growing rift between Austria and Great Britain. So long as there had been a danger that the Russian Emperor's idea might materialize, Metternich had shared Wellington's views as to the inexpediency of the affair of Spain being made the subject of a fresh treaty and of summoning another Conference to Paris, as the Tsar suggested, for the purpose of perfecting the work begun at Verona ; for there was little enough to attract Austria in the idea of a Conference presided over by Pozzo di Borgo and supported by the presence of an overwhelming Russian force. But now, having by the intervention of the French minister got rid of the greatest danger of all to Austria, Metternich—to use Wellington's phrase—' turned short round upon the remainder of the question ' and ' took up the Emperor of Russia's idea of having at least a treaty and all the ultra views of the French Government.'

The motive for this *volte face* was again not ' European,' but purely Austrian. The German Powers had no interest in the particular question of Spain ; they did not want war, and least of all a war which would have involved the passage of a Russian army across their territories ; but they were above all anxious to distract Alexander's attention from the affairs of Turkey, where lay the most immediate danger of Russian aggression,

[82] Wellington to Canning, *ibid*. Doubtless a move in the diplomatic game ; for Villèle's instructions to Montmorency clearly state that France could not allow the passage of foreign troops across her territory. (See Chateaubriand, *Congrès de Vérone*, i. 103.)

and for this purpose it was necessary to humour him in the matter of the intervention in Spain, if only to keep him 'grouped.' To preserve the ascendancy over Alexander's mind which he had acquired since the dismissal of Capo d'Istria seemed to Metternich worth the risk of a breach of the good understanding· between Austria and Great Britain—a breach which, if it could not be avoided, his vanity made him believe he would soon be able to repair.

During the discussions on the answer to be returned to the French questions he had laboured to persuade Wellington to hold a common language with the other Allies. The fundamental divergence of views between Great Britain and the continental Courts had been revealed in the 'confidential communication' that passed between them during the first days of the Conference, and when, on October 30, the answers of the Powers to the French note were handed in, the divergence was patent to all. 'The three continental Powers replied that they would act as France should in respect to their ministers in Spain, and would give that country every countenance and assistance she should require, the cause for such assistance, the period, and the mode of giving it being reserved to be specified in a treaty. The minister of Great Britain replied that, having no knowledge of the cause of dispute, and not being able to form a judgment upon a hypothetical case, he could give no answer to any of the questions.'[83]

Wellington's reply was so far non-committal as to give occasion for further attempts to reach an understanding. Hitherto, he reported, the continental Powers had carefully refrained from using any language or taking any action against which it would have been necessary for him to protest,[84] but there were now signs

[83] Memorandum of Wellington, Verona, November 12, 1822. F.O. : Continent, Verona, Wellington, November 22, 1822.

[84] 'Nearly up to the last moment he (Metternich) assured me repeatedly that he concurred in all my opinions and views' (Wellington to Canning, November 22).

of ' a different mode of proceeding.' He himself had suggested, as the best means of averting a rupture between France and Spain, the selection of a single Power as mediator, and with this Metternich agreed. But the only Power whose mediation would have been accepted by Spain was Great Britain, which was too much interested in the dispute to be acceptable to France. This solution thus being impracticable, Metternich proposed to the Conference that all the Powers should speak, so as to prove to the Spanish Government that in whatever action she might take France would have the support of Europe ; at the same time he disclaimed any intention of interfering in the internal affairs of Spain. The question of a treaty, though pressed by Montmorency, was shelved, and it was ultimately decided that the Allies should, through their ministers at Madrid, ' hold a common language, but in separate notes, though uniform in their principles and their objects.' This was settled in the Conference of October 31. On the following day it was arranged that dispatches to the ministers should be substituted for notes, as allowing greater latitude. These were to be at once drawn up by the four Courts and to be communicated to Wellington, who was then to declare what line his Government would take.[85]

As to this there could not be much doubt. In the discussions between the Powers the attitude of Wellington had been throughout quite unequivocal. He had urged the Powers to confine their attention to the ' external ' causes of quarrel between France and Spain, to abstain from menace, and ' above all not to approach Spain in the form of enemies, bound in a treaty of defensive alliance against her.' As for Great Britain, she could not be a party to any general declaration against Spain, to any hostile interference in her internal affairs, or to any defensive alliance between the Powers. The adoption of the principle of intervention by the four Powers led to Wellington's formal withdrawal from the

[85] Wellington to Canning, November 22.

conferences, and the character of the notes to be sent to Madrid was discussed in his absence.

This attitude of the British representative increased the irritation of the continental Powers against Great Britain, which, they complained, was again making, as at Laibach, ' an unnecessary display of difference of opinion upon a theory ' ; and the outcome of their deliberations showed little disposition to meet her views. On November 12 Wellington wrote to Canning that he had seen Montmorency's draft note to Spain, and that it was ' highly objectionable.' But this was not all. The Emperor Alexander had by no means given up his idea of collective intervention ; he still expressed his desire for an allied occupation of Spain, and at the Conference of November 17, as a concession to his views, a *procès verbal* had been drawn up defining the objects and principles of the Alliance with regard to Spain. The duty of Wellington, in accordance with his instructions, was now clear, and in a formal note, in the course of which he reiterated the British principle of non-intervention, he definitely refused to sign the *procès verbaux* of October 30 and November 17. The breach with the continental Allies was complete.

But, as Castlereagh had foreseen, it was the Alliance that had moved away from Great Britain, which had merely ' adhered to her course.' This is clearly brought out in a letter of Canning of September 16, 1823, to Sir H. Wellesley, the British ambassador at Vienna, who had reported a conversation in which Metternich complained of the speeches in Parliament and the support allowed in England to revolutionary movements. ' The pretensions of Prince Metternich in respect to this country,' he wrote, ' appear to me to be perfectly unreasonable ; they must be founded upon some strange misconception of our obligations, our interests, and our feelings. . . . England is under no obligation to interfere, or to assist in interfering, in the internal concerns of independent nations. The specific engagement to interfere in France

is an exception so studiously particularized as to prove
the rule.   The rule I take to be, that our engagements
have reference wholly to the state of territorial possession
settled at the peace ; to the state of affairs between
nation and nation ; not (with the single exception above
stated) to the affairs of any nation within itself.   I
thought the public declarations of my predecessor . . .
had set this question entirely at rest. . . . What is the
influence which we have had in the Alliance, and which
Prince Metternich exhorts us to be so careful not to
throw away ? We protested at Laibach ; we remonstrated at Verona.   Our protest was treated as waste-
paper ; our remonstrances mingled with the air.   Our
influence, if it is to be maintained abroad, must be secure
in its sources of strength at home : and the sources of
that strength are in the sympathy between the people
and the Government ; in the union of the public sentiment with the public counsels ; in the reciprocal confidence and co-operation of the House of Commons
and the Crown.' ' Our business,' he concludes, ' is
to preserve the peace of the world, and therefore the
independence of the several nations which compose it.
In resisting the Revolution in all its stages . . . we
resisted the spirit of change, to be sure, but we resisted
also the spirit of foreign domination.'[86]

Thus Canning revealed himself as the champion of
nationality, as opposed to the international system
on which it had been sought to establish the peace of
the world ; and in doing so he became, for all his essential
Toryism, the protagonist of those nationalist sympathies
which, during the century to come, were to inspire the
foreign policy of British Liberalism. He himself, however,
clearly did not realize the direction that would be taken
by the forces he helped to set in motion. For him
nationality was not a question of abstract ' rights,' but
a juridical status based upon long precedent or defined

[86] To Wellesley, September 16, 1823. In Stapleton's *George
Canning and his Times,* i. 374.

by international agreement in treaties, and for him, as for Metternich, a nation was but the aggregate of people bound together by a common allegiance. Like Castlereagh, he sympathized with the Greeks in their struggle for freedom ; like Castlereagh, he repudiated any obligation upon Great Britain to intervene on their behalf, maintaining that such intervention would be an unjustifiable interference with the right of the ' Turkish nation ' to manage its own affairs. If then the name of Canning, more than that of any other contemporary statesman, is associated with the birth of new nationalities in the Old World and the New, this was not due to any enthusiasm for the abstract idea of nationality, in the sense of an ethnical group claiming the right of untrammelled self-expression, but was the outcome of a policy wholly opportunist from the point of view of British interests.

The principle of national independence, as opposed to ' the spirit of foreign domination,' was not destined to make for peace. But even if Canning, himself the minister of a dominant Power, had foreseen this, it may be doubted whether it would have modified his attitude, which was determined first and last by what he considered due to the position of Great Britain. It was not only that her dignity had been wounded at Verona ; her material interests were also seriously threatened. The Alliance, of which the very *raison d'être* had been the fear of French aggression, had stultified itself by supporting France in her designs on Spain, and in doing so had been at no pains to safeguard the interests of Great Britain in the New World. The question of the Spanish colonies had been raised only to be shelved ; it must await the restoration of King Ferdinand VII to liberty and, possibly, the assembly of a Congress summoned to determine the whole relations of the Old and New Worlds. This was to imperil the commercial treaty signed by Great Britain with the Liberal Government of Spain and, worse still, to condone the piracies to which in the Spanish Main the ' contraband ' commerce of Great Britain with the new Latin American States was exposed at the hands of Spanish 'privateers.' In reply to Wellington's memorandum on these piracies in their relation to the whole question, Chateaubriand had drawn up a *note verbale* in which he deprecated the recognition in America of a political system hostile to that which ruled in Europe, and, in reference to the British grievances, declared that 'the principles of justice on which society is based ought not lightly to be sacrificed to secondary considerations.' Secondary considerations ! 'You know my politics well enough,' wrote Canning on November 5, 1822, to Sir Charles Bagot, the British ambassador in St. Petersburg, 'to know what I mean when I say that for Europe I should be desirous now and then to read England.'[87]

While resenting the dictatorial attitude of the continental Allies, with their tendency to deliver ' simultaneous sermons,' Canning neither broke, nor desired to break, the ties which bound Great Britain to them under the treaties ; and he was prepared to act even with Metternich, for all his loathing and contempt of him, on any points on which they were agreed. Two years after the close of the Congress of Verona he defined his attitude in this respect very clearly, in order to allay the misgivings of King George IV. His Majesty, who as Prince Regent had expressed his heartfelt agreement with the lofty moral principles of the Holy Alliance, had long regarded himself as one of the pillars of the European system ; his vanity was flattered by the increasing tendency— against which Canning protested—of the continental Governments to approach him direct, as though he too were an autocrat ; and he viewed with dismay the disruptive consequences of the erratic orbit followed by his meteoric minister. He reduced his misgivings to writing in a memorandum laid before the cabinet on January 27, 1825, in which he deplored the separation of Great Britain from her continental Allies and its cause,

[87] Stapleton, *op. cit.* p. 363.

the recognition of the Spanish American States. ' The late policy of Great Britain,' he said, ' has loosened these beneficial ties, by demonstrating a restless desire of self-interest in direct opposition to those wise and comprehensive principles by which the peace and general interests of Europe were bound together.' The King desired to know from the cabinet individually whether the great principles of policy established by his Government in the years 1814, 1815, and 1818 were or were not to be abandoned.[88] In reply, a cabinet minute stated that ministers fully recognized the principles of policy laid down in the years mentioned, in the sense repeatedly given to them by His Majesty's plenipotentiaries, and especially in the circular issued in 1821,[89] and in no other ; it added that ministers were deeply impressed with the obligation of preserving His Majesty's engagements, and with the advantages which might result from maintaining the system of confidence and reciprocal communication established with His Majesty's Allies.[90]

The King expressed himself satisfied with this answer ; yet three months later we find Canning again reassuring him, this time in language which gives the key to his whole attitude. ' My object,' he said, in an interview with Sir William Knighton, ' is to make His Majesty happy and comfortable, by placing him at the head of Europe, instead of being reckoned fifth in a great Confederacy.'[91] As for this Confederacy, the circumstances which gave rise to it, justified it, and held it together had, he said, gone by. More than two years before, indeed, he had welcomed its dissolution and the return to the healthy system of free competition among the nations. The ministers of the three autocratic Powers had delivered their simultaneous sermon at Madrid and, finding it produced no effect, had withdrawn, leaving the French representative, who had received no orders to withdraw, to make what profit he could out of the

[88] Stapleton, *op. cit.* p. 416.   [89] See pp. 210, 216, *supra*.
[90] Stapleton, *op. cit.* p. 420.   [91] Stapleton, *op. cit.* p. 433.

effect of their action.   To Canning it seemed that France, having gained what she could from the Alliance, was now, in however mean a way, bent on asserting her independence ; and he rejoiced in the fact. ' The issue of Verona,' he wrote to Bagot on January 3, 1823, ' has split the one and indivisible Alliance into three parts as distinct as the Constitutions of England, France, and Muscovy. . . . Villèle is a minister of thirty years ago— no revolutionary scoundrel : but constitutionally hating England, as Choiseul and Vergennes used to hate us— and so things are getting back to a wholesome state again. Every nation for itself and God for us all. Only bid your Emperor be quiet, for the time for Areopagus and the like of that is gone by.'

VI

THE GENESIS OF THE MONROE DOCTRINE

The French invasion of Spain—Ferdinand VII restored to power—
The question of the Spanish colonies—A Congress *ad hoc* proposed
—Attitude of the Emperor Alexander—Russia as an American
Power—Russian overtures at Washington—Attitude of Canning—
He suggests a concert between Great Britain and the United
States—Suspicious attitude of the American minister—The
question at Washington—Favourable attitude of President Monroe
—Influence of the Russian proposals—John Quincy Adams—
Victory of the principle of the isolation of the Americas—President
Monroe's Message of December 2, 1823—The Monroe Doctrine
—Effect on the Allied Powers.

INTO the further discussions that preceded the armed
intervention of France in Spain it is unnecessary for
our present purpose to examine. The hesitations of
the French Government, inspired by the fear of a rupture
with Great Britain, were ended when Montmorency was
succeeded in the Ministry of Foreign Affairs by Chateaubriand, from the first an enthusiastic partisan of the
war policy, and on April 7, 1823, a French army of 95,000
men, under the Duc d'Angoulême, crossed the Bidassoa.
The confidence of Chateaubriand in the issue was soon
justified. Of the implacable resistance which the Spanish
people had offered to Napoleon there was no sign ; on
September 30, Cadiz, the last stronghold of the Liberal
Government, surrendered ; and Ferdinand VII was once
more free to abuse his divinely consecrated authority.
Chateaubriand was right, too, in believing that Great
Britain, exhausted by her long struggle with revolutionary
France, would not embark on a fresh war in which the

European Alliance would have been ranged against her, instead of on her side. Whatever the sympathies of the British people, the Tory Government, quite rightly, had no great belief in the Spanish system as established by the unworkable Constitution of 1812 ; and, in any case, it repudiated any obligation or right to intervene, whether for the purpose of overthrowing or of supporting it. British interests, which alone determined Canning's policy, were threatened by the French intervention mainly through its possible effect on the question of the over-sea empire of Spain, involving as this did the newly acquired right of Great Britain to trade with Latin America, and British action would be eventually determined by the developments of this question. Powerful voices in Parliament denounced the revival by Louis XVIII of the aggressive policy of Louis XIV and urged the Government to prevent by arms the renewal of the Family Compact. But Canning realized that the Spain of Ferdinand VII was no longer the Spain of Philip V ; and when the determination of the French Government to embark on the war was announced, he contented himself with intimating at Paris that Great Britain would in no circumstances tolerate the subjugation of the Spanish colonies by foreign force.

The rapid success of the French arms brought the question forward more rapidly than had been expected. In overthrowing the revolutionary Government in Spain, France had acted as the mandatory of Europe ; but with the restoration of Ferdinand VII to liberty the mandate was at an end, for on the larger question of the Spanish colonial possessions no decision had been reached in the councils of the Allies. In view of the attitude of Great Britain, all-powerful at sea, it was clearly impossible for France to undertake alone to assist the King of Spain to re-establish the principle of legitimacy beyond the ocean. Yet the re-establishment of this principle seemed to her essential to the security of the very foundations of the restored order in Europe.

Chateaubriand, whose personal relations with Canning were intimate, exhausted the resources of his literary art in attempting to impress upon him the perils, upon which Richelieu had enlarged at Aix-la-Chapelle, of allowing the New World to develop upon lines antagonistic to the Old. Convinced that the motives of Great Britain in threatening to recognize the Latin American States were wholly material, he laboured to persuade Canning that, in seeking to restore these States to their legitimate allegiance or, failing this, to erect them into Bourbon monarchies, France was not actuated by any selfish motives and would be content to receive in the trade with the New World the same treatment conceded to Great Britain. It was the final proof of this disinterestedness that she was prepared formally to subordinate her interests to those of Europe, and supported the appeal of Ferdinand VII to a Congress of the Powers.

To this idea of a Congress the Emperor Alexander, needless to say, gave his whole-hearted support. The vast mass of his Empire stretched unbroken from the shores of the Baltic to those of the Behring Sea, and its frontiers in America were still sufficiently undefined to leave play for Russian ambitions along the Pacific coast. He had already asserted his position as an American Power by the *ukaz* of September 21, 1821, which declared all the coastlands of North America, as far south as fifty-one degrees of latitude, to be Russian territory.[92] He thus seemed to himself to be specially called to convert the Confederation of Europe into a Confederation of the World, and in spite of his discouraging experience with his allies at Aix-la-Chapelle, he pursued this ideal with characteristic obstinacy. The main obstacle in the path, so far as the New World was concerned, was the United States. Alexander had received the news of the recognition of the independence of the Latin

[92] This claim, which was at once contested by Great Britain and the United States, was in effect soon limited to the claim of Russia to declare the Behring Sea a *mare clausum*.

American republics with sorrow rather than with anger, and did not despair of persuading the Government at Washington of the error of its ways. On June 14, 1823, Count Nesselrode addressed to Baron Tuyll, the Russian minister in Washington, a letter telling him to inform the Government at Washington that in no circumstances would the Emperor receive any diplomatic agent accredited by any one of the *de facto* Governments of Spanish America. This was followed by a long dispatch, dated August 30, in which, after stating that the time had come when it would be useful to lay before the Government of the United States ' the decisions and ulterior views of His Imperial Majesty,' Count Nesselrode unfolded to the unsympathetic eye of the Secretary of State Alexander's vision of the Holy Alliance and its work, accomplished and yet to be accomplished.

The force of arms applied where needed (*déployée àpropos*) ; surrounded by all the guarantees demanded by the resolution to have to recourse to it ; tempered by all the measures and all the promises calculated to tranquillize the peoples as to their future ; supported, finally, by that power of union and of concord which in our days has created a new political system : the force of arms has only had to let itself be seen in order to unmask to the world a despotism too often disguised, either by the errors of theorists, perhaps themselves involuntarily deceived as to the true state of affairs, or by the bad faith of men of criminal designs who only sought the means to extend and propagate the same misfortunes.[93]

Of the effect, far other than that intended by its author, produced at Washington by this attempt to commend the Holy Alliance, with its principle of intervention by force in order to guarantee the peace of the world, I shall speak later. It was not laid before the Secretary of State until October 4, and, meanwhile, other and more fateful negotiations had been opened between Great Britain and the United States in Europe.

[93] In Worthington Ford's ' Genesis of the Monroe Doctrine,' *Massachusetts Hist. Society Proceedings*, Second Series, xv. 402.

Ten days before the date of Nesselrode's dispatch, on August 20, George Canning sent to Richard Rush, the American minister in London, as the outcome of conversations, an ' unofficial and confidential ' letter in which he suggested that Great Britain and the United States should come to an understanding on the question of the Spanish American colonies with a view to a concerted attitude in opposition to the designs of the continental Powers. ' We ourselves,' he wrote, ' have no disguise.'

1. We conceive the recovery of the colonies by Spain to be hopeless.

2. We conceive the question of the recognition of them, as independent States, to be one of time and circumstances.

3. We are, however, by no means disposed to throw any impediment in the way of an arrangement between them and the mother country by amicable negotiations.

4. We aim not at the possession of any portion of them ourselves.

5. We could not see any portion of them transferred to any other Power, with indifference.[94]

Three days later he wrote again, urging as an additional reason for a concert between the two Governments the news that had just reached him, that, as soon as the military objects of the French in Spain were achieved, a proposal would be made for a Congress, or a conference of some sort, with special reference to the affairs of Spanish America.

Richard Rush received these communications without enthusiasm. As a doctrinaire republican he was outraged by Canning's view that monarchy was the type of government best suited to the Latin American nations ; he noted that Great Britain had for years past acted in general harmony with the European Alliance ; he suspected that her motives in the matter of the Spanish colonies were wholly ' selfish ' ; and he concluded that,

[94] Ford, *loc. cit.* p. 415.

her particular interests once secured, she would again join in the general conspiracy of monarchs against liberty. The pledge of sincerity which he demanded, namely, a definite promise that Great Britain would acknowledge the independence of the Spanish American States, Canning refused to give. ' It is France that must not be aggrandized,' he reported to Washington, ' not South America that must be made free ' ; and in confirmation of his doubts he pointed out that, after Canning's conference with the Prince de Polignac early in October, ' the fresh discussion since the fall of Cadiz ' had been ' brought to a sudden pause.'

In view of the urgency of the crisis and of the *non possumus* attitude of Rush, who insisted on the recognition of the Latin American States out of hand, Canning had indeed recognized the necessity of attempting to come to an understanding with France, and early in October, in conversations with Polignac, certain bases of agreement were reached. Polignac, on behalf of his Government, agreed that the recovery by Spain of her colonies was hopeless ; he declared that France had no intention of assisting Spain to recover them, though she would be glad to see the dispute settled by an amicable arrangement between the mother country and the colonies ; he disclaimed for France all idea of deriving exclusive commercial advantages from the colonies, her object being, like England, to be placed on the most favoured nation footing, after Spain. On the other hand, France could not recognize the independence of States established on radically unsound principles, and urged the necessity for a Congress, in which Great Britain should take part, for the settlement of the whole matter. This represented a certain amount of concession to the British point of view ; and, though Canning resolutely refused to listen to the suggestion of a Congress, the extreme tension of the situation was relieved.

Meanwhile, however, the centre of interest in the discussion had been transferred to Washington. Rush's dispatch of August 19, enclosing Canning's proposals, reached the State Department on October 9. Upon President Monroe these proposals exercised a profound influence. He shrank, indeed, from the prospect of entangling the United States in European politics by an alliance with any Power, but, ' if a case exist in which a sound maxim may and ought to be departed from,' he conceived the present to be such a case, since it seemed that Great Britain was starting on a new career, in which she would be ranged with the United States on the side of liberty against despotism.[95] The alliance, however, was not destined to be realized. This was due not so much to the fact that Rush's suspicions were reflected at Washington, where Canning was regarded as a master of machiavellian statecraft, as to the determination of the American cabinet to profit by the occasion to assert a principle to which Great Britain would never have given her consent—the principle, foreshadowed in the letter of Pozzo di Borgo quoted earlier,[96] of the isolation of the Americas. And by a singular irony it was the well-meant advances of the Emperor Alexander that hastened the very consummation it was his object to avoid. President Monroe himself not only inclined to favour a concert with Great Britain, but even seriously considered the expediency of sending representatives of the United States to Europe with authority to attend a Congress summoned to discuss the South American Question.[97] The chief opponent of this policy was John Quincy Adams, the Secretary of State; and it was the language of the Russian dispatches, with their lofty assumption of the divine right of universal intervention in the interests of ' legitimacy,' which gave him the opportunity of ' speaking out.' In the end it was his masterful will that prevailed over the irresolution of President Monroe, and the famous Message to Congress

[95] Monroe to Jefferson, October 17, 1823. Ford, *loc. cit.* p. 375.
[96] See p. 85.
[97] Monroe to Jefferson, December. Ford, *loc. cit.* p. 411.

of December 2, 1823, in which the ' Monroe Doctrine ' was defined, was essentially his work.

The Monroe Doctrine, proclaimed as a counterblast to the pretensions of the Holy Alliance, was a declaration of policy of which the full significance was only realized in our own day. It was based on two underlying principles : (1) That no non-American Power should be allowed to intervene in the affairs of the American States, and that the American continents should be henceforth closed to colonization by such Powers ; (2) that the United States, in their turn, should refrain from intervening in the affairs of Europe. The isolation of the Americas was commended as reasonable owing to the double barrier that lay between the Western and the Eastern Hemispheres, the physical barrier of the ocean, and the moral barrier of the fundamental difference of the principles upon which their political systems were established.[98] This was a principle which went far beyond anything that Canning had contemplated when he made his first advances to Rush. That the United States should prefer to make their declaration of policy without any concert with Great Britain troubled him little, since the result was equally favourable to his plans. So far as the Monroe Message repudiated the principle of intervention and the idea of the Spanish colonies being transferred to any other Power, it gave expression to views with which he not only agreed, but which had actually been inspired by

[98] In the ' draft of observations on the communications recently received from the minister of Russia,' prepared by the Secretary of State, occurs a sentence which, more explicitly than in the Message of President Monroe itself, defines the attitude of the United States towards Alexander's idea of a universal union. It reads as follows : ' In the general declarations that the allied monarchs will never compound, and never will even treat with the revolution, and that their policy has only for its object by forcible interposition to guarantee the tranquillity of all the States of which the civilized world is composed, the President wishes to perceive sentiments, the application of which is limited, and intended in their results to be limited, to the affairs of Europe ' (Ford, *loc. cit.* p. 408).

him. It was otherwise with the claim of the United States to oppose the colonization by any European Power of the vast unoccupied spaces of the American continent, and against this he at once protested. The question, however, was only to become of pressing importance later, in connexion with the Oregon boundary dispute ; and, for the present, the uncompromising attitude of the United States Government was a valuable factor in securing the success of British policy.

The Allied Powers did not, indeed, at once give up the idea of a Congress, but they showed an immediate disposition to recede from their extreme position. Metternich, who was anxious to keep on good terms with Great Britain, suggested that those Spanish colonies which had succeeded in throwing off the yoke of the mother country should be recognized, and that the Powers should confine their intervention to those in which the struggle was yet doubtful.[99] With this idea the Emperor Alexander expressed his agreement, but it did not appeal to the King of Spain, who stood obstinately upon his rights, nor to France, which, under the disguise of zeal for legitimacy, was still hoping to secure an extension of her colonial possessions in America.[100] This divergence of views led to mutual suspicions. Chateaubriand noted that Russia was more prodigal of talk about the necessity of harmony and concerted action than of promises of material help, and he suspected Alexander of a desire to weaken France by entangling her in difficult enterprises over-sea and leaving her without support.[101]

[99] Carlos A. Villanueva, *La Santa Alianza*, pp. 86 *seq.*

[100] In January 1824 an unofficial French agent, M. Chasseriau, was dispatched by Chateaubriand to Colombia, in order to counteract the influence of the British consular officers sent by Canning and watch over French commercial interests. In view of the attitude of France, however, M. Chasseriau was not allowed by the Colombian authorities to proceed to Bogotá. That the suspicions of the Colombians were justified is shown by the dispatches to General Donzelot, the Governor of Martinique, of December 17, 1823, and to Admiral Jurien, of March 1, 1824. (See Villanueva, *op. cit.* pp. 27 and 90.)

[101] To Talaru, April 14, 1824. *Ibid.* p. 84.

The decision of the Conference at Paris, on March 21, to abandon the idea of a Congress, tended to confirm this view, which the suggestion of Alexander to continue the conferences in secret did nothing to weaken.   This, commented Chateaubriand scornfully, was but a device to adjourn the whole discussion *sine die*, without the appearance of having been routed by Mr. Canning.   He himself continued to press the Spanish Government to urge upon Great Britain the necessity of a Congress, and it was not till June that another peremptory refusal on the part of Canning led even King Ferdinand to see the hopelessness of the project.   This occurred at about the same time as the rupture of Chateaubriand with Villèle and his retirement from office.   The idea of an intervention of the Holy Alliance in the affairs of America was at an end.

The ' sublime conception ' of the Emperor Alexander, the visionary good in the pursuit of which he had neglected his duties to his own people, had proved itself the stuff that dreams are made of.   His attempt to realize a Confederation of the World had ended in drawing the Old World, worn out as it seemed with cataclysmic convulsions, further apart from that New World of which the fiery youth proved a centrifugal force too strong to be resisted.   As for the Confederation of Europe, from the moment that Great Britain decided to ' revolve in her own orbit,' the harmonious cohesion of the European system became impossible, and after the Revolution of July 1830 it broke definitively into two opposing groups. On the one side were the two Western Liberal Powers, Great Britain and France, under whose active encouragement the forces of nationalism and constitutional liberty developed, amid wars and revolutions, until the system established at Vienna had been shattered.   On the other side were the three Powers who had signed the Troppau Protocol, Austria, Russia, and Prussia, united in a Holy Alliance which, under the influence of the ' Iron Tsar ' Nicholas I, narrowed and hardened into a close league of which the object was to crush out, within the limits of its sphere, all motions towards national independence or constitutional change. Its principles were applied for the last time in the fateful intervention of the Emperor Nicholas in Hungary, on behalf of the Habsburg Monarchy, in 1849. It did not survive the Crimean War and the death of the Emperor Nicholas, the last uncompromising champion of its principles. Thenceforth it was but a memory, accursed in the eyes of the triumphant Liberalism of the age, its original character and aims forgotten or distorted by the legitimate prejudices aroused by its later developments.

But though the experiment in the international organization of peace which we have been studying failed, as in the long run it was bound to fail, it was by no means wasted effort. Its temporary use I have already pointed out ; it preserved peace during the critical years following the fall of Napoleon, and so gave to Western Europe the opportunity for that marvellous industrial and economic development which was to change the face of the world. It did more than this. It set the precedent for that Concert of Europe to which the world owed more than sometimes, in its more impatient moments, it was willing to allow, and it established the tradition of that sense of common interests among nations which has been, and will be, the strongest influence making for peace. It gave a new sanction to international law, the outcome of this feeling, and so made possible the developments which led to the Conferences at The Hague, which, whatever the bitter disappointments they prepared for the world, at least did much to gain acceptance for those principles of international solidarity which constituted the moral force behind the Allies in their successful struggle against German militarism. The life of the Emperor Alexander of Russia was, to all appearance, a tragic failure. But the wonder is, not that the shadowy world of his ideals collapsed in utter ruin, but that so much that was noble in it survived and survives.

VII

THE FEDERATION OF THE WORLD

The substitution for the reign of force,
for the clash of competing ambition, and
the groupings and alliances of a precarious
equipoise, of a real European partnership.
—MR. ASQUITH.

THE LEAGUE OF NATIONS

Criticism of pacifist proposals before the war—Danger of an international system to national liberties—The principle of intervention—President Wilson and Mexico—Comparison with the action of the reactionary Powers at Troppau—Light thrown by the international experiment after 1815 on the programme of the League of Nations—Parallel between the proceedings at Paris and those at Vienna—The ' dictatorship exercised by the Great Powers '—Criticism of the Covenant of the League—Objections by British statesmen to similar proposals a hundred years ago—The reservation of the Monroe Doctrine—Significance of this—Criticism of President Wilson's claim that the United States have been *par excellence* the champions of the principle of ' self-determination '—The Monroe Doctrine as a doctrine of conquest—The American attitude defined in the controversy with Colombia—Reason why the United States, in spite of their policy of expansion, have not developed into a military power—The history of the United States does not show that democracies are pacific—A democratic international government would not necessarily make for peace—Mirabeau on the warlike temper of popular assemblies—A democratic international system is inconsistent with nationalism—Falseness of the analogy between the suggested international federal system and such federations as the United States—The cosmopolitan ideal conceived as the culmination of the historical process of human grouping—Criticism of this—The stability of any international system must always depend on the balance of power—Limits of willingness to obey law, whether national or international—Criticism of the principle of ' self-determination ' as a guarantee of peace—A vivid sense of the community of interests between nations the only guarantee of peace—The only proof of this would be universal free trade—Danger of surrendering or curtailing national sovereignty in the absence of such a guarantee.

In the concluding section of the previous edition of this book I attempted to apply the lessons of the international experiment which followed the Congress of Vienna to the plans for the organization of peace which were then

before the world. I pointed out that the new Holy
Alliance, of which the pacifists were dreaming, would
be confronted with much the same problems as those
which faced the Emperor Alexander and his allies.

They too propose to establish their international system
on the principle of the preservation of the *status quo*—
indeed, there is no other practical principle conceivable ; they
too would apply the principles of the Troppau Protocol, by
empowering the Universal Union, in the event of any State
violating or threatening to violate the public law of the world,
to bring it to reason ' by peaceful means, or if need be by arms.'
Now it might be possible that, as Sir Frederick Pollock
points out,[1] ' contests for supremacy or predominant influence,'
which in their very nature cannot be ' disposed of by
argument,' might be effectually prevented by a coalition of
Powers of superior collective strength which ' should be
prepared to enforce the principles which now stand universally
acknowledged by the Second Peace Conference of the Hague.'
This would, in effect, be to apply the principle which the
Grand Alliance directed against France, that of a coalition
ad hoc.   But if an attempt were made to expand this coalition
into a ' universal union ' and to base its action, not on the
exigencies of circumstances as they arise, not on the particular
joint interests recognized by all the parties to it, but on the
general right of the world-organization to coerce its refractory
members—what becomes of the sovereign independence of
nations ?   Especially it would be the small States whose independence would be prejudiced ; for though international
law recognizes in theory the equality of all sovereign States,
no international system which should attempt to translate
this theory into practice would survive.   If, on the other
hand, the voting power of the central ' directory ' were to be
proportioned to the size and importance of its constituent
States, the result would be precisely such a hegemony of the
Great Powers as was exercised by the Grand Alliance after
1815.   Nor is it extravagant to suppose that the new Holy
Alliance, thus constituted, would develop, *mutatis mutandis*,
very much on the lines of the old.   It would begin by repudiating the principle of intervention in the internal affairs

[1] *Cambridge Modern History*, xii. 719.

of the constituent nations, only in the end to find itself compelled to intervene : for, in new forms, the old difficulty of drawing a sharp distinction between external affairs and ' internal affairs having an external effect ' would be sure to emerge.

The truth is, to cite Sir Frederick Pollock once more, that the effective working of an international federal system demands a far greater uniformity of political institutions and ideas among the nations of the world than at present exists. This truth was realized by the sovereigns and statesmen of the Holy Alliance, and they attempted to secure the necessary uniformity by forcing their own model on the European States, not primarily in the interests of despotism, but in the supposed interests of the general peace of society. It has quite recently received a fresh and striking illustration in the attitude of President Wilson towards the revolution in Mexico and similar conditions in other Latin American States, an attitude developed logically out of the assumption by the United States, under the Monroe Doctrine, of the duty of policing the Americas.[2] Like the signatory Powers of the Troppau Protocol, he too demands ' guarantees of legal stability and order ' before he will recognize a *de facto* Government ; like them, he proposes to reconcile the guilty State to his system ' by peaceful means, or if need be by arms ' ; he differs from them only in his conception of what constitutes the guarantee required. The sovereigns of the Holy Alliance found this in the submission of the peoples to their Governments *ab antiquo* ; by President Wilson it is assumed to depend upon the will of the people ' properly expressed and registered.' From the point of view of our present inquiry it matters not which conception of ' legitimacy ' be the more reasonable. The important thing is that for any international organization, whether dominated by a group of Powers or by a single Power, a certain uniformity of political system is essential, and that, sooner or later, this uniformity would be enforced by armed intervention. The moment of such intervention, moreover, will be determined always by the interests of the dominating Power or Powers. ' This abyss of iniquities which we call

[2] See my article ' The New Monroism ' in the *Edinburgh Review* for January 1914.

politics,' wrote the beautiful and unhappy Empress Elizabeth of Russia in 1817, ' is vainly covered with a tissue of brilliant phrases, since it is easy for anyone of the least intelligence, whose heart is in the right place, to see through this tissue and to recognize that, in spite of *evangelical treaties*, in spite of *the reign of justice*, it is always the weaker who are sacrificed to the interests of the more powerful.'[3]   This was true enough when it was spoken ; is there any reason to suppose that it is less true of the present age, or will be less true of the age to come ?

The new age has been born ; the new Holy Alliance is in existence. Again we may ask what light is thrown upon its problems by the experience of a hundred years ago. So far as the proceedings of the Paris Conference are concerned the parallel is striking. Statesmen at the outset were loud in denouncing the spirit and the methods of the Congress of Vienna. President Wilson, especially, made himself the champion of a new diplomacy which was to have no secrets from the public, and he embodied this principle in those Fourteen Points which have been accepted as a supplement to the decalogue. But political human nature, as might have been expected, proved too strong for the idealists, and the proceedings of the Conference seem in general to have followed very closely the precedents of Vienna. The public sessions, to which alone the Press was admitted, were mere full-dress parades ; the real work of the Conference was done, as at Vienna, in secret meetings of the representatives of the Great Powers, in informal conversations, and by a series of committees *ad hoc* ; and, as at Vienna, though the theoretical equality of all sovereign States was admitted, the ultimate decision on all questions was reserved for the Great Powers alone. It could not be otherwise ; and if the democratic world has cause for complaint, this is not in the fact that statesmen had to bow to the inevitable, but that they had consciously

[3] The Grand Duke Nicholas Mikhailovch, *L'Imperatrice Elizabeth*, ii. 633.

or unconsciously, in the passion of speech-making, misled the peoples into a belief in the impending realization of an unrealizable ideal.

As to the spirit of the Conference, we may say with truth that it displayed little of the petty personal motives which from first to last deformed the proceedings of the Congress of Vienna. The plenipotentiaries in Paris were in too serious a mood to dance ; and if to an impatient world their progress seemed irritatingly slow, this was not due to the interruption of business by frivolity, but in part to the vast complexity of the problems to be solved, in part doubtless to the insistence in certain quarters on priority being given to the settlement of general principles on which opinions differed and of which the practical application was largely a matter of speculation. But if the selfish rivalry of dynasts, big and little, was absent, the far more serious rivalry of nations was conspicuously present ; and, as at Vienna, the only forces making for compromise were the overwhelming need for peace and, in the last resort, the fiat of the superior Powers.

The Covenant of the League of Nations, accepted by the representatives of the Powers on April 28, though it appears to consecrate that principle of the Universal Union for which the Emperor Alexander contended, is in effect, like the Quadruple Alliance of 1815, a continuation for the purpose of preserving peace of the coalition of the Powers associated in the war. It is true that provision is made for the representation in the Assembly of all the lesser States, and these are to have as well elected spokesmen in the Council of the Great Powers. But though this arrangement gives the weaker nations the right and the opportunity to make their opinions heard, the ultimate decision is in all cases reserved to the Great Powers alone. All questions in dispute have in the first instance to be brought before the Council, where the representatives of the Great Powers are in the majority ; and though by the terms of Article XV the Council may refer a dispute to the Assembly, the opinion of the Assembly is only to be decisive ' if concurred in by the representatives of those members of the League represented in the Council.' The rights of the smaller States are further in appearance safeguarded by the terms of Article IV, which provide that ' any member of the League not represented on the Council shall be invited to send a representative to sit as member at any meeting of the Council during the consideration of matters especially affecting the interests of that member of the League.' It is interesting to note that this principle was consistently acted upon a hundred years ago,[4] and that it did not prevent the minor States from resenting and protesting against the ' dictatorship exercised by the Great Powers.'

The League of Nations, then, as it emerged from the Peace Conference, is to all intents and purposes an alliance of the Great Powers ; and no one can doubt that, if peace is to be preserved, such an alliance will for a long time to come be very necessary. Where it is open to criticism seems to me to be precisely in those points which Castlereagh criticized in the similar schemes for a ' universal guarantee ' put forward at Aix-la-Chapelle in 1818. He objected—and I think rightly—to the meetings of the Powers being put forward as a regular system, on the ground that, so far from allaying unrest, this would tend to increase it, because States dissatisfied with the settlement effected would have a perpetual opportunity for reopening the discussion. It was for this reason also that he opposed the conversion of the Conference at Aix-la-Chapelle into a Congress, as this ' might give rise to ideas of change not desirable to encourage.' [5] Bathurst, in the name of the British Government, also objected

---

[4] The Allied Sovereigns may in all such cases pursue the course which they have hitherto adopted, of placing themselves in relation with the particular State upon whatever may constitute the object of common interest to be treated of. Castlereagh to Earl Cathcart, March 27, 1818. *Wellington Supp. Disp.* xii. 445.

[5] To Cathcart, March 27, 1818. *Ibid.*

to ' a new treaty,' on the ground that it would ' set the mind of Europe again afloat,' would offend excluded Powers, and would lead to quarrels as to their future admission.[6] The last objection is very applicable to the League of Nations. The experience of 1818 proved how impossible in the long run it is to isolate a Great Power, however dangerous it may be considered to come to terms with it ; and it was the military recovery of France, culminating after her admission to the Alliance in her claim to ' restore order ' in Spain as the mandatory of Europe, which ultimately broke up the League. The Germans are diligent students of history and very clever in applying its lessons.

The constitution of the League of Nations, in spite of the imposing machinery it has set up, provides no means by which such a breach is to be avoided. Council and Assembly are essentially meetings of diplomatists ; their decisions will be arrived at by the usual diplomatic methods and determined by the usual international considerations ; votes will most certainly, as in the old Hungarian Parliament, be ' weighed, not counted ' ; the *liberum veto* will be overcome as it was in the old Polish Parliament—by the threat of consequences ; and the stability of the whole elaborate international edifice will depend, after as before, on the balance of power. The most that can be hoped is that, as Gentz believed, the organization will help to keep the balance in equilibrium. The Secretariat and the international Archives will doubtless serve a very useful purpose in facilitating the progress towards an international juridical system. But the most difficult problem connected with such a system, the constitution of an international court, was shelved at Paris. Nor is this surprising, since it is a problem which the best brains of both hemispheres have for years past laboured in vain to solve.[7]

[6] To Castlereagh, November 13, 1818. F.O. : Continent, Aix, Castlereagh, November 1818.

[7] See, e.g., the numerous projects published in the *Rapports* of the Organisation Centrale pour une Paix Durable at The Hague. The

This being the general character of the League of Nations, as designed under the Paris Covenant, it may be of value to test some of its provisions by the principles laid down as fundamental by the British Government a hundred years ago. The Covenant of the League expressly repudiates the principle of ' intervention ' (Art. XV), and in this respect it honours the British tradition. But the Holy Alliance equally repudiated it, yet on occasion intervened. Controversies in the councils of the League as to what are or are not ' disputes solely within the jurisdiction of domestic law ' are likely to be lively,[8] and the old principle of ' vicinage ' opens up endless possibilities of trouble. I doubt, moreover, whether British statesmen have fully realized all the possible consequences of the admission as a member of the League of ' any self-governing State, Dominion or Colony.' This provision, in view of the new self-

fundamental difficulty is the creation of a Court representative of all interests without being too large to be effective. The experience of Courts of Arbitration has been that the arbitrators appointed as representatives of the parties to the suit have always acted as the advocates of the view of their own nationals, and that the decision has therefore in practice always been given by the neutral umpire. It may be doubted whether any nation would be willing to submit its vital interests to the arbitrament of a single foreign jurist, however eminent.

[8] The truth of this has already been illustrated by the vigorous attempts, backed by the weight of the American Congress, to assert the right of the Paris Conference to intervene in the Irish Question. During his propaganda campaign in the autumn of 1919 President Wilson, indeed, in order to counter Irish-American opposition to the League, definitely asserted that, under Article XI of the Covenant, the United States would have the right to raise the Irish Question. In other words, he formally committed himself to Metternich's principle of intervention in 'internal affairs likely to have an external effect.' It is impossible to exaggerate the dangers to international peace and good will inherent in such a principle. Its full implications have been forcibly stated by opponents of the Covenant in the United States, in a way calculated to appeal to the American imagination. Senator Knox, for instance, pointed out in his speech of June 18 in the Senate that the concession of this claim would involve the recognition of the right of the League to intervene in order to support the claim of the negroes to equal treatment in the United States.—*The Times*, June 19, 1919.

consciousness of the British Dominions beyond the Seas, was probably inevitable ; but its consequences may none the less be portentous. When in 1818 it was proposed that the German States, which had adhered separately to the Holy Alliance, should be admitted as such to the suggested general league of mutual guarantee, Castlereagh objected that this ' might dissolve the Germanic Confederation ' of which the States would be ' subject to a double jurisdiction, the German and the European.'[9] This objection may have little weight at present, or for many years to come, in the case of the British Dominions, which are bound to the Empire by double ties of sentiment and interest. It is easy to imagine, however, what would happen if an exuberantly Sinn Fein Ireland, endowed with ' Dominion self-government,' were to be represented in the International Assembly.

A shrewd criticism of Castlereagh on the projected league of guarantee was that it would destroy ' all moral guarantees in the minor States,' which would be placed in a position to agitate and make themselves unpleasant in every way without running any risk in so doing.[10] This, it appears to me, will be equally true of the League of Nations. There will not be a petty State with a real or imagined grievance but will carry it to Geneva, where a host of international jurists will be deeply interested in keeping it alive. The litigious spirit, in the case of individual persons, is held in check by the cost of litigation ; no such check would operate in the case of self-assertive nationalities. Great Britain especially, with her world-wide relations, might thus be exposed to an infinitely irritating juridical guerilla warfare, which would prove extremely costly and certainly not tend to create a peaceful atmosphere. The United States, which in this respect is threatened mainly by the alarm

[9] To Bathurst, November 9, 1818. F.O. : Continent, Aix, Castlereagh, No. 29.
[10] To Bathurst, *ibid.*

and jealousy of the Latin American republics, has very wisely contracted out of the League in respect of the whole Western Hemisphere.

The true character of this momentous exception, against which at Paris representatives of the minor Latin American States protested in vain, is disguised in the Covenant of the League by the ambiguous definition of the Monroe Doctrine as a ' regional understanding.' Now, as a matter of fact, the Monroe Doctrine has been understood in a great variety of ways by American statesmen, and the substitution of the phrase ' regional understanding,' new to diplomacy, for the older phrase, also very modern, of ' sphere of influence,' only serves to disguise from the world the nature of the concession made by the Powers to the spirit of the old Adam.[11] President Wilson, of course, claimed that the League of Nations grew naturally out of the Monroe Doctrine, that it was but an extension of the Doctrine to all the world, and that in making his proposals for the League he was acting strictly in accordance with tradition and policy of the United States as a nation and in fulfilment of all that it had ' professed and striven for.'   This claim is worth examining, since the President's views have received widespread acceptance among people wholly ignorant of American history.

The belief that the United States is the pacific nation *par excellence*, and as such entitled to take the lead in the League of Nations, has not been confined to Americans. ' Perhaps historians will look back to the United States,' says Mr. Delisle Burns, ' as an example of a nation which has not been formed by war, so much at least as earlier

[11] The ' explanation ' by the British Government, that in every case it would be for the League to decide whether a particular case did or did not fall under the Monroe Doctrine, was vigorously criticized by Senator Knox, in the speech already referred to, as involving a derogation from the sovereignty of the United States by submitting its policy to the discretion of foreign Powers.   Nominally this would be so ; but in fact the decision of the League would be that of the United States.

nations have.'[12] It is doubtless true that in the case
of the United States there was no such deliberate policy
of ' blood and iron ' as proved so fatally effective in the
case of Germany. Yet the American nation owes its
very being to conquest ; it was nurtured in warfare—
with the Indians, with the Dutch, with the Spaniards,
with the French ; by bitter war with the mother country
it won the right and power to walk alone ; and its mighty
growth has throughout been made possible by war or
by the threat of war. It preserved its unity by one of
the bloodiest wars in all history. The Monroe Doctrine,
according to President Wilson, is the doctrine ' that
no nation should seek to extend its polity over any other
nation or people, but that every nation should be left
free to determine its own polity.' He does not indeed
in this respect claim an absolutely pure record for his
own country. ' Like other nations,' he said in his address
to the League to Enforce Peace, ' we have ourselves no
doubt once and again offended against that principle
when for a little while controlled by selfish passion, as
our franker historians have been honourable enough
to admit.' Once and again ! The truth is that nearly
the whole history of the territorial growth of the United
States, from the Louisiana Purchase in 1803 to the most
recent adventures in Central America, is that of their
expansion at the expense of neighbouring peoples and
States. Even the original, pure doctrine of Monroe was
not put forward in the spirit of international altruism,
and its abiding significance is accurately defined by
Senator Lodge.

We stand by the Monroe Doctrine for the same reason
that England upholds Afghanistan, and takes the Shan States
from China, because it is essential to our safety and defence.
The Monroe Doctrine rests primarily on the great law of self-
preservation.

But whatever the doctrine of Monroe himself may

[12] *The Morality of Nations.*

have been, it has gone through a series of the most remarkable transmutations to fit the *Realpolitik* of various
Presidents and Secretaries of State, until at times it has
assumed the character not of a doctrine of peace, but of
a doctrine of conquest. The latest American historian
of the Monroe Doctrine, with honourable if disconcerting
frankness, draws attention to ' the contrast between the
principle that foreign nations must not annex American
territory and the equally well-established principle that
the United States may annex what she pleases.' [13]   On
this latter principle the United States has consistently
acted from the beginning. There never was a more
startling assertion of ' the right to hand peoples about
from potentate to potentate as if they were property,'
which President Wilson rightly denounces, than the
Louisiana Purchase. Though the French First Consul
was the seller, the annexation of Louisiana, says Professor Bushnell Hart,[14] was practically an enormous
expansion of the United States at the expense of Spain.

Once started in this direction, two other provinces seemed
desirable. West Florida was annexed by military force in
several instalments from 1810 to 1814. East Florida was
ceded by the treaty of 1819. . . . The Administration felt
strong enough to refuse the boundaries claimed by Spain in
West Florida and Texas, and to make the most of the so-called
purchase of East Florida from an unwilling vendor.

It was, however, with the inauguration of James
K. Polk as President, on March 4, 1845, that the Monroe
Doctrine became in the minds of Americans definitely
a doctrine of conquest. To quote Professor Hart again :

Instead of the peaceful doctrine that America ought to
remain as it was, the United States now began systematically
to re-arrange the map of North America at the expense of
her neighbours, and to maintain with all her might that there
was a mysterious thing called the Monroe Doctrine which
prevented any one from interfering with the Latin Americans
—except ourselves.' [15]

[13] Bushnell Hart, *The Monroe Doctrine*, p. 368.
[14] *Ibid.* p. 15.   [15] *Ibid.* p. 112.

Texas was annexed in 1845 ; war with Mexico followed in 1846, and ended in 1848 with the annexation of New Mexico and California. In 1846 the Oregon dispute with Great Britain was compromised and the vast territory of the North-West added to the United States. It is no wonder that in the years to come ' the spirit of the country was honestly for expansion, and against recognizing too many rights of weaker neighbours.'

In all this process there was no pretence of consulting the populations concerned ; and when in 1844 John Quincy Adams urged in Congress that ' there was no power to transfer the inhabitants of one country to the sovereignty of another without their consent,' he was overruled on the ground of the universal practice of nations, it being pointed out that Adams himself had not consulted the people of Florida when he annexed that territory. The contrast between the theory and practice of American politics could hardly be better illustrated. Nor in the years before the war had there been any essential change in this respect. Professor Bushnell Hart has very clearly traced the stages by which the Monroe Doctrine developed into the ' American Doctrine,' which implied not only the complete isolation of the Americas but also the right of the United States to dominate them, a claim which received its most uncompromising expression in the declaration of Secretary Olney, during the Venezuela boundary dispute in 1895, that ' to-day the United States is practically sovereign on this continent, and its fiat is law upon the subjects to which it confines its interposition.'[16] The outcome was concisely summed up in 1913 by Professor Hiram Bingham, who drew attention to the alarm and resentment caused in the Latin American countries by the latest developments of United States policy :

In 1895 we declare that we are practically sovereign on the continent ; in 1898 we take a rich American island from a European Power, and in 1903 we go through the form of

[16] Hart, *op. cit.* p. 203.

preventing a South American republic from subduing a revolution in one of her distant provinces, and eventually take a strip of that province because we believe we owe it to the world to build the Panama Canal.'[17]

It is, indeed, in connection with this latter enterprise that the limitations of the pacificist idealism so widespread in America were most vividly illustrated, namely, by the reply made, early in 1913, by President Taft's Government to the demand put forward by the Government of Colombia that the whole question at issue between it and the United States should be submitted to arbitration. The American Minister at Bogotá, Mr. Du Bois, was instructed to inform the Colombian Minister for Foreign Affairs

that the Government of the United States could not submit to arbitration the questions relating to the separation of Panama, considered in its political aspect, though ready to accept arbitration in questions of a juridical nature arising out of it, because the people of the United States would never consent to submit to an arbitral judgment such transcendent acts of international policy, a thing which no country in the world had hitherto done.'[18]

President Wilson did not, and could not, reverse this decision after his inauguration in March of the same year ; and though the limitations here stated were done away with in the Wilson ' pacific settlement treaties,' for which Mr. W. J. Bryan as Secretary of State was largely responsible, these treaties are only valid for a term of years, and might therefore be dropped by any future American Government.

In making these comments on the true character of American foreign policy in the past I have no intention of condemning this policy, which has been on the whole

[17] ' The Monroe Doctrine an exploded Shibboleth,' *Atlantic Monthly*, June 1913, p. 724.
[18] *Boletin del Ministerio de Relaciones Esteriores*, Bogotá, 1913, tom. iv., num. 13 and 15, p. 981.

amply justified by its beneficent results for the United States and the world at large. But the true issue, as between the standpoints of idealism and realism in politics, has been obscured by the fact that the United States has obtained these results without developing great military power. Now this has been due in the past, not to her pacific spirit, but to the peculiarity of her geographical position ; and the sanction of force behind her policy has been no less real because it was potential rather than actual. ' The action of the United States in her quarrels with her neighbours,' says Professor Bushnell Hart, ' has usually been of writing-paper mixed with possible blood ' [19] ; and if writing-paper so often prevailed, this was because no other Power thought it worth while to accept a challenge thrown down by a nation with such vast and inestimable reserves of strength.

It is necessary to insist on these points because the claim is made, and very widely accepted without question, that democracies are by their very nature inclined to peace and averse from aggression ; and the inference is drawn that the League of Nations will be made finally effective for its purpose when its constitution is modelled on democratic lines by the creation of an elected ' Parliament of Man ' with an Executive responsible to it. It is urged that the fruitful cause of wars has been that diplomacy has worked in secret, and that this will cease when international discussions are conducted in the full light of publicity. But even if secret diplomacy be wholly an evil, which I am not prepared to admit, there is no conceivable method by which, even under a completely democratic system, the publicity of all negotiations could be assured. In all democratic legislatures more business is transacted behind the scenes than on the floor of the chambers, and secret diplomacy is very busy in the lobbies. Under the unwritten law of the British Constitution the proceedings of the regular meetings of the Cabinet have to be reported to the Sovereign. When

[19] *Op. cit.* p. 325.

Ministers do not wish to report to the Sovereign they hold a Cabinet *dinner*. In the same way it is impossible to prevent diplomatists, be they never so democratic, from arranging matters in quiet talks over a glass of champagne or a pot of beer. Indeed, it is notorious that the Labour leaders, who are loudest in their denunciations of secret diplomacy, use precisely the same methods, there being a tendency for all the more important business, even of the congresses, to be debated and decided by them *in camera.*[20] Nor is it possible to agree with the suggestion that the publicity given in the press to the deliberations of the international parliament would create and maintain a wholesome current of international opinion which would clear up misunderstandings before they became dangerous. For the popular press—which alone produces a wide effect—has long ceased to report the debates even of national parliaments, and would certainly only report the deliberations of the international assembly when these became exciting enough to provide 'good copy.' Questions of the most delicate character would thus be thrown open to public discussion, without the great public being provided with the data necessary for forming an opinion upon them. This would certainly not make for peace.

Nor is it true that the atmosphere of an assembly composed of elements differing widely in language, in interests and in ideas would be favourable to calm and impartial discussion. In the history of democratic assemblies there is nothing to justify any such assumption. Mirabeau, in the great speech in the National Assembly of May 29, 1790, in which he insisted on the reservation to the Crown of the right of declaring war, cited numerous instances in which popular assemblies had been hurried by the influence of oratory and group excitement into precipitating wars which diplomacy would have avoided ; and but for his premature death, he would have seen

[20] Robert Michels, *Political Parties : A Sociological Study of the Oligarchical Tendencies of Modern Democracy.*

his arguments admirably illustrated by the action of the Legislative Assembly in 1792. Mr. Willis Fletcher Johnson, in his 'America's Foreign Relations,' points out how the country was again and again saved from disastrous enterprises by the fact that the President and Secretary of State, in whom under the Constitution the effective control of foreign affairs is vested, refused to be carried away by gusts of popular passion, which were reflected in Congress, and even how on occasion they deliberately neglected to lay before the Foreign Relations Committee of the Senate documents calculated to inflame this passion.

The truth is that the creation of an organized international or supernational system on the democratic model depends on the development of a common sentiment and a common will among the peoples ; it is wholly inconsistent with the often exaggerated group-consciousness which we call nationalism.[21] It has, indeed, been argued that in the federation of the United States of America we have an outstanding example of how a series of rival and often mutually jealous State-groups may be combined in an organization for common purposes by the application of democratic principles. But there is no true analogy between the American Federation and the League of Nations conceived as an effective supernational government. The object of the American Federalists was not to create an international system, but to preserve a national consciousness already in existence, and to perfect a national organization of which the foundations had already been laid. They believed that the prosperity of the American people depended on their ' continuing firmly united,' and that ' an inheritance so proper and convenient for a band of

[21] Discussing the question of the creation of an international General Staff, Sir Frederick Pollock wrote : ' Obviously there are plenty of difficulties in this operation ; but it seems no less obvious that they are of a kind that can be overcome if there is a general will to overcome them ; and if there is not such a general will there cannot be any League at all.' ' The American Plan for Enforcing Peace,' *Atlantic Monthly*, May 1917.

brethren, united to each other by the strongest ties, should never be split into a number of unsocial, jealous, and alien sovereignties.' [22]   They have been justified in their belief ; for the strength of the United States is rooted in the American consciousness that the Congress no longer represents a plurality, but a unity. This consciousness is so strong that it contentedly ignores the rules of grammar. Officially the United States *is* a Nation.

The groups into which men form themselves are, in fact, only effective in so far as they grow out of a common need and are directed by a common will ; and this is as true of States as of Trade Unions, of federations of States as of States. Moreover, when a body politic, whether State or federation of States, is made up of many groups, it is essential to its stability and permanence that the interests of its constituent groups should be subordinated to those of the whole in all matters affecting the commonwealth.   There must, in brief, be a general will exercising in the last resort that absolute dominion which, as Sir William Temple pointed out long ago,[23] is of the very essence even of democratic government. Without this the body politic will simply dissolve into its elements —a truth made disquietingly clear by the developments of the Russian revolution. And if this be true of the State, it is equally true of federations of States ; and it is true also of the League of Nations. President Wilson's ' organized major force of mankind ' is either an empty phrase, or it implies the effective supremacy or sovereignty of a general will over the wills of all the national and other groups within the League.

This is a consummation which from the point of view of people with an ' international mind ' is devoutly to be wished. The *Nation*, which is in England perhaps the most distinguished representative of this mind, saw, or affected to see, the main obstacle to a world-federation

[22] *The Federalist*, No II.
[23] *Essay on the Original and Nature of Government*, 1672.

in ' the clamour of some special interests for preferential
treatment in Africa or Asia, or some misunderstanding
of a phrase, like Freedom of the Seas.'[24] But the obstacles
to any effectively organized international system, as
even Mr. Bertrand Russell has seen and admitted,[25] lie
very much deeper than any mere clamour of particular
economic interests of individual persons or groups of
persons within the nations. They lie in the fact of the
existence of the nations themselves as they have developed
during the last hundred years—that is to say, as intensely
self-conscious groups bound together not only by carefully
cultivated separate traditions, customs, and habits of
life, but by jealously guarded economic interests. We
may deplore this segregation ; but it exists, and though
the war may have done much in the way of regrouping
and of modifying the sentiments and relations of certain
nations towards each other in the direction of amity
and co-operation, it has still more certainly intensified
old antagonisms between the nations opposed to each
other. This was admitted during the war by Mr.
Bertrand Russell, who did not share the illusion of his
brother pacifists that a system of international government could be presented ready-made to the Peace Conference with any hope that it would be effective, even if
accepted. ' We have,' he said, ' still a very long road to
travel before we arrive at the establishment of an international authority ' ; and the very first step in this
long road is that people must rid themselves of their
' group morality '—that is to say, of that loyalty to their
own nation which for ' nine citizens out of ten ' carries
a higher obligation than any considerations of abstract
justice or the good of humanity. The cosmopolitan
ideal is thus conceived as the logical culmination of the
long process of development by which men formed themselves into groups for certain ends, and these groups

[24] War and Peace Supplement for May 1917.
[25] 'National   Independence   and   Internationalism,'   *Atlantic
Monthly*, May 1917.

are again grouped in larger sovereign aggregations until, with the final realization that the ties uniting human interests as a whole are far more numerous than those which divide them, one group is made supreme over all.

This ideal of the world as it ought to be, and perhaps might be but for ' the fault and corruption of the nature of every man,' must appeal to all people of good will. But it has very little to do with the League of Nations considered as an expedient of practical politics. The amount of mutual understanding which, together with the general will to maintain peace, which Mr. Russell predicates as necessary for his ' international authority ' would, in fact, make such an authority unnecessary. A purified diplomacy would suffice for the conduct of the friendly business between harmonious groups inspired by a sense of the community of their sentiments and interests. The immediate question is, rather, how to preserve peace in a world of narrow sympathies and conflicting interests, of slow or violent economic and social shrinkages and expansions, of racial, cultural, and religious antipathies—in short, in the world as it is and is likely yet to be. In such a world will the League of Nations be a guarantee of peace ? Will it indeed—to quote Mr. Asquith—mean ' the substitution for the reign of force, for the clash of competing ambition, and the groupings and alliances of a precarious equipoise, of a real European partnership ' ? To think so is to suppose that it is possible to establish an international system in which the harmony of the general will is more pronounced than it is even in national States ; for in these too it is force that in the last resort gives dominion ; in these too there is a clash of competing ambitions ; in these too there are groupings and alliances (of organized interests and parties) and an equipoise which, so long as there is liberty and movement, must always be precarious.

Nor, if we descend from the regions of abstract specu-lation to the real world of politics, is it by any means clear that the formation of a general union is the logical culmination of the processes that have led to the grouping of men in communities and junctions of communities. As Mr. Hammond has shown, the almost universal process in such groupings has been that of war and conquest. He gives, indeed, five examples of ' voluntary junctions of equal communities,' namely, in ancient Achaia, mediæval Switzerland, the Dutch Netherlands, North America, and Switzerland in 1848. But even of these he notes that ' in all cases before their junction they had been precluded by their position from conquering one another, i.e., either by geographical obstacles or, in the case of America and the Netherlands, by subjection to powerful foreign rulers who effectually prevented them from contending with one another.' [26]

Moreover, whatever may have been the origin of the cohesion of particular federal groups, so far as this has been due to a common will it has been the result, above all, of a sense of particular interests as opposed to those of other groups, and of pressure exercised by these other groups. The league of the Swiss cantons was originally formed against the oppressions and aggressions of German feudal neighbours ; it was enlarged and cemented by successful resistance to the imperial ambitions of the House of Austria. Defence against Spain and later against France, was a sufficient bond of union in the loosely-knit confederation of the United Netherlands. The thirteen original States of the American Union began by quarrelling among themselves to the point of war ; and if, fourteen years after the Declaration of Independence, the Federal Constitution of the United States was at last ratified by all of them, this was because ' the interest of every State demanded that the central government should be strong enough to ensure the federated States against foreign enemies.' [27] Instances might be multiplied ; but those cited will suffice to show

[26] B. E. Hammond, *Bodies Politic and their Governments*, p. 469.
[27] Hammond, *op. cit.* p. 487. Also *The Federalist*, Nos. I and II.

that bodies politic, whether States or confederations of States, whatever the original sympathies which drew them together, are essentially combinations for the assertion and defence of their common interests against other competing groups outside.

There are examples enough in history to show that when this competition ceases to be keenly felt the group tends to lose its sense of community, freer play being given to the centrifugal forces of the conflicting interests within it. This is conspicuously true, of course, of that loosest of all forms of political group—the international alliance ; and it is true in varying degrees of all the others. In the days when Great Britain held the undisputed mastery of the seas, and something like a monopoly of the world's trade, the British Empire was all but allowed to fall to pieces ; it needed the challenge of Germany to draw it together in a strong group-consciousness. So long as the threat of French domination on the North American Continent continued, the English colonies on the Atlantic sea-board were well content to form part of the British Empire ; it was not until after the conquest of Canada that they became conscious of their separate rights and interests as against the mother country and, striking for independence, threw off her protecting aegis. The splendid isolation of the United States beyond the ocean brought its dangers in turn ; in the absence of any external pressure the interests of the States and groups of States within the Union drew apart, until the great federation was all but shattered by the war between the North and South. In short, the tendency of federations, or of other more or less loosely compacted political groups, has been to break up in the absence of any need for common defence against external enemies. It seems to me idle to suppose that the world-league, of which the very *raison d'être* is to remove the apprehension of war, will prove more stable.

Those federations which have survived have done so because, as in the case of the United States, they have developed a common sentiment far stronger than any which may divide their constituent States, a sentiment based on the consciousness of interests, traditions and ideals distinguishing them from other political groups. They have survived, in short, because they have become nations. Seeing the world as it is, it is difficult to believe that any such powerful cement of sentiment could be found to bind together even the civilized peoples, not to mention the semi-civilized and the uncivilized. In the absence of such a sentiment the stability of the League of Nations must depend on a system of checks and balances, and this in the long run is unlikely to prove any more effective in keeping the peace than were the expedients of the old diplomacy.

The advocates of a supernational system base their hopes on the development as between nations of that almost instinctive respect for law which characterizes the citizens of civilized national States. But in doing so they seem to me to exaggerate the effect even of national sentiment on the respect for law within the bounds of the nation itself. It is of course true that people are more ready to obey laws which they regard as in a peculiar sense their own than those imposed by an alien authority; it is true also that in a well-ordered community the law-abiding habit becomes instinctive, as an almost unconscious submission of the individual to the general will; and it is not impossible that, with the growing sense of the interdependence of nations, the development of a general will may produce a similar habit of submission to international law—as, indeed, has to a large extent already been the case. But it is too much to say that this will guarantee peace and unselfish co-operation to such an extent as to make it unnecessary for nations to reserve to themselves in the last resort the right to safeguard their own interests— that is to say, to preserve their sovereignty. All history proves that there are limits to the willingness of the citizen to submit to the national law imposed by the community,

and these limits may be defined by precisely those terms,
' vital interests ' and ' honour,' applied to the questions
hitherto for the most part excluded from the cases which
States have declared themselves willing to submit to
arbitration. The question of ' honour ' in the case of
individual persons in their relation to the State is comparatively unimportant, though not wholly so, as the
trouble caused by ' conscientious objectors ' in all ages
proves. But the question of the vital interests of individual persons, or of groups of persons, has been and
is a frequent cause of trouble inside States, and has led
to innumerable civil wars. For an illustration we need
not look beyond the United Kingdom at the present
time. The Protestants of North-East Ulster proved
themselves during the war intensely loyal to Great
Britain and the Empire ; but they would undoubtedly
resist with all their power any attempt to sacrifice what
they believe to be their vital interests by subjecting them
to the domination of the less advanced Catholic majority
of the rest of Ireland.

If it be argued that such troubles would be avoided
were the democratic principle of ' self-determination '
everywhere applied, the answer is that experience does
not endorse this. The Latin American republics, for
instance, have unexceptionable democratic constitutions ;
save in a very few instances, their boundaries are demarcated in accordance with national sentiment ; yet
in most of them civil war is endemic. The erection of
the principle of self-determination into a political dogma
to be enforced by the power of the world-league would,
indeed, increase the risk of trouble ; for under this
system national States will tend to close their frontiers
against the immigration of people of alien race,[28] and,
in the absence of the safety-valves hitherto provided by

[28] It cannot be denied, for instance, that from the German point
of view the misgivings excited for years before the war by the mass-
immigration of Slavs all along the eastern marches of the Empire have
been amply justified.

the comparatively free movement of populations, the pressure of the natural increase within the artificial boundaries of national States will gradually accumulate explosive forces exceedingly dangerous to the world's peace.

That the lurid memories of the Great War will for a long time to come incline the majority of men to peace is certain. It is very generally admitted that, in order to make this peace secure, a League of Nations in some form is a necessity. The only difference of opinion, but it is a fundamental one, is as to the nature of this League. Everyone desires the growth of a friendlier spirit and a freer intercourse between nations, but opinions differ as to the means by which these desirable ends are to be attained. I cannot believe that they will be attained by an attempt to unite the nations, differing as they do in interests, in temperament, and in ideas, by artificial bands. Generally speaking, the looser the legal ties which bind people together the less likely they are to quarrel ; for what human nature, individually and collectively, most resents is the sense of constraint. The British Empire has remained united in sentiment precisely because of its loose organization, and it may be doubted whether it would long survive any serious effort to give it the character of an organized State. The same is in a far greater degree true of the Society of Nations. Its only trustworthy foundation would be a vivid sense of community of interests, and the only final proof of the existence of such a sense would be, in my opinion, the throwing down of the economic barriers between its constituent groups. The mere delimitation of boundaries on national lines will not effect the desired end ; for every frontier line drawn is in essence a declaration of war and nothing in this will be altered by the fact that the last word as to the to be or not to be of war will be spoken in the councils of the League, in which interest and opinion on the questions at issue may be violently divided. In short, I agree with the Belgian

writer M. Henri Lambert in holding that without universal
Free Trade ' the Grand Supernational Council will have
more need of peace than peace will have of the Grand
Supernational Council.'

' Le temps viendra sans doute,' said Mirabeau in the
speech already cited, ' où nous n'aurons que des amis
et point d'alliés, où la liberté de commerce sera universelle,
où l'Europe ne sera qu'une grande famille ; mais l'espér-
ance a aussi son fanatisme.' This seems to me to be
equally true to-day. The surrender by Great Britain
of her sovereignty—that is to say, of the power to determine herself what line it would be right, just and expedient
to follow in given circumstances—is to stake her whole
fortunes on a prospect which, as Castlereagh said a
hundred years ago, is at best one of speculation and
hope.

APPENDIX

THE ACT OF THE HOLY ALLIANCE

In the name of the Most Holy and Indivisible Trinity.

Their Majesties the Emperor of Austria, the King of Prussia, and the Emperor of Russia, having, in consequence of the great events which have marked the course of the three last years of Europe, and especially of the blessings which it has pleased Divine Providence to shower down upon those States which place their confidence and their hope in it alone, acquired the intimate conviction of the necessity of settling the steps to be observed by the Powers, in their reciprocal relations, upon the sublime truths which the holy religion of our Saviour teaches ;

They solemnly declare that the present Act has no other object than to publish, in the face of the whole world, their fixed resolution, both in the administration of their respective States, and in their political relations with every other Government, to take for their sole guide the precepts of that Holy Religion, namely, the precepts of Justice, Christian Charity and Peace, which, far from being applicable only to private concerns must have an immediate influence upon the counsels of Princes, and guide all their steps, as being the only means of consolidating human institutions and remedying their imperfections. In consequence, their Majesties have agreed on the following articles :—

ART. I. Conformably to the words of the Holy Scriptures which command all men to consider each other as brethren, the Three contracting Monarchs will remain united by the bonds of a true and indissoluble fraternity, and, considering each other as fellow-countrymen, they will, on all occasions and in all places, lend each other aid and assistance; and, regarding themselves towards their subjects and armies as fathers of families, they will lead them, in the same spirit of fraternity with which they are animated, to protect Religion, Peace, and Justice.

ART. II. In consequence, the sole principle of force, whether between the said Governments or between their subjects, shall be that of doing each other reciprocal service, and of testifying by unalterable goodwill the mutual affection with which they ought to be animated, to consider themselves all as members of one and the same Christian nation; the three allied Princes, looking on themselves as merely delegated by Providence to govern three branches of the One family, namely, Austria, Prussia, and Russia, thus confessing that the Christian world, of which they and their people form a part, has in reality no other Sovereign than Him to whom alone power really belongs, because in Him alone are found all the treasures of love, science and infinite wisdom, that is to say, God, our Divine Saviour, the Word of the Most High, the Word of Life. Their Majesties consequently recommend to their people, with the most tender solicitude, as the sole means of enjoying that Peace which arises from a good conscience, and which alone is durable, to strengthen themselves every day more and more in the principles and exercise of the duties which the Divine Saviour has taught to mankind.

ART. III All the Powers who shall choose solemnly to avow the sacred principles which have dictated the present Act, and shall acknowledge how important it is for the happiness of nations, too long agitated, that these truths should henceforth exercise over the destinies of mankind all the influence which belongs to them, will be received with equal ardour and affection into this Holy Alliance.

INDEX

ACHAIAN League, 299

Adams, John Quincy, 224, 271, 291

Aix-la-Chapelle, Conference of, 158 *seq.* ; Declaration of, 176, 178 (text) ; and the Spanish Colonies, 241 *seq.*

Alexander I, Emperor of Russia, character of—33, 189 ; education, 49 *seq.* ; religious influences, 54, 55 *seq.* ; and Baroness Krüdener, 124 *seq.* ; and La Harpe, 34, 49 *seq.* ; Castlereagh on, 128, 162, 164 ; Caulaincourt on, 67 ; Czartoryski on, 46, 52, 57, 188 ; Bishop Eylert on, 47 ; Robert Gordon on, 188 ; Baron Vincent on, 10 ; effect of burning of Moscow, 56 ; militarism, 53 ; and murder of Paul I, 53 ; effect of Semyonovsky mutiny, 206, 207

and Castlereagh, 134 ('grouped'), 138, 243

and Constitutional Government, 35 *seq.*, 52 (Russia), 62, 186 (Poland), 113, 132 (France), 142 and *note* 27, 153 (Germany), 166 ; 194 (Carlsbad Decrees) ; 196

and France, 47, 51 (Revolution), 83 (Jacobinism), 72 (Bernadotte), 82, 123 *seq.* (Paris, 1815) ; 159, 190 (French Liberalism) ; 161, 163, 175 (at Aix), 250 (intervention in Spain), 256 *seq.* (at Verona)

Alexander I, and Germany, 60 ; 186, 194 (Carlsbad Decrees)

and the Grand Alliance, 68 *seq.* (Langres, 1814) ; 145 (draft of treaty of 20 Nov. 1815) ; 164 *seq.* (Aix-la-Chapelle, 1818) ; 216 (Troppau) ; 215 (Laibach) ; 252 *seq.* (Verona)

and the Holy Alliance, 24 (Henry IV's Grand Design), 34 (Projet of St. Pierre), 141 (proclamation), 143, 165, 195, 199 *seq.* (universal union) ; 215 (at Laibach), 216 (Troppau Protocol)

and Metternich, 70, 209, 192, 206 (Troppau), 232, 257

and Napoleon, 34 (murder of Enghien), 46 (Tilsit), 47 (Moscow), 48, 69 (Langres), 70, 76

and Nationality, 89, 112

and the Neapolitan Revolution, 198 *seq.*

and Pitt, 35 *seq.*

and Poland, 51, 111 (Kosciuszko), 61 (Czartoryski), 68 ; 103, 104 *seq.*, 110 (Vienna Congress), 186 (Constitution)

and Russia, 52 (reform projects) ; 53 *note* (on state of Russia)

and Spain, 195, 250, 251 (European intervention), 255 (Verona) ; 238 *seq.*, 241, 267, 273, 274 (Spanish colonies)

on Treaties, 106

Alexander I, and Turkey, 219 seq., 221 seq. (Greek insurrection), 223, 232

and the United States, 229 (Behring Sea), 267 (*ukaz* of 1821), 268 seq. (Holy Alliance)

plot to kidnap, 190

Alliance, the, 74 (Treaty of Chaumont), 84 (nature and scope of), 87 seq. (question of constitution), 115 (as fixed at Vienna), 136 (and French Monarchy), 145 (discussed at Paris, 1815), 147 (Treaty of 20 Nov., 1815), 152 (principles) ; 159 seq. (question of admission of France) ; 161 seq. (discussed at Aix-la-Chapelle) ; 164 (Russian memorandum on) ; 176, 177 (suggest league of guarantee); 177 (Quadruple Alliance, 1818) ; 199 seq. (Russian memorandum, 1820) ; 203, 204(Castlereagh's comments); 208 seq. (Troppau Protocol) ; 217 (first rifts) ; 219 seq. (Eastern Question) ; 224 (and the United States) ; 229 (attitude of England at Verona defined) ; 236 (and the Spanish Colonies) ; 254 seq. (and the Spanish Question) ; 259 (breach at Verona), 274 (breach after 1830) ; Canning on, 227, 260, 263 ; Castlereagh on, 172, 227, 243; Gentz on, 120

Alsace Lorraine, 132

Amphictyonic Council, 23, 24

Angoulême, Duc d', 265

'Anti-Machiavel,' The, 8

Arbitration, difficulty of impartial, 285 note 7 ; United States and, 292

Argentina, 246, 247

Asquith, Mr., 298

Austria,and the Eastern Question, 221, 225 ; and France, 69, 109, 110, 130 (Russian influence), 135 ; and Great Britain,256 seq. (Verona); and Germany,153, 193 ; and Italy, 198 (treaty with Naples), 201 (revolution in Naples) ; general policy, 71, 72 ; and Poland, 108 and *note* 38 ; and Prussia, 99, 103, 107, 136 ; and Russia, 69, 71, 72, 130 (French entente), 256 (Spanish intervention). [*See also under* Metternich]

Ayacucho, Battle of, 234

Bacon, on Machiavelli, 5

Baden, succession question in, 180

Balance of Power, 16, 21, 74, 83, 101, 301

Barbary Pirates, 179, 181

Barclay, Sir Thomas, on The Hague Conferences, 13

Barrier Fortresses, 130, 136

Bathurst, Henry Bathurst, 3rd Earl, 76, 167, 231

Bavaria, and Constitutional Government, 153 ; and Baden succession, 180 ; and Mainz, 103, 107 ; and occupation of France, 135

Beaufort, M. de, and the Holy Alliance, 12

Behring Sea, Russian claims, 229, 267 and *note* 92

Bennigsen, Field-Marshal Count Levin August von, 102

Bernadotte, Jean Baptiste (Charles XIV of Sweden) Alexander I. and, 56 ; 72, 190 *note* 9

Bernstorff, Christian Günther, Count, 163, 213, 253

Berri, Duc de, murder of, 194, 249

Bethmann-Hollweg, German Chancellor, 3

Bielfeld, Baron de, on the Reason of State, 4

Bingham, Hiram, on Monroe Doctrine, 291

Blacas, M. de, 214

Blücher, Gebhard Leberecht von, Prussian Field-Marshal, 70

Bolivar, 234, 245 *note* 72 (Legion).

Bourgeois, Léon, on The Hague Conventions, 13

British Empire, 300; and constitution of the League of Nations, 303

Bryan, William Jennings, 292

Bucharest, Treaty of, 151, 219

Buenos Aires, 233, 247

Burghersh, Lord, 253

Burke, Edmund, 41

Burns, Delisle, 288

CALIFORNIA, 291

Canada, effect of conquest of, 300

Canning, George, and Alexander I, 264; and the Alliance, 227, 260, 262 *seq.*, 269 (Anglo-American understanding); and France, 270 (Spanish colonies); and George IV, 262, 263; and Metternich, 227, 259, 262; and the Monroe Doctrine, 272, 273; and the Spanish colonies, 248 *seq.*, 266 *seq.* (French occupation of Spain), 269, 270

Capo d'Istria (Capodistrias), Count Giovanni Antonio (Joannes), early career, 62; and Alexander I., 63, 194, 224 *note* 52, 232; and the Alliance, 162, 169, 200 and *note* 31, 213; and the Carlsbad Decrees, 186, 193; French policy, 191 (Lebzeltern's comments); and the Greek revolt, 220, 221, 224; in Italy, 187; at Laibach, 214, 215; as reactionary, 208; and Switzerland, 62

Caraman, Marquis de, 205, 253

Carbonari, 188

Carlsbad Decrees, 186, 193, 194

Castlereagh, Robert Stewart, Viscount (2nd Marquess of Londonderry), at Allied headquarters, 1813, 65 *seq.*; and Treaty of Chaumont, 73 *seq.*; on the Châtillon negotiations, 76; at Congress of Vienna, 95 *seq.*; and secret Treaty of 3 January, 1815, 109, 110; and continental policy, 135; and the Treaty of Alliance (20 November, 1815), 147 *seq.*; at Aix-la-Chapelle, 158 *seq.*; Instructions for Verona, 228; foreshadows Canning's policy, 231; death of, 226

Castlereagh, and Alexander I, 82, 83 (must be 'grouped'), 155; 104 *seq.* (at Vienna); 130, 134 (French policy); 162, 164 (at Aix-la-Chapelle), 169 *seq.*; 222 (Greek Question); 244 (Spanish colonies)

and the Alliance, 29 (system of guarantees), 70; 104 and *note* 32 (selfishness of the Powers); 143, 145 *seq.*, 155 *seq.*, 391 (proposed compromise, 1818), 167 (Russian project, Aix), 170 (international Russian police), 172 (on true bases of alliance), 173 (on the universal union), 175 (Holy Alliance); 176, 177 (general guarantee), 210 *seq.* (Troppau Protocol), 222, 225 (Holy Alliance and Eastern Question); 287 (danger of 'double jurisdiction')

on Austria, 71

and the Balance of Power, 101

and the Carlsbad Decrees, 186, 193

and the Eastern Question, 222 *seq.*

and France, 90, 91, 107, 109 (at Vienna); 120 (after Waterloo); 129 (report on attitude of Powers); 130 *seq.* (question of dismemberment); 135 *seq.* (British policy towards France); 139 (resignation of

Talleyrand and Fouché) ; 174
(admission to Alliance) ; 190
(French armaments)

Castlereagh, on Intervention, 173,
191, 202 (Naples), 211 seq.
(Troppau Protocol),243(Latin
America)
and Germany, 103 (Confederation) ; 135, 138 (German
Powers).
and Metternich, 108, 154, 203
(Intervention) ; 222, 224, 225
(Hanover meeting).
and Naples, 202
and Poland, 98, 104 seq.
and Prussia, 103, 107, 122, 132
on Russian danger (1814), 102
and the Saxon Question, 98
and Spain and her colonies, 236
seq., 241 (at Aix), 247
and the sanctity of treaties, 106
and the United States, 224, 225
Sorel on, 66

Catherine II, Empress of Russia,49

Catholic Reaction, 54

Caulaincourt, Armand A. L.,
Marquis de (Duke of Vicenza),
67, 69

Charles III, King of Spain, 234

Chateaubriand, Vicomte de,
54, 253 seq. (at Verona) ; 262,
267 (perils of the New World);
265 ; 273, 274

Châtillon, Conferences of, 70, 73
seq.

Chaumont, Treaty of, 74 seq. ; and
1st Treaty of Paris, 90 ; renewed at Vienna, 115; and
Treaty of 20 November,
1815, 145 seq. ; 160 (Metternich on) ; 173 (Castlereagh
on) ; 175

Chile, 247

Clancarty, Earl of, 100, 115

Clanwilliam, Earl of, 253

Clay, Henry, 224

Cobenzl, Count Ludwig von, 4

Cochrane, Lord (Earl of Dundonald), 245

Colombia, 247 (independence) ;

and the United States, 292
(Panama)

'Confederation of Europe,' and
German Confederation, 209,
212

Confederation of the Rhine, 60

Consalvi, Cardinal, 113

Constantine Pavlovich, Grand
Duke, 53, 102, 187 and note 3

Constitutional Government, Alexander I and, 35 seq., 52, 62,
113, 132, 142 and note 27,
153, 166, 186, 194, 196 ; the
Holy Alliance and, 142 ;
Vienna treaties and, 113 ; in
America, 234

Cromwell, Thomas, 5

Crucé, Éméric, 24

Cuba, 246, 291

Czartoryski, Prince Adam, and
Alexander I, 35, 46,111, 187 ;
on Alexander's character, 52
57, 189 ; on Austrian perfidy,
72 ; on La Harpe, 49

Decazes, Duc, 156 ; on Pozzo di
Borgo, 189 ; Alexander I on,
194 note 23 ; Lebzeltern on,
190

Democracy, and the League of
Nations, 293

Diplomacy, effect of a permanent,
20 ; 'secret,' 293

Dominions, as independent members of the League, 286

Du Bois, Mr., 292

Eastern Question, The, 219 seq.

East Florida, 239, 290

Elizabeth Feodorovna, consort of
Alexander I. of Russia, 124,
282

Empeytaz, H. L., 127

Enghien, Duc d', murder of, 34

Federations, National, and the
League of Nations, 295 seq. ;
and sovereignty, 296 ; origins
and essential conditions of,
299

Ferdinand IV, King of the Two
Sicilies, 214 seq.
Ferdinand VII, King of Spain, 152,
194, 234, 241, 246, 265, 273
Finland, Annexation of, 46
Florida Treaty, 247
Foreign Enlistment Act, 245
Fouché, 121, 122, 139
France, Alexander I and, 36 (1804),
69 (Langres),72,82 seq.,130 seq.
(1815), 190 (Liberal reaction) ;
and the Alliance, 88 seq. (1814),
159 seq. (Aix-la-Chapelle) ;
Austria and, 72, 160 ; and the
German States, 89, 90 and note
24 ; Castlereagh and, 107, 120 ;
Wellington and, 120 ; question
of fate of (1813), 64 ; Treaty of
Chaumont and, 74 seq; First
Treaty of Paris, 86 ; and the
Congress of Vienna, 95 seq.;
question of dismemberment
of, 129 seq.; Second Treaty of
Paris, 140 ; reaction in, 156 ;
Allied occupation of, 135, 137,
140, 156 seq. (evacuation) ;
Committee of Ambassadors
in, 129, 185 (suspended) ; and
Spain, 248 seq., 254 seq.
(Verona) ; 265 (invasion) ;
and Latin America, .235,
241 seq. (Aix-la-Chapelle),244,
267, 270 (Canning's atti-
tude) ; 273 and note 100
Francis I, Emperor of Austria,
120, 158, 208, 253 .
Frankfort, Conference of, 185 ;
Declaration of, 77
Frederick II, King of Prussia, 4,
6, 8
Frederick William III, King of
Prussia, 59, 108, 123, 158, 253
Frederick William (IV.), Crown
Prince of Prussia, 208
Freedom of the Seas, Great
Britain and, 84, 85 and note 6
(Gentz) ; 297
Free Trade, as a condition of
peace, 30 (Voltaire), 303, 304
(Mirabeau).

French Revolution, and the ideal
of universal peace, 31

GAGERN, Baron, 98 note 25
Gentilis, Albericus, on Machiavelli, 5
Gentz, Friedrich von, on the
European Confederacy, 21 ;
on Freedom of the Seas, 85
note 6 ; on Talleyrand, 88 ;
on the Congress of Vienna, 93
seq., 101, 114 ; on Napoleon's
outlawry, 119 ; on Great
Britain, 85 note 6, 120 ; on
Prussia, 120 ; at Verona, 253
George IV, King of Great Britain,
and the Holy Alliance, 143 ;
222 ; Canning and, 262, 263
Gerard, Bishop of Cambrai, 18
German Confederation, 102 (Hardenberg's views) ; 113 (Constitution) ; 153 (question of
Constitutions) ; as a warning,
171 ; and the Alliance, 177 ;
185 (Treaty of Frankfort) ;
186 (Carlsbad Decrees) ; dependence on ' Europe,' 193 ;
as model for a Confederation
of Europe, 209, 212 ; 287
Germany, religious reaction in, 54;
Constitution of, 75 (Chaumont), 113 (Vienna) ; France
and, 89 ; and the dismemberment of France, 132, 136 ;
Metternich and, 192 seq. ;
menace of Slav immigration
into, 302 note 28 ; the United
States and, 16 (Roosevelt's
view).
Golitsin, Prince Alexander Nikolaievich, 55
Golovkin, Count, 191, 200
Gordon, Sir Robert, on Alexander I, 188 ; on Metternich,
188, 190 note 9 (spy system),
193 (German Policy) ; on the
Troppau Protocol, 209 ; at
Laibach, 214
Gouvion St. Cry, Marshal, 190, 249

' Grand Design ' of Henry IV, 22 ; and Alexander I, 33

Great Britain, Alexander I and, 35 *seq.*

and the Alliance, 65 (1813), 84 (sacrifice of conquests) ; 144, 172 (Holy Alliance) ; 226 (system of guarantees), 227 *seq.* (Canning's policy)

and the Barrier Fortresses, 136

and the Carlsbad Decrees, 193

and the Eastern Question, 220, 221 (Turkey) ; 230 (Greek insurrection)

and France, 135 (Castlereagh's policy), 157 (evacuation), 160 (at Aix-la-Chapelle), 265 *seq.* (invasion of Spain)

and the Freedom of the Seas, 85

and Intervention, 196 (Spain), 202 (Naples), 209 *seq.* (Troppau Protocol), 258 (Verona).

and the League of Nations, 287

and Naples, 198, 202, 214

and the Netherlands, 65, 130

and Poland, 104

and Russia, 35 *seq.*, 155

and the Slave Trade, 85

and Spain, 196, 261 (Verona).

and the Spanish colonies, 235 *seq.*, 245 and *note* 72, 248 *seq.* (Verona), 269

and Treaties, 203

and the United States, 85 (peace negotiations), 271 *seq.* (Monroe Doctrine). [*See also* Castlereagh]

Greece, insurrection of, 220 *seq.*, 230 (Verona).

Gregorios, Orthodox Patriarch, murder of, 223

Grégoire, Abbé, 191

Grey of Falloden, Viscount, and the League of Nations, 12

Grotius, Hugo, 8, 24

Hague Conferences, 12, 13

Hammond, B. E., on Federations, 299

Hanover, Prussian designs on, 132 ; conference at, 222, 224, 225

Hardenberg, Prince, and the German Confederation, 102 ; and Mainz, 107 ; and Metternich, 108 ; and the Saxon Question, 110 ; and the Alliance, 163

Hart, Bushnell, on the Monroe Doctrine, 290, 291; on American foreign policy, 293

Henry IV, King of France, 22

Hesse, William I, Elector of, 152, 180

Hetairia Philike, 220

Holy Alliance, The Act of the, 305 (text) ; proclamation of, 141 ; character of, 142 ; and Instructions to Novosiltsov, 35 *seq.* ; Abbé de Pradt and, 41 ; Saint - Simon on, 32 ; Sorel on, 10 ; Castlereagh and, 172, 210 (Troppau Protocol), 225 (Eastern Question) ; George IV and, 262 ; and the Greek Question, 221, 222 ; as reactionary force, 207 ; Metternich and, 160, 215, 216 (Laibach), 225 (Eastern Question) ; and the United States, 268, 272 ; and the Peace Rescript of Nicholas II, 12 ; after 1830, 274 ; comparison of League of Nations with, 280 *seq.*

Holy Roman Empire, as an ideal, 19 ; and the ' Grand Design,' 22 ; Abbé de St. Pierre on, 25, 26 ; Leibnitz on, 28 ; restoration demanded at Vienna, 98 *note* 25 ; Protest of Roman Church against abolition of, 27, 113

Holstein, Russia and, 102

Humboldt, Baron Alexander von, 253

Humboldt, Baron Wilhelm von, 133

INDIA, Gentz on British rule in, 85

Inquisition, the, 152

International Court, difficulty of constituting, 285 and *note* 7

Internationalism in 1815 and 1919, 14

International Law, in eighteenth century, 10 ; Abbé St. Pierre on, 25 ; Pitt and, 40 ; and nationalism, 112 ; moral sanction of, 301

International Parliament, 293 *seq.*

International Rivers, 86

Intervention, Principle of, Alexander I and, 195 (Spain), 216 ; debates on (1815), 145 ; Canning on, 259 ; Castlereagh and, 146, 173 (limits defined), 191, 193 (Carlsbad Decrees), 202, 208 *seq.* (Troppau Protocol), 236 (Spanish Colonies), 243 ; Metternich and,195, 202, 209; at Verona, 254 *seq.* ; United States and, 272 and *note* 98 ; the inevitable outcome of an international league, 280, 281 ; the Covenant of the League and, 286 ; President Wilson and, 281 (Mexico), 286 and *note* 8 (Ireland), 289

Ireland, President Wilson and intervention in, 286 and *note* 8 ; attitude of Ulster, 302

Italy, 75 (Treaty of Chaumont) ; 186 (Treaty of Frankfort) ; Russian propaganda in, 187 *seq.* ; Revolution in Naples, 197 ; Conference of Laibach, 213 ; Conference of Verona, 228

JESUITS, 152

Jews, 180

Johnson, Willis Fletcher, on the warlike temper of Congress, 295

Jung-Stilling, Heinrich, 55, 124

Junin, Battle of, 234

KANT, Immanuel, 13, 31

Kaunitz, Count, Circular of 1791, 41

Knox, Senator, on the League of Nations and MonroeDoctrine, 288 *note* 11

Kosciuszko, Tadeusz, 51, 111

Koshelev, Alexander Ivanovich, 55

Kotzebue, August von, 189, 192

Krüdener, Barbara Juliana, Baroness von,55; and Alexander I, 124 *seq.*; Castlereagh on, 127 ; and the Holy Alliance, 141

Kutusov (Golyenitsev-Kutuzov-Smolyenski), Prince Mikhail Ilarionovich, Field-Marshal, 59, 60 *note* 19

LABOUR organizations and ' secret diplomacy,' 274

La Ferronnays, Comte de, 205, 253

La Harpe, Frédéric César de, and Alexander I, 34, 49 *seq.* ; at Langres, 69 ; in Italy, 187 ; Robert Gordon on, 188, 189

Laibach, Conference of, 213 *seq.*

Lambert, M. Henri, 304

Langres, Conferences at, 68 *seq.*

Latin America, and the Monroe Doctrine, 291 *seq.*; civil wars in 302. [*See also* Spanish Colonies]

Law, limits of respect for, 301

League of Nations, The, covenant of, 283 *seq.* ; character of, 285 ; and the Balance of Power, 301 ; conditions of success of, 303 ; question of democratic constitution of, 293 ; and national federations, 295 *seq.* ; and intervention, 280, 281 ; Mr. Asquith on, 298; Mr. Bertrand Russell on, 297, 298 ; President Wilson on, 288, 296

Lebzeltern, Baron, on Louis XVIII, 190 ; on Alexander I and Turkey, 223 *note* 50

Legislative Assembly, French, warlike temper of, 295

Legitimacy, Principle of, 88, 89; Talleyrand and, 97; Holy Alliance and, 281; President Wilson's conception of, 281

Leibnitz, and St. Pierre's *Projet*, 28; and the Holy Roman Empire, 28; and the system of guarantees, 29

Liége, Prussian designs on, 132

Lieven, Count (afterwards Prince), 253

Liverpool, Earl of, and the dismemberment of France, 130, 133

Lodge, Senator, x (Lodge Resolution); on the Monroe Doctrine, 289

Loewenhielm, Baron, on Vienna Congress, 108

Londonderry, 2nd Marquess of. [See Castlereagh, Viscount]

Londonderry, 3rd Marquess of. [See Stewart, Lord]

Longwy, defence of, 122

Louis XIV, and the Reason of State, 6; 'family compact,' 249

Louis XVIII, King of France, 81 (first restoration); 120 *seq.* (second restoration); protests against dismemberment, 138; and the reactionaries, 156; and the execution of Ney, 156 *note* 5; and the 'family compact,' 249; Alexander I and, 83; Lebzeltern on, 190

Louis, Baron, 190

Louise, Queen of Prussia, 124

Louisiana Purchase, 234, 290

Lützow, Count, 224

Luxemburg, 132 (Prussian designs), 137, 139, 140

Machiavelli, influence of, 5

Mahmud II, Sultan of Turkey, 220

Mainz (Mayence), 103, 107

Malta, 86

Marie Louise (Ex-Empress of the French), Duchess of Parma, 253

Maritime Code, excluded from the scope of the Alliance, 85

Mediatized Princes, 89, 180

Metternich, Prince, at Langres, 68 *seq.*; at Vienna, 100 *seq.*; at Aix-la-Chapelle, 158 *seq.*; at Troppau, 205 *seq.*; at Laibach, 215 *seq.*; at Verona, 253 *seq.*

and Alexander I, 70, 72, 187, 188, 194, 199, 206 (Troppau meeting), 209, 224, 232 (Alexander's principal adviser), 257 (at Verona)

and the Alliance, 159 (at Aix-la-Chapelle); on the Holy Alliance, 10, 166, 208 (at Troppau), 215, 216 (Laibach); 209 (Troppau Protocol)

and Canning, 227

and Castlereagh, 222, 224, 225 (Hanover meeting); 239 (American policy)

on the Treaty of Chaumont, 73

and the Eastern Question, 221 (Greek revolt), 225 (Austria and Turkey)

and France, 133 (1815); 160 161 (admission to Alliance, 1818); 190, 191 (Liberal reaction)

and Germany, 186 (Carlsbad Decrees), 192 *seq.* (revolutionary movements), 193 (German Confederation)

and Great Britain, 155 (suggests separate alliance), 195 (change of attitude), 256 *seq.* (at Verona)

and Intervention, 191, 192 (France), 196 (Spain); on the principle of, 202 *seq.*, 258

and Nationality, 261

and Naples, 197 *seq.*, 201

and Poland, 108 and *note* 38

Metternich, Prince, and Prussia, 108
  and Russia, 189 *note* 5, 191 (policy in France), 195, 224
  and the Saxon Question, 109
  and Spain, 196 (opposes intervention), 256 *seq*. (at Verona); 239, 273 (Spanish colonies)
  Castlereagh on, 71 ; Sir Robert Gordon on, 188
Mexico, Independence of, 247 ; the United States and, x, 291 ; President Wilson and, 281
Michels, Robert, 294 *note* 20
Mirabeau, on democracy and war, 294 ; on a European Confederation, 304
Moltke, on Russia, 101
Monaco, 180
Monroe, James, President of the United States, 224 ; and the Latin American Republics, 247 ; and Canning's overtures, 271 ; and the European Alliance, 271 ; message to Congress of December 2, 1823 (Monroe Doctrine), 272
Monroe Doctrine, The, Original principles of, 272 ; developments of, 290 *seq*. ; and the 'Lodge Resolution,' x ; and Mexico, 281 ; the Latin American States and, x, 291 *seq*. ; President Wilson and, 289 ; and the Covenant of the League of Nations, 288 ; Professor Hiram Bingham on, 291 ; Professor Bushnell Hart on, 290 ; Senator Lodge on, 289
Montesquieu, on British statesmanship, 4
Montevideo, Portuguese occupation of, 237
Montmorency, Vicomte Mathieu de, 250, 253 *seq*.
Moscow, burning of, 47
Murat, Joachim (King of Naples), 64, 82

Muraviev, Mikhail Nikolaievich, 49
Mysticism, 55

NAPLES, Revolution in, 197 ; the Alliance and, 198, 214 (Laibach)
Napoleon I, Emperor of the French, and Alexander I, 34, 46 (Tilsit), 48, 70 ; as Antichrist, 56 ; and the Confederation of Europe, 24 ; victories in 1814, 70 ; and the Conferences of Châtillon, 73 ; abdicates, 81 ; returns from Elba, 115 ; outlawed, 119 ; 112 ; appeal at Aix for release of, 180 ; plot to restore, 190 ; and Louisiana, 290
'Nation, The,' 296
Nationality, as a force making for war, 7, 15, 16 ; ignored by St. Pierre, 27 ; Pitt and, 39 ; Alexander I and, 46, 60, 63, 89, 112 ; Canning and, 260, 261 ; Mr. Bertrand Russell on, 297 ; President Wilson and, 289 ; and the League of Nations, 297
Neipperg, Count, 253
Nesselrode, Count, Russian Chancellor, 162, 262
Netherlands, The, 75 (Treaty of Chaumont) ; 86 (First Peace of Paris) ; 186 (Treaty of Frankfort) ; and the German Confederation, 103 ; Great Britain and, 65, 107, 130 ; Prussia and, 132 ; and Luxemburg, 140 ; the old Federation of, 299
New Mexico, 291
Ney, Marshal, execution of, 156 and *note* 5
Nicaragua, United States and, x
Nicholas I, Emperor of Russia, 274, 275
Nicholas II and the Holy Alliance, 12

Novosiltsov, Nikolai Nikolaievich, 35 (Alexander's Instructions), 52

OLDENBURG, Duke of, 180
Olney, Secretary, Declaration of, 291 (Monroe Doctrine)
Oregon, 291

PANAMA Canal, and the Monroe Doctrine, x ; 292
Paris, Fall of, 81 ; First Peace of, 86 ; Second Peace of, 128 seq:, 140 ; Conference of (1919), 282, 283
Parliament and the Alliance, 161, 167, 169
Parnell, John Stewart, on Nationality, 7
Paul I, Emperor of Russia, 46, 48, 53 (murder) ; Alexander I on tyranny of, 52 ; influence on Alexander, 53
Peru, 247
Pietism, 55
Pillnitz, Declaration of, and the Holy Alliance, 41
Pitt, William, and Alexander I's general union, 38 seq. ; and a system of guarantees, 144 ; and International Law, 40 ; and Legitimacy, 39 ; and Nationality, 39 ; and Prussia, 107
Pius VII, Pope, 152
Poland, 22 (Gentz on the partitions) ; 75 (at Chaumont) ; Alexander I and, 51, 61, 68, 97, 103, 111, 186 ; Grand Duke Constantine and, 102, 107 ; Constitution of, 186 ; Castlereagh and, 103 seq. ; Metternich and, 108 and note 38 ; Talleyrand and, 97
Pole, Cardinal Reginald, 5
Polignac, Prince de, 270
Polk, James K., President of the United States, 290
Pollock, Sir Frederick, 280, 281 ; .

on the League of Nations, 295 note 21
Portugal, 87 ; 100 (Vienna) ; and Spain, 237
Pozzo di Borgo, General Count, Russian ambassador in Paris, 85 (Europe and America) ; on the Alliance (memorandum at Aix), 164 ; and British policy, 237 ; and France, 90, 123, 191 ; and Poland, 111 ; Decazes on, 189 ; Metternich and, 191 ; 253 ; 256
Press, influence of the, 294
Price, Dr. Richard, on the new league of peace (1789), 31
' Prince, The,' of Machiavelli, 5
Protosov, Alexander Yakovyevich, 49
Prussia, and the Alliance, 141, 166 (Holy Alliance) ; 176 (union of guarantee)
    and Austria, 108 (at Vienna) ; 136
    and France, 130, 135 (occupation), 137 (dismemberment), 139 (indemnities) ; Prussian outrages, 122 seq., 128, 129 and note 14
    and Luxemburg, 132
    and Naples, 198
    and the Netherlands, 103, 132
    and Russia, 107 seq. (Vienna) ; 132 seq. (dismemberment of France)
    and Saxony, 108 seq. (at Vienna) ; 102 (occupation)
    and South German States, 107
    and Spain, 250

RASUMOVSKY, Prince Andrei Kirillovich, Russian ambassador at Vienna, 100
Raynal, Abbé, on the United States, 235 note 57
Rayneval, M. de, 253
' Reason of State,' eighteenth-century theory of, 4 ; French Revolutionists and the, 6 ; 19

Republicanism, Alexander I and, 51, 63; Castlereagh and, 247; Kant on, 31, 32; Richelieu on, 242; in the New World, 234

Revolution, French, and perpetual peace, 31

Rhine, Confederation of the, 60

Rhine frontier, Prussia as guardian of, 107 (views of Pitt and Castlereagh); French aspirations towards, 107 and *note* 36, 134

Rhine, navigation of the, 86

Richelieu, Duc de, and proposed cessions by France (1815), 140; and the Allied occupation, 156; on the 'federal system' in Europe, 157 *note* 6; at Aix-la-Chapelle, 159, 175; and the Neapolitan Question, 201; 205 *note* 36; and the Spanish Colonies, 241; on the perils of the New World, 242; 244; 249 (resignation)

Riego Nuñez, Rafael del, revolt of, 194, 246

River Plate (Argentine), 247

Rohrbach, Dr. Paul, on national expansion, 7

Roosevelt, Theodore, on President Wilson's Fourteen Points, 15

Rousseau, on the *Projet* of the Abbé de St. Pierre, 24, 29; Alexander I and, 50

Ruffo, Cardinal, 198

Rumyantsev, Count Nikolai Petrovich, Russian Chancellor, 46

Rush, Richard, and Castlereagh, 241; and Canning, 269

Russell, The Hon. Bertrand, 297

Russia, under Paul I, 53 *note* 12; Alexander I and reform in, 52; suspected ambitions of, 101 *seq.* (Vienna), 171, 192, 196, 220 *seq.*

Russia, and America, 229 (Behring Sea); 238 and *note* 60; 267

and Austria, 69 *seq.* (1814), 109 (Vienna); 166 (Aix-la-Chapelle); 195; 223 *seq.* (Eastern Question)

and the Eastern Question, 219 *seq.*

and France, 130, 161 (rumoured alliance)

and Italy, 187 (Russian propaganda); 200 (Revolution in Naples)

and Poland, 104 *seq.*, 111

and Prussia, 108 *seq.* (Vienna)

and Spain, 195, 237; Spanish Colonies, 236 *seq.*

[*See also* Alexander I]

St. Pierre, Abbé de, 24 *seq.* (*Projet de paix*); influences Alexander I, 34

Saint-Simon, Comte de, on the Holy Alliance, 32

Sand, Karl, 192

San Gallo, Duke of, 215

San Martin, José de, 233

Sarrelouis, 137, 139 and *note* 23

Savoy, 186

Saxony, at Vienna, 98, 102, 103, 108, 109 *seq.*

Schwarzenberg, Karl Philipp, Prince, Austrian Field-Marshal, 70, 71

'Self-determination,' probable effects of principle of, 302

Semyonovski Regiment, mutiny of, 206 and *note* 38

Senate, Foreign Relations Committee of, 295

Sicily, Metternich on Constitution of, 198

Slave Trade, 85, 179, 180, 229

Soltikov, Prince Nikolai, 49

Sorel, Albert, on Alexander I, 10; on Castlereagh, 66; on results of conference of Châtillon, 77; on Treaty of

Chaumont, 75 ; on the ' war of nationalities,' 60

Sovereignty, and the Universal Union, 280 ; fundamental to bodies politic, 296, 301

Spain, 55 (Treaty of Chaumont) ; 86 (Treaty of Paris) ; 100 (Congress of Vienna); Riego's revolt (1820), 194 ; Alexander I and, 195 ; Metternich and, 196, 197 ; 241, 242 (Aix-la-Chapelle) ; Great Britain and, 245 seq. ; and Portugal, 237 ; question of intervention in, 249 seq., 254 seq. ; United States and, 234, 290

Spanish Colonies, 233 seq.; at Aix-la-Chapelle, 241, 242 ; Alexander I and, 267, 273 seq. ; 230 seq. (Castlereagh's Instructions) ; 266 seq. (1823) ; United States and, 269 seq.

State, rise of conception of the, 19 ; essential nature of the, 296, 300 ; exclusiveness of the national, 302

Stern, Professor Alfred, on the Holy Alliance, 10

Stewart, Sir Charles, on Alexander I, 82, 83

Stewart, Lord (3rd Marquess of Londonderry), on Metternich, 194 ; at Troppau, 205 seq., 209 ; at Laibach, 213, 215 seq. ; at Verona, 253

Stourdza, Alexander Scarlatovich, 138, 189

Stourdza, Roxandra (Countess Edling), 125

Strangford, Lord, 253

Strassburg, claimed by Germany, 138

Strogonov, Count Paul Alexandrovich, 52, 223

Sully and the ' Grand Design ' of Henry IV, 22

Sweden, 87 ; 95, 100 (Vienna) ; and Treaty of Kiel, 180, 181

Switzerland, Alexander I and, 35, 62 ; 75 (Treaty of Chaumont) ; and the German Confederation, 103 ; 299 (origins of the Federation)

TAFT, William Howard, President of the United States, and arbitration, 292

Talleyrand - Périgord, Charles Maurice de (Prince of Benevento), and Legitimacy, 88 ; policy at Vienna, 91 ; and the Congress, 96 seq., 100 ; and Alexander I, 97 ; and the Polish-Saxon question, 98 seq., 104 ; at the second restoration, 121 ; and Allied control of France, 129 ; on the restored monarchy, 130 ; resigns, 139

Tatishchev, Ivan, 237

Temple, Sir William, on sovereignty, 296

Teplitz, Treaty of, 160

Texas, 290, 291

Treaties, St. Petersburg, 1805 (Third Coalition), 40 ; Convention of St. Petersburg (1797), 104 ; Tilsit (1807), 46 ; Kalisch (1813), 59 ; Teplitz (1813), 160 ; Chaumont (1814), 74 ; Paris I (1814), 86 seq. ; secret treaty of January 3, 1815, 110 ; Vienna Final Act (1815), 112 seq. ; Paris II (1815), 140 ; Treaty of Alliance (November 20, 1815), 147, 161 ; Frankfort (1819), 185 ; Vienna Final Act (1820), 193; Austria and Naples (June 12, 1815), 198 ; Bucharest (1812), 219 ; Treaty of Neutrality (Great Britain and Spain, 1814), 245; Florida Treaty (United States and Spain, 1819), 240, 247

Treaties, Castlereagh on, 173 ; Great Britain and obligation of, 203 ; principle of inviolability proclaimed, 59

Troppau, Conference of, 205 *seq.* ; Protocol, 208, 210 *seq.* (Castlereagh's criticisms), 215 *seq.* (at Laibach)

Truce of God, The, 18

Turkey, Alexander I and, 37, 219 *seq.*, 232 ; and the Alliance, 84, 142, 220 (at Vienna), 225 ; Austria and, 221 *seq.* ; Great Britain and, 221, 222 *seq.* (Hanover Conference), 230 (Instructions for Verona)

Tuyll, Baron de, 268

ULSTER, and the question of ' vital interests,' 302

United States, The, Alexander I and, 267, 268 ; and the Alliance, 242, 243, 271 *seq.* ; and arbitration, 292 ; and Colombia, 292 ; and Great Britain, 85 (1814), 271 *seq.* (Monroe Doctrine) ; and the League of Nations, 288, 289 ; and Russia, 229 (Behring Sea) ; and Spain, 234, 240, 247, 290 ; and the Spanish Colonies, 244, 247, 269 *seq.* President Wilson on the tradition of, 288 ; expansion of, 290 *seq.* ; fear of, 234, 235 *note* 57, 239 ; compared with the League of Nations, 295 ; causes of federation of, 299

Universal Union, Alexander I and, 37, 164, 195, 199 *seq.*, 267, 268 ; Castlereagh on, 173 ; Great Britain and, 66 ; Holy Alliance and, 143 ; United States and, 272 *note* 98 ; involves intervention, 280 ; realized in the League of Nations, 283

VATTEL, Emerich de, on the European Republic, 20

Venezuela, 291 (boundary dispute, 1895)

Verona, Congress of, 226 *seq.* (preliminaries) ; 252 *seq.*

Victor Emmanuel I, King of Sardinia, 152

Vienna, Conferences of (1822), 226

Vienna, Congress of, 93 *seq.* ; question of French representation at, 90 *seq.* ; constitution, 100 ; Final Act, 115 ; Turkish Question at, 220 ; precedents followed in Paris (1919), 282

Vienna Final Act (1820), 193

Villèle, Vicomte de, 249 ; and intervention in Spain, 250, 254, 255 ; Canning on, 264 ; 274

Vincent, Baron, on Alexander I, 10, 154

Voltaire, on the *Projet* of St. Pierre, 30

WAR, as ordeal by battle, 7 ; Voltaire on, 30

Wellington, Duke of, 100, and Alexander I, 251, 255 ; and Castlereagh, 120 ; and France, 120, 121 (in Paris), 128 (Prussian outrages), 130 and 133 (dismemberment), 140 (army of occupation), 156 (supports moderates), 157 (evacuation), 158 (indemnities), 254 (Spanish Question) ; and an international force, 177 ; and intervention, 258 *seq.* (Verona) ; and Metternich, 232 ; and Spain, 257 ; and Spanish Colonies, 242, 243 ; and the United States, 243 ; at Vienna Conferences (1822), 231, 232 ; at Verona, 228 (instructions), 253 *seq.*

Wessenberg, Baron, 100

West Florida, 235, 290

Westphalia, Congress of, 20, 26

Wicquefort, on Machiavelli, 5

William, Prince of Prussia (afterwards German Emperor), 253

Wilson, Woodrow, President of the United States, on the moral superiority of Americans, 15, 288 ; on America's motives in entering the War, 16 ; and arbitration, 292 (Colombia) ; on 'international consciousness,' 14, 15 ; and intervention, 281 (Mexico), 286 note 8 (Ireland), 289 (Monroe Doctrine) ; and the League of Nations, 12, 288, 296 ; and Mexico, x, 281 ; and the Monroe Doctrine, 288, 289

Württemberg, King of, and Constitutional Government, 153; and the 'dictatorship' of the Powers, 170, 181 ; and the Carlsbad Decrees, 194

YPSILANTI, Prince Alexander, 220, 221

ZAÏONCZEK (Zajączek), General Joseph, Viceroy of Poland, 187

Zea de Bermudez, Chevalier de, 195.

DATE DUE

Rason			
DE 1 2 '67			
OCT 28 '68			
Б H			
NOV 1 5 '68			
H 9			
APR 1 0 '69			
I N			
JUN 2 6 '69			
I N			
JUL 1 0 '69			
I N			
JAN 2 2 '73			
Б H			
NOV 9 '78			
FEB 4 '86			
FEB 1 1 '86			
GAYLORD			PRINTED IN U.S.A.